FALDO/
NORMAN

FALDO/ NORMAN

The 1996 Masters:
A duel that defined an era

ANDY FARRELL

First published 2014
by Elliott and Thompson Limited
27 John Street
London WC1N 2BX
www.eandtbooks.com

ISBN: 978-1-90965-370-2

A CIP catalogue record for this book is available from the British Library.

Typeset by Marie Doherty
Printed in the UK by TJ International

CONTENTS

INTRODUCTION

Everyone who saw it has their own memories of that fateful day. You only have to mention the 1996 Masters, and Faldo/Norman, and they come tumbling out. Television viewers recall simply how difficult it was to watch, how the prolonged agony became so disquieting. Those who were on the course remember the unnatural hush, people looking at their feet as the final two players passed by, spectators flooding for the gates well before the finish.

The outcome had appeared certain when Norman led by six strokes at the start of the day but the reversal of fortunes was so dramatic that Faldo eventually won by five. 'It was a wedding that turned into a funeral,' someone said of the atmosphere. Others' instinct was immediately to mention the press conference afterwards when Norman fronted up to every last question about how devastating it must be for the green jacket to slip through his hands yet again, repeating as often as was required that he would be fine, thank you.

My own memories are less about the golf and more about technological failure and human ineptitude. A freelance golf writer at the time, the Saturday of that Masters was the first time I had done the main report for a national newspaper from a major championship. The five-hour time difference with the UK creates its own problems – and in 1996 there was no broadband or Wi-Fi to come to your aid, e-mail and mobiles not yet standard parts of the kit – but having to use four different machines to file each of the four editions to the *Independent on Sunday* only added to the chaos. The initial problem was the failure of the modem on my battered old Apple Mac, while another laptop, kindly but unwisely lent by a colleague, died when I spilt Coca-Cola on it. A borrowed Tandy, that clunky but indestructible pre-laptop word processor, enabled me to file the 'on the whistle' close-of-play report.

Sunday was taken up with retyping a myriad of stories destined for *Golf Weekly* magazine while the brief from *The Independent* for a sidebar story on Norman's previous Masters disasters appeared simple enough. Alas, midway through the afternoon it became increasingly apparent that the way I had written the piece would not stand up. As I was frantically rewriting, Martin Johnson, who was sitting next to me in the Augusta press room and had exactly the same brief for the *Daily Telegraph*, was in relaxed mode. The old pro did not have to change a single word.

It is fair to say that retreating from a post-round huddle with Colin Montgomerie, who had delivered a five-star woe-is-me rant after taking a triple-bogey eight at the 15th for the second day running, on this particular occasion I was less than sympathetic and inclined to observe that Monty did not know the half of it.

It was more than a decade later that the first germ of an idea for this book emerged after seeing the original stage version of *Frost/Nixon* in London. Peter Morgan's play set up the series of interviews as a battle of wills, almost as a sporting duel. But rather than boxing or fencing, it suggested to me the long-drawn-out psychological warfare of golf. And the notion that a supposedly dominant participant should ultimately capitulate under the sustained pressure and perseverance of his opponent suggested one tournament above all others: the 1996 Masters. It seemed obvious this was a story worth retelling.

Looking back, the events of Sunday 14 April 1996 not only sealed the verdicts on both men – Norman, the great showman whose go-for-broke golf let him down too often when it mattered most; Faldo, feared and respected rather than loved but at his best when the pressure was at its greatest – but also on an era of the game. After Tom Watson, the latest in a long line of American golfing legends, had dominated in the early 1980s, a new group of international stars had emerged – including Seve Ballesteros, Bernhard Langer, Sandy Lyle, Ian Woosnam and Nick Price. Faldo and Norman, both having been ranked as the world's best player for lengthy spells and after numerous head-to-head contests, were the last men standing from that new generation.

A year on from their climactic encounter at Augusta, the game would have a new superstar. Tiger Woods had the power of the Australian and the precision of the Englishman, which proved an all-conquering combination for so many years. No matter whether the Tiger era is over, enough golfing history has been made in the meantime that it is relevant to be reminded of an earlier age.

So why write this book now? The 20th anniversary in 2016 might have been a more logical moment. But then Adam Scott won the Masters. After so many disappointments, usually involving Norman, Australia had a wearer of the green jacket. And the connections with 2013 did not stop there. Justin Rose won the US Open to become the first Englishman to win a major championship since Faldo 17 years earlier. Phil Mickelson, who pipped Frank Nobilo for third place in the 1996 Masters, won the Open Championship at Muirfield after two decades of trying, while it was at Muirfield that Nobilo became a member of the BBC television commentary team. Now a respected pundit for the Golf Channel in America, Nobilo had had an initial BBC outing back in 1996 when he joined Steve Rider as a guest after his round, offering eloquent observations on Norman's collapse and presaging his future career. At the US PGA in 2013, Jason Dufner equalled the major championship record of 63, just as Norman had done at the 1996 Masters. And there was even a golfer, Inbee Park, trying to win her fourth major championship of the year at St Andrews, where Masters founder Bobby Jones started his Grand Slam in 1930.

It was time indeed to return to the story of Faldo/Norman and the duel that defined an era of the game when an Englishman and an Australian vied to be the best player in the world.

Tea Olive

Hole 1
Yards 400*; Par 4

At start	Hole	1	2	3	4	5	6	7	8	9	Out	Status
	Par	4	5	4	3	4	3	4	5	4	36	
−13	G. Norman	5										−12
−7	N. Faldo	4										−7

G REG NORMAN came to the 1st tee with a six-stroke lead. This was the final round of the 60th Masters and everyone standing around the tee box – no need for grandstands at Augusta National as there are at the Ryder Cup and even the other major championships these days, the players are separated from the public by a simple rope line – believed that he was going to win.

So did virtually everyone else who had come onto the grounds that morning, now lining the 1st fairway or staking out the prime positions around the course. For those just yards away around the 18th green, nothing could be more certain than the identity of the winner who would salute them at the end of the afternoon. Television viewers might have thought something similar, except coverage of the climax of golf's first major of the year did not start for another hour or so. But make no mistake, this was going to be a parade, at the end of which the Norman Conquest of Augusta would finally be complete.

Perhaps only two people were not thinking along these lines. One was Norman himself. He could not afford to. He still had a

---

* Hole yardages stated in chapter headings refer to the course as played in 1996.

tournament to win. He led by six strokes but they had only played 54 holes, there were 18 still to come. A quarter of the marathon still to be raced. Norman told himself to treat the round as if he had no lead at all. If he wins on the day, then he wins the title. Keep it simple.

Another person who did not think it was a foregone conclusion was the other player standing on the 1st tee. Nick Faldo did not think he would win. But he had not ruled out the possibility that he could win. If nothing else, out of sheer bloody-mindedness, he was going to pretend he could win and see what happened.

Most people, however, chose to believe the evidence of the leaderboard, which showed Norman at 13 under par for the first three rounds. He had equalled the course record of 63 in the first round to lead by two strokes, and then followed up with a steady 69 in tricky conditions on Friday to extend his lead to four strokes. On Saturday he again added two strokes to his lead after returning a 71 to the 73 of his nearest opponent, Faldo. Norman appeared to be striking the ball as well as ever and, just as importantly, had the assured look of a player who was in control of his game and his mind. Not even playing alongside his old rival in the third round had disturbed his equilibrium.

But Faldo had not gone away. His putting had gone through a wobbly patch on the back nine on Saturday but had come good just at the right time, producing a birdie at the 17th hole and a par-saver at the last to ensure he again played alongside the leader on the final day. Faldo and Norman had spent 20 years crossing swords on the fairways of the professional game. In the previous decade they had each in turn been the best golfer in the world. Following on from Tom Watson and Seve Ballesteros in the early 1980s, Norman and Faldo had become golf's premier rivalry.

In 1986 a ranking system was introduced by Mark McCormack's International Management Group, then agents to Norman and Faldo, among others. It has since evolved into today's Official World Golf Rankings but in its first decade of existence it showed Norman's dominance of the game. In all, the Australian spent 331 weeks as number one; Faldo was the next best on 97 weeks.

It was during that year (1986) that Norman won his first major championship, the Open at Turnberry. He won it again at Sandwich in 1993, the greatest performance of his career as he raced clear of all the best golfers of the day, including Faldo.

But in between Norman's twin triumphs, Faldo won five majors – the Open three times and the Masters twice – putting him alongside Ballesteros as Europe's most successful player. When it mattered most, Faldo came out on top more often. Wasn't it Norman's hero Jack Nicklaus, the game's greatest major winner with 18 titles, who said that he could play his game longer than others could play theirs? Let the other guy make more mistakes than you.

Faldo also learnt to do just that, by stifling his natural flair, completely revamping his swing and absorbing himself in the task at hand to the exclusion of all else. His reputation for being almost machine-like was sealed by his 18 pars in the final round of the 1987 Open at Muirfield, his first major victory. At other times, when not quite on his game, he wore his perfectionism so fussily that Brough Scott wrote in the *Independent on Sunday* in 1991: 'Everyone suffers on a Faldo round, Faldo most of all. Anything less than perfection gets a terrible black mark. Out on the course it will never be easy to love him. For he does not love himself.'

A choice between watching Norman or Faldo was no contest. When Norman arrived in Europe, the 'Brisbane Bomber' was right up there with Ballesteros in the thrill-a-minute department: his Scandinavian looks from his Finnish mother, Toini, combined with the surfer boy image straight from central casting by the

Australian tourist board (long before *Crocodile Dundee*, this). 'Norman is a sight worth seeing on a golf course,' wrote John Hopkins in the *Sunday Times* in 1984, 'and not only for his guardsman's walk, his parchment-coloured hair and a voice that echoes around the fairways. He hits the ball as if his life depends on it. From the top of his backswing, when his powerful shoulders are fully turned, he brings his club down at high speed, often grunting with the effort, and swinging so hard that his hands are swept through, up and around his head until his body position resembles a reverse C. When his dander is up, he creates such an impression of power that you wince when he makes contact.'

Now, on Sunday 14 April 1996 both men stood side by side awaiting their opening shots of the final round of the Masters. The date was significant: the last three winners on April 14 had all been non-Americans: Ian Woosnam in 1991, Bernhard Langer in 1985 and Gary Player in 1974. Further confirmation that Norman was on to a good thing arrived with news that the previous five winners of the Masters had played in the final pairing on the last day (as would the next 12). It was the perfect spring day in Georgia, ideal golfing conditions and both men were dressed similarly, in black trousers and white shirts, Faldo with vertical stripes, Norman with dark geometric shapes and, of course, his trademark hat.

It was a black wide-brimmed synthetic straw hat, a golfing version of the Akubra bushman's hat. In his youth, Norman had had a scruffy old straw hat that he wore down at the beach or while fishing or boating. He continued with the old favourite when he took up golf, even if his mother (the golfer in the family) thought it inappropriate for the golf club. It seems a distant past, compared to the modern ubiquity of golfing caps, when the game's stars went bareheaded, as Faldo was this day. In fact, Faldo always looked a bit odd when he later adopted a cap, his distinctive features hidden as they are for virtually all today's leading players, a strange uniformity prevailing.

Norman, by contrast, looked eye-catching whether showing off his yellow mane or sporting the Akubra. Of course, the latest version featured his 'Great White Shark' logo, the nickname bestowed long ago on his debut in the Masters having not just stuck but become a brand in itself. The hat, as so much with Norman, suggested that anything other than winning was not an option. But the more inevitable not winning became that day, the more incongruous the hat became. Curiously, Norman won his two majors hatless, his most distinctive feature unhidden, albeit under the softer rays of the British seaside sun.

Was Norman a talented showman or one of the golfing greats? This was the day that should have put an end to such questions but actually only intensified them. David Davies wrote in the 1999 book *Beyond the Fairways*: 'So, what is he, this blond-haired, icy-blue-eyed man with broad shoulders, flat belly, slim hips and long legs and who is likely to be wearing a big hat, a garish shirt and tight trousers? Is he a great golfer or a charismatic clothes horse? Is he the most imposing player in modern professional golf or a total poser? The questions follow him around the world.'

Norman's ability to make money, whether on the golf course or in his increasingly successful business ventures, was not in question. Nor was his liking for speed and expensive toys – the cars, yachts, helicopters, jets – nor his energy and zest for life. Good on him. But golfing greatness required something more, something to add to the two claret jugs and to balance the scale against the times he came so close but ultimately failed, sometimes by his own hand, sometimes due to terrible misfortune. Victory at Augusta, the scene of so many previous Masters disasters, was his due. He had been sized up for a green jacket, the symbol of a Masters champion, so often but now it seemed certain that finally he was going to be able to wear one.

From the opening tee shot that Sunday a different story started to unfold, centred around not one but two players. It was uncomfortable, sickening, traumatic at times, and through it all a pensive grimace was glued to Norman's face. It had been there ever since his eyes first started turning left, following the ball, from his very first drive of the day.

As it turned out, the 'most imposing player in modern professional golf', as Davies put it, was to be not Norman but Tiger Woods. Just a year later Woods burst onto the scene by winning the 1997 Masters by a record 12 strokes and his tenure at the top of the world rankings has lasted twice as long as that of Norman's. And it would take another 17 years for an Australian, Adam Scott, finally to win the Masters, in 2013.

While Norman and Faldo have moved on to new careers with success, the impact of their epic duel at the 1996 Masters has had a lasting effect. Their influence lives on in the new generation of players who have followed each of them, such as Scott and Justin Rose. Norman heads a number of companies under the umbrella of Great White Shark Enterprises and in the syntax of Twitter has found the perfect expression of his personal mantra: #AttackLife. Sir Nick Faldo, for he was knighted by the Queen in 2009 for services to golf, has created a worldwide junior tournament scheme as well as becoming one of the game's leading television commentators. Each April the Englishman is ensconced in a tower above the 18th green at Augusta National to analyse and comment for the American broadcaster CBS.

It was below Faldo on the final green that Scott holed a

25-footer and bellowed: 'C'mon Aussie'. It got the 32-year-old into a playoff with Angel Cabrera which Scott won at the second extra hole when he holed a 15-footer for birdie in the dark and rain on the 10th green. 'An unbelievable, magical moment – he is now officially the Wizard of Oz. What a couple of putts they were!' Faldo exclaimed as a nation on the other side of the world celebrated over breakfast. 'From Down Under to on top of the world,' added CBS's Australian commentator Ian Baker-Finch.

Australians had won the other three golfing majors, and winning the Open Championship remains the dream for any young Aussie golfer, as it was for Norman. But not winning the Masters was getting ridiculous. Too many good players had failed in the quest and Norman's near misses had almost traumatised a nation.

'Between the Bangles and the Boomtown Rats, it's pretty much set in underwater-cured concrete that Mondays have a bit to answer for. They certainly have for Australian golf fans, especially during the mesmerising but frequently demoralising heyday of Greg Norman,' wrote Patrick Mangan in *So Close – The Bravest, Craziest, Unluckiest Defeats in Aussie Sport* (Norman could have multiple entries in all those categories).

Scott had watched the 1996 Masters as a 15-year-old golf-mad Shark fan and was crying by the end. After his victory he said: 'Part of this belongs to Greg. He inspired a nation of golfers. He was the best player in the world and was an icon in Australia. He has devoted so much time to myself and other Australian players who have come after him. He has given me so much inspiration and belief.' Norman had long since gone from being Scott's hero to his mentor and the champion said he was looking forward to celebrating over a beer with him. Norman, who was watching at his home in Florida, was delighted. 'There was more pressure on Adam because no Australian has ever won the Masters. It was a monumental feat and I'm so happy for him.'

This is what Scott's victory meant: within 24 hours the members of the Australian Golf Writers Association had unanimously agreed, halfway through April, that Scott would be their player of the year – nothing could top this. Scott was also honoured with Australia's top sporting award, The Don, named after cricket legend Don Bradman. When he returned home in November he received the keys to the City of Gold Coast and there was a 'Wear Green for Adam Scott Day' at the Australian PGA Championship. 'The whole of Australia was buzzing with excitement following Adam's momentous victory at Augusta,' said Brian Thorburn, CEO of the PGA of Australia. 'We wanted to provide a welcome home befitting his achievement whilst also giving fans the chance to celebrate.'

When Scott received a congratulatory text from his friend Rose, Scott replied that the Englishman was next. 'This is our time,' he wrote. 'He's a wise man,' Rose said after winning the US Open at Merion, hitting a four-iron at the final hole from beside the plaque commemorating Ben Hogan's one-iron in 1950. Both Scott and Rose could go on to win more majors. Perhaps they will be the new Norman and Faldo, although the old duo themselves might be in competition again once Fox take over televising the US Open in 2015. When the announcement was made that the US Golf Association was dropping NBC and Johnny Miller, Norman admitted he had been approached to become the lead analyst for Fox's first venture into golf.

Rose was the first Englishman to win the US Open since Tony Jacklin in 1970 – Faldo never managed it – and the first Englishman to win any major since Faldo at the 1996 Masters. 'It was always a matter of time before one of us broke through,' Rose said. 'But I'm glad it was me.' Rose had had lunch with Faldo two weeks before. 'He's a classy guy,' said Faldo. 'No matter how many times he got knocked down, he still had self-belief.'

Scott won on his 12th appearance and at 32 was exactly the average age for a Masters winner. Norman was two months past his 41st birthday in April 1996 and was making his 16th appearance at Augusta. No one would have been older or taken as long to win their first Masters had the Shark won that year (although at 41 years and three months, Mark O'Meara would have taken the age record anyway in 1998).

Only three players, Horton Smith, Gene Sarazen and Fuzzy Zoeller, have won on their Masters debut, and the first two of those were in the first two years of the tournament. Charl Schwartzel became only the third player to win on his second appearance in 2012.

It took Woods three goes, Arnold Palmer and Ballesteros four each, Nicklaus and Gary Player five and Faldo six, which turns out to be the average number of appearances before a first Masters win. In all, Norman appeared 23 times in the Masters, with eight top-five finishes. Gene Littler and Tom Kite, who had nine top-fives, hold the record for the most appearances without winning (26). Without the winner's lifetime exemption, all the other qualifications for receiving an invitation eventually run out. Faldo chooses not to play any longer; Norman does not have that choice.

For Norman, the Masters was his favourite tournament of the year and Augusta National one of his favourite courses. Winning this event became something of an obsession, particularly after having had a chance to get into a playoff with Nicklaus in 1986, but flailing his approach deep into the crowd, and in 1987 when he was in a playoff down at the 11th when Larry Mize did the unthinkable and holed an outrageous chip from well off the green. 'From the last day of the 1986 tournament, from the very moment I missed the putt for the par, for the next year, 24 hours a day, I thought about the Masters,' he said. 'Every day it was on my mind. More than anything else in my life, I wanted to win that one.' Trying to get the Mize chip out of his head was even worse.

But the 1996 Masters was all about Norman. Even the introduction to the final round on the BBC coverage hardly mentioned Faldo. Over pictures of Norman's highlights from the third round, Steve Rider said: 'The icy nerve of Greg Norman, six shots clear after 54 holes of the US Masters, form that rarely wavered, a putter that rarely failed. He's led throughout. He's always looked in control. Even the treacherous 16th held no fears and yesterday produced a vital birdie. They say yesterday was the day he won the US Masters. Today is surely not the day he's going to lose it. It's happened before, though. In 1986, needing a four to tie at the last he took five and Nicklaus won the title.'

Cue the video of Norman's four-iron diving right of the green and Peter Alliss's commentary: 'That really was a dreadful shot. Put to the test and found wanting, I'm afraid.'

Rider again: 'In 1987 victory looked assured. He was in control of a playoff only for Larry Mize to produce his miracle and Norman was second at the Masters once again.' Cue video with Alliss's succinct: 'And they say the meek shall inherit the earth...'

Rider, over a caption with the leaderboard: 'Greg Norman, the world number one, seems poised to put all that agonising history behind him. In yesterday's third round he opened up a six-shot lead over his nearest rival Nick Faldo. Greg Norman arrived at Augusta National a few hours ago ahead of what most people are expecting to be a triumphant march to his first major title in the United States. Once again playing alongside Nick Faldo, admitting he was in need of a miracle but in the last round of the Masters, the miraculous can happen.'

That morning's newspapers had trodden a similar line between proclaiming Norman as the winner and not wishing more of the unthinkable on him. 'Shark smells blood' was the headline in the *Augusta Chronicle*, with the subheading: 'Pursuers can only hope for complete collapse by Norman, who holds six-shot lead going into the final round'.

Those who did not see the result as a foregone conclusion were certainly in the minority, although some time after the 1996 Masters, the sports columnist Ian Wooldridge admitted of Faldo's victory: 'Shamefully, I confess that on the previous evening, emboldened by several martinis, I'd backed Nick to do it and thereby won the biggest bet of my life.' (Details unknown but Ladbrokes had Faldo at 7-1 before the final round, Norman at 1-8.)

Ron Green, in the *Charlotte Observer*, wrote: 'Greg Norman won the Masters on Saturday. Now, if he can only keep from losing it. Don't worry, he won't lose this time. Surely, not this time. He has a six-shot lead over Nick Faldo, who doesn't score a lot of 65s and 66s, the kind of scores he'll need to even have a chance of catching Norman. Phil Mickelson is another shot back, but he drives his ball into the camellias too much and has to play trick shots to make his pars. Nobody else is in the game. It will be Greg Norman against himself out there Sunday on those rolling fairways where so many of his demons have been born. It is a formidable opponent.'

Meanwhile, Australian journalists were up late on Saturday night concocting tributes for their Monday morning newspapers, which would arrive on readers' doormats as the final round was taking place. The *Sydney Morning Herald* may have indicated that Norman was Australia's greatest sportsman since Bradman. They changed their tune after the following day.

On Saturday evening, after his third round, Norman was asked if he had 'thought about the ceremony and the jacket, and will you think about that tonight?' Norman was not falling for the cart-before-the-horse trick. He replied: 'No, I haven't. I never have in the past. When you've got the lead in a tournament, you don't think about the end result. You just think about what you're doing at the time and relax and chill out. If you get ahead of yourself, it is not going to work. So, I'll wake up tomorrow and do what I've been doing and get ready for the 1st tee.'

Temptation was everywhere, however. After a late practice session, Norman went back to the locker room, where a friend said: 'Your last night in here.' Masters champions use a different changing room upstairs in the clubhouse. Another longtime friend of Norman's, Peter Dobereiner, the great golf writer for *The Observer* and *The Guardian*, was attending the Masters for the last time. He died in August that year, with Norman paying a handsome tribute: 'To think of golf without Peter Dobereiner is like a bunker without sand, a fairway without grass, a flag without a green. His dry humour, wonderful understanding of the game, coupled with his deep love for the sport, is going to be sadly missed.' But now, standing at the urinals in the (downstairs) locker room at Augusta, Norman could do little more than force a smile when Dobereiner remarked: 'Well, Greg, not even you can fuck this one up.'

What Norman and Faldo did during the final round of the 1996 Masters is a matter of record. But what happened before their 2.49 p.m. tee time remains open to speculation. Not least for Norman himself. Asked on the Sunday evening if his routine had been anything different the night before or that morning, Norman replied: 'No, nothing different. Everything was pretty much the same. I did the same process.' Asked if he had slept well, he answered: 'Yeah, I slept great. By the time you get back and eat, you don't get to sleep until 12, 12.30 a.m. But I wake up every morning at nine. I had a lot of good night's sleep. That wasn't my problem.'

During the week, Norman's back had played up and he had to curtail his practice on Wednesday. But after treatment from both Fred Couples's back specialist and then his own trainer, he was fine once the tournament got under way. He did not mention it in his Sunday night press conference, but when interviewed for the ABC TV documentary programme *Australian Story*, which aired in Australia in September 2013, Norman said: 'Again, there's more to it than people realise. Because I did have bad back issues that morning and I tried to walk it off but I couldn't. I told my coach, "Today's not going to be easy."'

This made news around the world along the lines of Norman suddenly changing his story. That is not true and is unfair in the sense that he would not have wanted to discuss the full extent of his back issues during the tournament. In 2009, on the eve of his return to the Masters after a six-year absence, Norman told Jeff Rude of *GolfWeek*: 'My timing was off. I knew on the driving range before I teed off. My back was bad on Saturday, and I woke up Sunday morning very stiff. I went for a one and a half mile walk to try and loosen it up. But on the range, my turn wasn't good. You look at all the shots from the 1st hole on – they were just three or four yards out. The more I pushed it, the harder it was. So you feel like water going through your fingers. It's just disappearing.'

Augusta National, with its hills – proper ski-slope inclines – is no place for someone with a bad back to walk all week. In *Breaking the Slump*, also published in 2009, Jimmy Roberts wrote that Norman woke up with a stiff back. Norman told him: 'No matter what I tried to do in a short amount of time on the range, I couldn't get the club squared up.'

In his *GolfWeek* piece, Rude quoted Norman's then coach, Butch Harmon, who had masterminded his rise back to being world number one after a couple of poor years at the start of the 1990s, as saying he had noticed his man 'didn't have it' on the range on Sunday. Harmon said: 'He was definitely a different person physically and emotionally. He fought his back all week but played within himself. Sunday, it was like he tried to push everything. There was a tremendous amount of anxiety in his body that day.' However, in a *Golf World* interview published in September 1996, Harmon, while saying Norman's whole nervous system was out of synch, also said: 'I never anticipated it would happen that way. I didn't see anything before the round on Sunday – whether it be swing mechanics, personality or nerves that gave me any indication that would happen. I was in a state of shock.'

Lauren St John, in her 1998 book *Greg Norman – The Biography*, wrote: 'Out on the range, Norman felt nervous but, as he later told his wife, Laura, "It was the right kind of nerves." He didn't feel the curious deadness that had come over him at St Andrews in 1990, and he didn't feel as jittery and nauseous as he had at Turnberry in 1986. He felt hopeful and relaxed. Watching him, Butch Harmon thought his ball-striking was almost perfect. A constant stream of people came up to wish Norman the best.' Ken Brown, the former Ryder Cup player, was covering the Masters for BBC Radio and remembered watching Norman on the range. 'He was flushing everything,' he recalled. Norman's last shot before leaving the driving range and short game area to go through to the other side of the clubhouse, and the putting green and the 1st tee, was to hole a bunker shot.

Norman himself wrote in his autobiography, *The Way of the Shark* (2006), about his back problems on the eve of the tournament. But in light of future comments, this is strange about the Sunday: 'I recall walking up feeling hopeful and relaxed. My back was still in good shape, so I knew I had an opportunity to fulfil one of my career dreams.'

Painting the scene before the final round, the 1996 *Masters*

Annual reported: 'On the practice tee, Norman was the picture of relaxation. He chatted with fellow competitor Frank Nobilo and the two made a date for a practice round at the next Tour stop. Norman seemed in no hurry to get down to business, trying on three brand-new shark-emblazoned golf gloves before finding the one that felt just right. Then he worked methodically through a half dozen irons and woods, pausing now and then to joke with his caddie Tony Navarro and coach Butch Harmon. At one point, Norman playfully poked a finger into Harmon's forehead and all three men laughed heartily. If Norman was less than comfortable with his swing or his situation, he didn't show it.

'Throughout the previous three days, the tournament had buzzed with talk of the "new Norman", the wiser, more serene warrior whose competence had at last matched his confidence. The fellow striping skyscraper two-irons to the back of the range was that Greg Norman.

'A few steps away, Nick Faldo toiled in a more studious mode. He, too, was flanked by his caddie and his coach but there was no byplay with Fanny Sunesson and his few exchanges with David Leadbetter focused on swing mechanics, Leadbetter stepping in at one point to check club position as Faldo froze at the top of the swing. Team Faldo, it seemed, had serious work to do.'

In fact, Faldo had spent his morning on the phone with his parents, which was atypical on the Sunday of a major, and got so caught up with the NASCAR motor racing on the television that there was no time for his usual hour-and-a-half warm-up session. Sunesson told him he had 57 minutes till their tee time when he walked onto the range at last. 'In reality, this break in my usual routine was probably a good thing for me as it meant that I just had to get on with my practice,' Faldo wrote in *Life Swings*, his autobiography, 'whereas Greg had been down there early, talking to everyone.'

Even Faldo. As the pair waited on the 1st tee, they chatted. 'Oh, we were talking about photographers,' Norman reported. 'The way they do it here at the Augusta National is the best. Like everything else they do here, it's the best championship we play. We get to play the game without having to ask photographers to move. Sometimes they don't know they're in the line of sight of where you want to play. But here they've got them situated in fixed positions. Nick said it would be great if we can get this at the British Open and would speak to Michael Bonallack.' The Masters remains unique in excluding press and photographers from inside the ropes, something the then secretary of the Royal and Ancient was probably used to players complaining about at the Open.

Then there would be no more talking until the 18th green. Phil Harison, the starter for 60 years until his death in 2008, announced: 'Fore, please, Greg Norman now driving.' It was a pull into the trees on the left between the 1st and 9th fairways. He had a direct route to the green but his recovery was a fraction short for the tight line that he attempted to play. The ball toppled back into the bunker on the left and from there he came out seven feet past the hole. Faldo had driven safely and then hit a nine-iron to the heart of the green. His 25-foot putt, slightly uphill, came up a touch short but it was a sure four. Norman missed his putt, the sort he had been holing all week, but this one did not come close to touching the hole.

It was a different day, a different Norman: that much was obvious already. Quite when he realised he was in trouble, well before the round or on this 1st hole, will remain shrouded in doubt. The scoreboard reflected only a minor change, and his lead was still commanding at five strokes. Was it to be a momentary blip or was it game on?

Pink Dogwood

Hole 2
Yards 555; Par 5

At start	Hole	1	2	3	4	5	6	7	8	9	Out	Status
	Par	4	5	4	3	4	3	4	5	4	36	
-13	G. Norman	5	4									-13
-7	N. Faldo	4	4									-8

A BOGEY WAS NOT the best start but it was nothing to panic about, either. After an opening hole that is designed to wake up any golfer not immediately on top of their game, the 2nd offers a chance to even up the scorecard. It is a big, sweeping hole that swings from right to left, downhill, so it does not play as long as the yardage suggests.

It usually plays as the second or third easiest hole on the course but that does not mean it is without danger. A ravine on the left is referred to as the 'Delta ticket counter' as a trip in there on the first couple of days can lead to a rescheduling of flights for Friday evening and a weekend at home. It was the last of the par-fives at Augusta to concede an albatross, Louis Oosthuizen holing out for a two from 253 yards with a four-iron – before losing to another spectacular shot in the playoff by Bubba Watson in 2012.

Norman had already given a hint of encouragement to Faldo, who was happy to receive any tiny crumb of comfort, so this was the time to recapture the initiative. Yet Faldo, having gained the honour and already driven off at the 2nd hole, certainly noticed a change in the leader. So much for the mantra of only 'playing your own game'. Inside the ropes at a major championship is as intimate as a boxing ring.

Perhaps Norman was still fretting about the frailty of his back or the lack of coordination he felt in his swing on the very first shot of the day. 'As we stood on the second tee,' Faldo wrote in *Life Swings*, 'I could feel the nervousness emanating from Greg. He gripped and regripped his club time and again, as though he could not steel himself to hit the ball. "Obviously, something is going on in Greg's mind," I thought to myself. Courageously – and the White Shark has never been less than courageous on a golf course – he matched my birdie four on the second where he showed sublime touch from off the back of the green, which suggested that he had pulled himself together.'

Norman certainly had no problem with his tee shot, outdriving Faldo by 50 yards. His second shot, however, trickled through the back of the green into the first row of spectators. Once the folding chairs and the people had been pushed back, and with two stewards raising the gallery rope above his head, Norman putted down stone dead and then tapped in for his four.

Faldo had hit a five-wood for his second shot into the front-right bunker – the hole was cut on the right wing of the green as it usually is on Masters Sunday – and played a fine recovery shot to two feet. Norman was back to even par for the day but Faldo had kept his deficit at five. Given the power and the touch shown by Norman here, it was one of the day's many contradictions that Faldo should be the one to birdie all four of the par-fives. It is also sobering to think that Norman played the par-fives in three under and still managed to score a 78.

'Greg Norman has always been the guy who is going to win the Masters one year. It's been that way since his first appearance at Augusta National, sporting a gold neck chain and unbelievably white blond hair,' wrote Robert Green in *Golf International*. 'Norman, Augusta and Sunday have come to represent one of golf's more unsettling *ménages a trois* – not so much the Great Triumvirate, more the Folies-Bergère.'

Norman made his debut at Augusta in 1981 and led after an opening round of 69. So far he had played mainly in Australia and Europe and this was only his second major in America. After the round he talked about his outdoors, seaside life growing up in Queensland and it was a headline writer for the *Augusta Chronicle* who christened him the 'Great White Shark'. It was better than his initial nickname of the 'Brisbane Bomber', but Norman was at first uncomfortable with it. Soon, however, he embraced being one of golf's leading predators, in a line of succession from the Golden Bear to Tiger Woods, and it was a unique brand to let loose on the corporate world when he started to tee it up as a businessman.

That first year, Norman was lying third after three rounds but owing to a quaint Masters custom of the time, that meant he was paired with the leader on the final day. Before pairing players by score on the weekend became de rigueur, tournaments such as the Masters would more likely spread the leaders out, at one point entrusting the third-round leader to elder statesman Byron Nelson for the final round. For Norman, it meant he had the best seat in the house as Tom Watson held off Jack Nicklaus and Johnny Miller, while his own fourth place was an encouraging start. Was it also an omen? It was the first of ten times in major championships that he played in the final pairing in the final round and he only won once.

That victory came at the Open Championship in 1986, the

year Norman did what became known as his 'Saturday Slam', lead-ing after 54 holes at all four majors. At Augusta, Norman led by one from a large group of players that included Seve Ballesteros, Nick Price and Bernhard Langer. When Norman had a double bogey at the 10th, it looked as if Ballesteros, after an eagle at the 13th, would win a third green jacket. But just ahead of the Spaniard, something extraordinary was going on. Jack Nicklaus, at the age of 46, was making one last charge at Augusta and the galleries were roaring their heads off.

Ballesteros could hear it all, especially the cheers for Nicklaus's eagle at the 15th and then the birdie at the 16th, just before Seve faced his second to the 15th. He hit a miserable four-iron that never had a chance of clearing the pond in front of the green, a moment accompanied by a strangulated cheer. Ballesteros was done and Nicklaus added another rousing birdie at the 17th. The 'Olden' Bear had come home in 30 for a closing 65 and his sixth green jacket.

Except Norman had not given up, despite his gallery having shrunk considerably. He birdied the 14th hole, the 15th, then the 16th and the 17th for four in a row and a tie with Nicklaus at nine under. A birdie to win, a par for a playoff. Despite having hit his driver at the 18th all week, and the fact that he had become the best driver in the game – long *and* straight – he hit a three-wood off the tee and then had 175 yards to the green. He and his caddie Pete Bender agreed on a four-iron but Norman sailed it well right of the green into the gallery and over towards the 10th hole. He chipped back down but could not make the 16-footer to tie.

'I let my ego get the better of me,' he said afterwards. 'I was going for the flag. I was trying to hit it too hard and too high and spun out of it.' In *The Way of the Shark*, Norman said the idea had been to hit an 'easy four-iron' rather than a hard five. After all, it was none other than Nicklaus, after they had played together in the Australian Open years earlier, who had advised Norman to learn to 'hit more delicately with longer clubs to gain additional control', rather than to hit hard every time. But instinct had taken over. It was either the wrong shot or the wrong club, but it was certainly muddled thinking. The result was not pretty.

A year later Norman again suffered disappointment on the 72nd hole at Augusta. On that occasion, he did hit a driver off the tee and put his second on the green. His birdie putt from 22 feet looked as if it would fall but just stayed out. 'I couldn't believe it,' Norman said. 'I could feel the ball going into the hole.' A par meant a playoff with Ballesteros and Larry Mize. Seve departed after the first extra hole, trudging up the hill from the 10th green in floods of tears having again been denied his third Masters title.

Norman and Mize went on to the 11th and the American, who grew up in Augusta and had worked on the scoreboards at the tournament during his youth, shovelled his approach well wide of the green. Norman had an eight-iron and simply made sure he found the green. He was convinced there was no way Mize could get up and down. Imagine how shocked he was then when Mize holed his chip from what was measured as 140 feet.

Norman was not even looking, as he concentrated on how to nudge his putt down to tap-in range. But he soon found out when he was hit by a wall of sound and looked up to see Mize running around in excitement and the crowd going nuts in the background. After all that, there was no way Norman would hole his putt to stay alive. 'This is probably the toughest loss I've ever had,' he said. 'I couldn't believe my eyes.' It happened just eight months after Bob Tway had holed a bunker shot at the 72nd hole to deny Norman at the previous major, the 1986 US PGA. No one had ever suffered such a brutal double-whammy. 'All I can say is that at least I was there for both of them.'

Norman was not quite there in the 1988 Masters, finishing fifth only after a closing 64 from too far back. But the next year he again came to the last hole needing a birdie to win and a par to get in a playoff. He hit a one-iron off the tee and then went with the five-iron for his approach, this time coming up short on the upslope in front of the green. 'It just didn't fly, it hung up in the breeze,' he said. He did not get up and down and missed out on the playoff, in which Nick Faldo beat Scott Hoch for his first Masters title.

A good weekend in 1992 got Norman up to a tie for sixth and he said: 'If I can figure out a way to play the first two rounds better, I might be able to win this S.O.B. one of these days.' Two years later he was a shot out of the lead at the halfway stage but slumped to 18th place. Two years after that, he had certainly figured out how to play the first two rounds – indeed, the first three rounds – but to no avail once again.

Norman's ability to grasp defeat from the jaws of victory was not confined to Augusta National. 'There's no place I play where I haven't screwed up at some point,' he once told the *Sunday Telegraph*. At Sunningdale during the 1982 European Open, an earthworm emerged from the ground behind his ball just as he was about to hit and in trying to adjust his shot, Norman ended up in the gorse and that was that. His first runner-up finish in a major came at the 1984 US Open at Winged Foot when he birdied the 17th to tie for the lead but then at the last, as was to be repeated at Augusta two years later, pushed his second with a six-iron into the grandstand on the right. This time he holed a remarkable 45-footer for his par and Fuzzy Zoeller, who thought it had been for birdie, waved a white towel from back down the fairway in a salute of surrender. In fact, Zoeller tied with Norman and the next day they played an 18-hole playoff. Norman was never at the races, losing with a 75 to a 67 and waving his own white flag as the pair marched down the 18th fairway.

Two years later at the US Open at Shinnecock Hills, Norman was leading after 54 holes for the second major running. But he was not feeling well, was diagnosed with pneumonia and had no answer to the fast greens and strong winds of the final day. Five bogeys in eight holes from the 8th meant a 75 as he dropped to a tie for 12th place, six strokes behind the 43-year-old Ray Floyd, who had charged through the field with a 66. For the second major running, Norman had lost to a player who had become the oldest ever to win that championship.

At Turnberry a few weeks later, Norman did hang on to win his first major title and that was the year he went on to complete the 'Saturday Slam' by leading after 54 holes at Inverness in the US PGA. The closest anyone had got to such a feat was Ben Hogan in 1953, when he had led after three rounds of the three majors he contested that year. Of course, Hogan won all three of them. At Inverness, with rain delaying much of the final round until Monday, Norman's four-stroke lead started disappearing early on the back nine. He ended up coming to the 18th tied with Tway and both men missed the green. Norman was in the better spot, with a relatively straightforward up-and-down, while Tway was in a deep bunker front-right of the green. When Tway holed his shot, Norman had to match him with his chip from just off the fringe and ended up taking a bogey.

Lee Trevino once said: 'God never gives a golfer everything, he always holds something back. Jack Nicklaus didn't get a sand wedge and Greg Norman didn't get any luck.' It is undeniable that Norman was hugely unlucky on occasions and not for the reason that you might surmise from Gary Player's assertion that 'the harder I work, the luckier I get'. Norman was not just one of the most talented golfers in the world, he was one of the hardest-working.

But it is also undeniable that Norman had a habit of getting in his own way. At Inverness, he came home in 40. A shot saved here and there, and by his own description it was only a matter of inches in most cases, and he would have been out of reach of Tway's dagger to the heart. 'Greg does all right until the head comes off and the turnip goes on,' Australia's Jack Newton told *Golf Digest*. 'I don't think it is bad luck. He has some bad breaks but you make your own luck. Technically, there isn't much wrong, either. The biggest flaw in his game is his course management. The bottom line is, it sucks.'

Johnny Miller, former US Open and Open champion, said: 'Greg can only play one way, and that's aggressively. When he tries to play conservatively his brain short-circuits. His wires get crossed and the sparks start flying. The worst thing you can tell Greg to do is to swing smoothly and just hit it down the middle. It won't work – he'll hit it in the bushes every time.' Yet, time and again on the last day of a major championship, it is a conservative approach, as demonstrated often by Nicklaus and followed diligently by Faldo, that gets the job done. Norman's habit of going for broke was only ever rewarded with two major titles.

Dan Jenkins wrote in his report of the 1986 Open that until his victory at Turnberry Norman's 'suitcase had flown open on Sundays. He can let it soar in a peculiar direction now and then. Greg's feet seem to move on most swings with any club in his hands. He addresses his putts on the toe of the clubhead. He sprays his irons both right and left when he goes bad. He often makes you wonder about his judgment. Despite those things, his power can be awesome and his touch at times is enviable. At Turnberry he managed to keep all of it together for a spell, and there were moments when it looked like everybody else in the game could forget golf and go play polo with Prince Charles.'

By winning the Open, Norman did fulfil one of Peter Dobereiner's prophecies. Writing in a 1984 profile, he stated: 'A few more guesses are in order at this stage of his career as, at the age of 29, he is poised at the crossroads. Will he take the *Pilgrim's Progress* path to greatness and spiritual fulfilment? Or will he be diverted into the lush byways of winning millions of dollars without causing a flutter among the record books? Well, I will wager my Scottish castle, my Black Forest shooting estate, 20 of my most attentive handmaidens that he will win at least one major championship. Beyond that I would prefer to hedge my bets. It all depends on that core of ambition and determination residing so deeply within him that even he cannot unravel its secrets.'

Typical of the heady mixture of brilliance, carelessness and misfortune was the final day of the 1989 Open at Royal Troon. Norman birdied the first six holes and posted a 64 to end up in a playoff with compatriot Wayne Grady and America's Mark Calcavecchia. Norman then birdied the first two holes of the Open's inaugural four-hole playoff. But a bogey at the par-three 17th left him tied with Calcavecchia and then at the 18th Norman spanked a driver into a bunker 310 yards away, something he never considered possible. He found another bunker with his next, went out of bounds over the green with his third and picked up. Calcavecchia's second birdie at the 18th of the afternoon gave him his sole major title.

'Destiny has a funny way of saying, "Hey, this is the way it's got to be,"' Norman said. 'But we all accept fate. It's what keeps us coming back, hoping. You've got to think positively. I have to believe my time will come soon.'

The following March at Doral, the Shark destroyed the Blue Monster course with a closing 62 and managed to win a four-man playoff that included Calcavecchia by chipping in for an eagle at the first extra hole. But, still, the outrageous hits kept on coming his way. A few weeks later at Bay Hill, Robert Gamez holed a seven-iron from 176 yards on the 18th fairway for an eagle two to beat Norman by a stroke. A month after that, David Frost holed a 50-foot bunker shot at the last to again condemn Norman to a one-stroke defeat. 'If other guys hole their shots and beat me, I have no control over that,' Norman said rather wearily. 'At least it means I have been in contention.'

It is a contradiction in golf that a player who goes along quietly and ends up in the top ten at the end of the tournament has had a 'good week' while a player who is in contention but loses gets a whole heap of trouble, despite the fact that they have beaten all but one other player – or two or three if they have just missed out on a playoff. Norman always prided himself on putting himself 'there' – in contention, where it matters, the hottest part of the crucible. He won more than 90 times in his career, and you can't do that without putting yourself at the sharp end of things regularly and being able to handle yourself when you get there, but he got burned so often it was bound to have an effect.

'Why me?' would not be an unreasonable question, especially after the Mize chip-in of 1987. He put a brave face on it but said it felt like 'somebody had ripped that green jacket right off my back'. Considering his near miss the year before, his victory at Turnberry and then Tway's bunker shot at Inverness, in a parallel universe Norman might have won three majors in a row and even four out of five. Not even the Australian realised how long the 1987 Masters defeat lingered in his subconscious. 'I would not be telling the truth if I did not acknowledge that it took me much longer to get over that loss than I would care to admit,' he wrote in *The Way of the Shark*. 'For the longest time, I would tell everybody that I could take it all and keep going. But I was only kidding myself. The truth is that I tried to bury it deep within myself. But the longer I held it in, the deeper it buried itself inside me. And the deeper something like that gets inside you, the more it harms you.'

From the middle of 1990 – not long after the Gamez and Frost daggers and his third-round capitulation to Faldo at the Open at St Andrews – through most of 1991, Norman's form deteriorated and his enthusiasm for the game waned. He was burned out. Already interested in many areas of business, he contemplated doing what many others would like to do – ditch the day job to take up his hobby full-time, except the reverse of getting out of the corporate world to play golf. But that seemed like quitting, and he was not a quitter.

A devotee of Zen teachings and motivational gurus such as Tony Robbins, Norman would eyeball himself in the mirror or pull his convertible over to the side of the road near his Florida home and stare at the sky in contemplation. Vowing to become a more resilient person who could learn to expect the unexpected and to put bad breaks behind him and move on, Norman found his old passion for the game returning. He realised he still loved the game and the competition on Sundays, giving yourself a chance to win. Losing was not as good as winning, but it was surely better than finishing early on a Sunday afternoon without having the thrill of knowing the tournament was on the line. He wanted to be the best again and was prepared to start putting in the work again.

He also recalled some advice given to him by Nicklaus: 'Greg, you are one of the best – the number one, in fact. When you walk out on that 1st tee, people are going to try and elevate their games to your level just to beat you. And sometimes they will, whether it's with a phenomenal round or a miracle shot. I've been through it and I finally realised you have to take it as a compliment.' It was in a television interview with former Australian prime minister Bob Hawke in early 1992 that Norman finally admitted to the world how tormented he had been by the Mize chip-in and it was a moment of catharsis.

For his game he sought the help of Butch Harmon, the coach of his friend Steve Elkington. Harmon was convinced he could get Greg Norman to start being Greg Norman again. He began by getting Norman to let fly at a bunch of two-irons, to regain the feel of the ball soaring into the air, higher than most could hit such a club, and drifting it left or right as desired. There were technicalities to tinker with, merely applying the basics, but Harmon's main priority was rebuilding his pupil's confidence.

Harmon had Norman slightly abbreviate his swing into a more controlled action, a move that he would replicate with Tiger Woods at the end of the 1990s, which resulted in Woods playing some of the finest golf ever seen as he claimed all four majors at once in 2000–01. He tried something similar later on with Phil Mickelson without ever quite taming the left-hander's erratic genius. Norman had already been a fine driver of a golf ball and now he was supreme with the longest club in the bag, easily the straightest long hitter of his generation. His iron-play could be sparkling and he worked tirelessly on his putting. Everything was coming together.

Norman won the Canadian Open late in 1992 and at Doral in March 1993 he tied his own course record with a 62 and went on to win by four strokes from Paul Azinger and Mark McCumber at the top of an impressive leaderboard. But the quality of the leaderboard was even better that summer for the Open Championship at Royal St George's. The course at Sandwich is notorious for its lumpy, bumpy fairways that can drive a player to distraction with awkward bounces here, there and everywhere. But a couple of huge downpours during the week had taken the worst of the fire out of the links and shot-making of the highest order was rewarded handsomely.

With a round to play, Faldo was sharing the lead with Corey Pavin. Norman was a stroke behind alongside Bernhard Langer. Two shots further back were Nick Price and Australia's Peter Senior. One behind them were Fred Couples, Ernie Els and Wayne Grady and next on the leaderboard were John Daly and Fuzzy Zoeller. Eight of the leading 11 players were major champions and two of the others would later earn that status.

The final round was unmissable drama. Payne Stewart came in early with a 63 to match Faldo's course record from two days earlier. Norman began in similar vein with a nine-footer for birdie at the 1st and a 25-footer for a two at the short 3rd. He made another two at the 6th and hit a nine-iron to six inches at the 9th. Clearly, something special was unfolding. He birdied the 12th with a wedge to four feet and then got a four at the par-five 14th. He had just watched his playing partner, Langer, knock it out of bounds on to Prince's Golf Club on the right but did not hesitate to reach for his driver. A drive, a three-wood and a sand wedge later he was only six inches from the hole. At the 16th, he hit a five-iron to four feet for his third two of the day and even the aberration of missing his par putt from 14 inches at the 17th did not matter.

Out in 31, home in 33, his 64 remains the lowest score by an Open champion in the final round. His aggregate of 267 still stands as an Open record and he became the first champion to score all four rounds in the 60s. It was his finest performance on a golf course. He won by two from Faldo, who had tried everything he could, including almost holing in one at the 11th, for his 67, by three from Langer, by five from Pavin and Senior, by seven from Price, Els and Paul Lawrie, by eight from Couples, Grady and Scott Simpson and by nine from Stewart. Only one of that top dozen never won a major. 'Today, I saw the greatest championship in all my 70 years in golf,' said 91-year-old Gene Sarazen, who had won the Open next door at Prince's in 1932.

'Greg had a great day,' Faldo said. 'He was always just out of my range. So many guys had opportunities to win, they were all trying to raise their game and do something special. Greg has had a rough ride over the past few years so I'm sure he is happy to have his golf do the talking.' Langer said: 'He was invincible. It was fun to watch. People were saying he wouldn't win another major. I always thought he was too talented not to.'

'This win means more to me knowing I have beaten great players,' Norman said. 'Bernhard is the Masters champion and Nick is the most tenacious golfer on this planet. I probably played the best I have ever played in my life. Today I never mis-hit a shot. I have never hit the ball as solidly. I hit every drive perfect, I hit every iron where I wanted it to be to get on the green. I was playing a game of chess. This is the proudest moment of my life.'

As a double Open champion, Norman was back on his way to overtaking Faldo as the world number one. There was more superlative golf to come, such as at the Players Championship in 1994 when he took the Sawgrass course apart to win by four strokes on 24 under par. Off the course things were going well, too. He had split from IMG and set up his own businesses under the flag of Great White Shark Enterprises. Early in 1996, his stake in the Cobra equipment company realised $40 million when it was bought out by Fortune Brands, ultimate owners of Titleist and Footjoy.

Needless to say, there were still hiccups. Just a few weeks after the 1993 Open at Sandwich, there was another titanic battle for the US PGA, at Inverness (returning to the venue of Tway's miracle shot at the 18th in 1986). This time Faldo finished one shot behind Norman, who had become the first player to score eight successive major rounds in the 60s, and Paul Azinger. By strange coincidence, Azinger's caddie was Mark Jimenez, who had caddied for Tway seven years earlier. In the playoff, Norman's birdie putt at the first extra hole, which was the 18th, dipped into the cup and horseshoed out again. They went on to the second extra hole, the 10th, where Norman three-putted from 18 feet, lipping out from five feet for his par. It was another 54-hole major lead that had gone astray and in the process he matched Craig Wood for the unwanted distinction of having lost playoffs for all four major championships.

Two years later, at the 1995 US Open, Norman shared the 54-hole lead with Tom Lehman but his first major title on US soil remained elusive. Lehman scored a 74 and Norman a 73, but Pavin hit a wonderful four-wood onto the 18th green for a 68 and a two-stroke win. It was Norman's seventh runner-up finish in a major.

On Saturday evening at Augusta in 1996, leading again after 54 holes in a major but this time by six strokes, Norman was asked if he 'felt more confident than ever that you may finally see it through to the end?' He replied: 'Well, I don't live in the past. I feel comfortable. Those were good tournaments I played in the past. People played some great shots to win some of them. So I'm looking forward to getting out there tomorrow and playing some great shots and finish the tournament like I know I can.'

Flowering Peach

Hole 3
Yards 360; Par 4

At start	Hole	1	2	3	4	5	6	7	8	9	Out	Status
	Par	4	5	4	3	4	3	4	5	4	36	
-13	G. Norman	5	4	4								-13
-7	N. Faldo	4	4	4								-8

A T THE START of Masters week, Greg Norman was one of the favourites for the title but hardly an overwhelming one. He might have been the world number one but he had missed the cut in his past two tournaments and was only one of a host of players expected to contend. 'It's anyone's green jacket' was the headline on the front page of the *Augusta Chronicle*'s special Masters section. Even a 20-year-old college student and a 56-year-old former champion were sharing the billing with Norman, as the subhead on the preview of the South's oldest newspaper made clear: 'Wide-open 1996 Masters features a young Tiger, an aging Golden Bear and a Shark'.

Tiger Woods had yet to turn professional but he was already the centre of much attention. This was his second appearance in the Masters after finishing as the leading amateur in 1995, playing all four rounds and finishing tied for 41st. He returned in 1996 expecting to play a practice round with Arnold Palmer on Monday. But Palmer postponed until Wednesday so Woods played with Norman, with whom he shared a coach in Butch Harmon. At the 9th tee, Norman encouraged Woods to hit a drive over the trees on the left and down the 1st fairway. With the fairways mown towards the tee, the grass is usually growing against the ball when it lands. By going down the 1st fairway in the reverse direction, they could get the ball to run for ever down the hill and leave a shorter shot to the 9th green. 'He's exceptionally long,' Norman said. 'I think he's longer than John Daly. He flights the ball so well.'

On Tuesday, Woods again played a practice round with Norman, along with two former champions, Ray Floyd and Fred Couples. 'These guys know the course like the back of their hands,' Woods said. 'I was listening to Raymond give some pointers out there. Ray's been out here for a few years and has done pretty well here, and he was giving Greg some of his idiosyncrasies Greg didn't even know about. These guys have a lot of knowledge and are willing to share their knowledge. That's very nice on their part.'

The reason Palmer had passed on a practice round with Woods on Monday was that he had lined up someone else to join them on Wednesday. Jack Nicklaus got his first close-up view of the game's next superstar as they played nine holes on the main course and then moved over to the nine-hole, par-three course for the traditional pre-Masters appetiser. Nicklaus was impressed. 'Very, very impressed, to say the least. So was Arnold,' Nicklaus said. 'This kid is the most fundamentally sound golfer that I've ever seen at any age. Hits the ball nine million miles without a swing that looks like he's trying to do that. And he's a nice kid. He's got great composure. He handles himself very well.'

If that was not enough to get his audience excited, then Nicklaus added: 'Arnold and I both agree that you could take his Masters and my Masters and add them together, and this kid should win more than that.' Palmer won the Masters four times and Nicklaus is the only person to surpass that with six titles. Together, that's ten green jackets. Nicklaus was suggesting that Woods might win at least 11, an extravagant claim that has become even more so with time. Woods has been stuck alongside Palmer on four since 2005, but the magnitude of the declaration merely added to all the Tigermania.

Could he win this week, Nicklaus was asked? 'I don't know whether he is ready to win yet or not, but he will be your favourite for the next 20 years. If he isn't, there's something wrong.' About that, Nicklaus was spot on.

Woods had faced the media a day earlier, one of only nine players to be invited to the interview room for a formal preview interview. It was quite an honour for an amateur, though that is not a word he would probably use after being constantly rolled out as a professional. The room was as packed as it would be for a champion on Sunday night. 'I'm pleased to say I haven't got lost in the clubhouse like last year,' he said. There was more laughter and a flash of his gleaming smile when he added: 'One thing I forgot about the Masters is all the cameras people can bring to the practice rounds – and they fire them, too.'

The big question on everyone's lips was when he would turn professional. It was a question he was already fed up of answering. 'It does tend to get to you after a while if it keeps coming up repeatedly. But the answer's still the same.' Stanford University, where he was in his second year, was 'awesome' and, in any case, 'I have no place to play yet. I'm not exempt. I have no security.'

When the time was finally right, at the end of the summer, Woods would have no problem finding security or a place to play. In the meantime, Nicklaus was not only being asked about the young amateur's chances of winning, but his own. Ten years on from his dramatic sixth victory at Augusta when he swept past Norman and Seve Ballesteros with a stunning back-nine charge, he arrived having won his eighth major title as a senior at the previous week's Tradition tournament. He played down his chances of winning, though. 'My game felt awfully puny today,' he said after playing with Woods. Others thought he might have a chance. 'I'll bet Jack does,' said Nick Faldo.

This was Nicklaus's 38th appearance at Augusta but he could not accept becoming a ceremonial golfer, as Palmer had. The King, ten years older than the Bear, had been honoured by the city of Augusta with a statue unveiled in the Riverwalk area on the banks of the Savannah River. The inscription on the plaque, entitled 'Arnie's Charge', noted that when in contention 'he wore his determination and concentration just as surely as he wore his smile a few holes back. Once you saw it, you could never forget it. Now, it has been captured forever, for those who remember and for those not fortunate enough to have seen it for themselves.'

Nicklaus did at least contend in the par-three contest, the traditional Masters curtain-raiser on the club's gorgeous nine-hole course that started in 1960, recording his best finish of joint third with Ian Woosnam on 23, four under par. In his prime, Nicklaus used to skip the event to conclude his media duties and rest up for the tournament proper. Nothing to do with the supposed jinx on the winner of the par-three, who has never gone on to don the green jacket in the same week, a curse that persists.

Jay Haas was the victor on this occasion, beating Larry Mize at the second extra hole after they had tied on 22. Haas, with an ace at the 2nd, was one of four players to have a hole-in-one, along with debutant Mark Roe, Ian Baker-Finch (both at the 7th) and Sandy Lyle, at the 9th. He joined Sam Snead and Isao Aoki as the only two-time winners, having won the event as an amateur 20 years earlier. However, by finishing 36th on Sunday, he merely proved again that Wednesday's winner could be ruled out of contention for the green jacket.

He was about the only one. Almost everyone else was in with a chance. 'It's not likely you can pick anybody,' said Davis Love. 'It's whoever gets that magic. You always need to look toward guys who are really playing well.'

Since 1987, when Augusta native Mize shocked Norman, the winners had all come from the top of the game. The only exception to this trend had been Ben Crenshaw in 1995. Crenshaw had won the Masters in 1984 but 11 years later had little form in the run-up to Augusta and even less during the practice rounds. On the Sunday before the tournament, his great mentor Harvey Penick died and on the Wednesday of Masters week Crenshaw and Tom Kite, another of Harvey's 'special boys', returned to Austin, Texas, to act as pallbearers at the funeral.

Love, another player associated with Penick, had actually won the New Orleans tournament on the Sunday he died. This afforded him a last-minute invitation to the Masters and he continued his fine form to finish second – to Crenshaw, who dissolved into tears on the 18th green after completing a one-stroke victory. 'Fate dictated this championship, as it does so many times,' Crenshaw said. 'Someone put their hand on my shoulder this week and guided me through. I had a 15th club in the bag today, and it was Harvey.'

Norman finished three behind Crenshaw in third place but this was not a title he lost, as one report said, 'it was kept from him'. He said at the time: 'Maybe Harvey was up there looking down saying: "Hey, Ben, this one, I'm going to help you do that." Augusta National has a way of sifting out whoever it wants to sift out. Somehow, you have to do something special, as Ben did.'

Would the Australian finally do something special at Augusta? Would he ever win the Masters? That was the theme running through his lengthy pre-tournament press conference but the Shark was as gabby as ever. First up was a question about how he felt about the Masters: great player, great tournament, 'seems like a great mating'. 'Well, I don't know – it hasn't happened yet but you're right, it is the greatest championship around,' Norman began. 'Like I said, there's no other golf tournament anywhere in the world that generates the type of feeling like here at Augusta National. Any golfer, no matter what his stats or position in the world, whether a budding amateur or a professional, we all want to win it. And the guys who have experienced it have known that great feeling winning this tournament gives them and they want to get it back. So everyone has their reason for wanting to win it.'

Could he still win? 'Sure. I don't play golf if I don't think I can win.' Does he believe in karma? 'There's not a situation that I've been under where I haven't been able to experience or pull something out of it. Whether you call that karma or whether you call that self-analysis of a situation, I don't know. But I do believe certain things are meant to happen for you. Sometimes you don't feel like you have a chance to win and, boom, something happens. You get your good breaks and your bad breaks. But I like to feel that things are meant for a reason.'

Now aged 41, was his best golf still ahead of him, Norman was asked? 'I believe my best golf is in my 40s. But I used to believe my best golf was in my 30s. I believe if you just keep yourself halfway fit, you learn so much as time goes by in this game. As I get older, I think my life gets better. I think that gives you greater peace of mind and comfort. I honestly think my best golf will be in my 40s. I really do. It just depends on how far you want to push yourself.'

Is it possible to want something too much? 'I don't think so. I'd rather have that pressure being put on yourself than no pressure at all. That, to me, is a great stimulus. It's just how you approach it within yourself.'

With a bit more luck, a little less bad fortune, how many times did he think he could have won here? 'I don't think like that. I've had many good fortunes in my golfing life. So whether it's sound advice or smart work on my behalf, I don't think like that. My golfing skills have given me a lot to be thankful for on and off the course. My kids are happy and healthy. I've seen a lot of families who aren't happy and healthy, so those type of things I feel blessed for and with. So what happens on the golf course – when you let one get away from you, it's not going to make a bit of difference in your life at all. I've been very lucky in many aspects of my life and I just hope it keeps going that way.'

One more try from the media: 'Surely, it gets to a point when you say, "I've got to win this thing"?' 'No, it doesn't. You guys are missing the point. Yes, there's a lot of things you'd like to do in life that you probably will never, ever get a chance of doing. But you appreciate what you've done. And my career's not over yet.

'You guys are making this sound like this is my last time I'm ever going to get a chance to win in the Masters. But my golfing career is not over. I don't feel like it has to be cast in stone that I have to win the Masters. We all would like to have things we've never had. And, obviously, I haven't won the Masters, I haven't won the US Open, I haven't won the PGA. I'd like to have them all. You just have to chase that elusive rainbow, pot of gold at the end of the rainbow. If you get it one day, you feel a great sense of satisfaction.'

Norman was right, it was not his last chance at seeking his pot of gold at Augusta, or rather, a green jacket. But the magic never happened. He did get to put on a jacket and tie for the now-discontinued International Players Dinner on the Monday night but it is the green variety that is required for the Past Champions Dinner on Tuesday night. Defending champion Crenshaw was the host and served up a Texas barbecue in contrast to Olazábal's paella and tapas the previous year. There were 27 former winners present for the 1996 dinner, including 81-year-old Herman Keiser, who won 50 years earlier in 1946.

Following their duels in 1993, Norman and Faldo had not collided again in the eight major championships since. Both players had tied for fourth at the 1994 US PGA but were out of contention and finished eight strokes behind Nick Price. By dint of also having won the Open at Turnberry a few weeks earlier, the Zimbabwean became the new world number one but his major tally of three stalled there.

No other players had truly established themselves as dominant major contenders, although Colin Montgomerie had managed to lose two playoffs in the previous two years. Perhaps the most significant win around this time came from Ernie Els at the 1994 US Open at Oakmont, where he beat Montgomerie and Loren Roberts in extra holes and Curtis Strange declared the 24-year-old South African was the 'next god of golf'. Els had a good chance to win a second title at the 1995 US PGA, but did not even make the playoff in which Steve Elkington defeated Montgomerie.

Elkington then had the only set of clubs he had used throughout his professional career stolen from his car and his form had dipped, so the winner of the last major was not thought a likely contender at Augusta. The other major champions from an eclectic couple of years were Olazábal, who missed the 1996 Masters while suffering from rheumatoid polyarthritis, Crenshaw, who was just as out of form as the year before, Corey Pavin and John Daly, who had beaten Costantino Rocca in a playoff to win the 1995 Open at St Andrews.

Faldo was no better than 24th in any of the majors in 1995 and while Norman lost out to Pavin at the US Open at Shinnecock Hills, he won the money list on the PGA Tour for only the second time in his career and regained the world number one crown from his friend Price. Bookmakers in Las Vegas were quoting Norman as the narrow favourite for the 1996 Masters but in London Fred Couples led the betting following his victory at the Players Championship.

For many years until 2006, the Players was the anchor event of the Florida swing of tournaments in March and the main warm-up event for the Masters, played two or three weeks earlier. Defying years of back problems since winning the Masters in 1992, Couples charged to victory at Sawgrass with an eagle at the 16th hole thanks to an approach shot that bounced the right way off the bank by the water and a 30-foot putt. He then holed from 25 feet for a birdie on the island green of the 17th hole. The crowd were going nuts and Montgomerie, who had been leading, had little chance once his second at the 16th splashed into the lake.

However, Montgomerie, who had already won the first three of his incredible seven-in-a-row order of merit titles on the European Tour, was now second on the world rankings, a career high. After a winter in his garage-turned-gym, a slimmed down version of the Scot emerged after a long winter's break to win his first event of the year in Dubai in March, in the process hitting his famous shot with a driver from the fairway over the water to the 18th green. His record at Augusta was poor, but he was so heavily backed with British bookmakers on the eve of the Masters that he started as the co-favourite with Couples.

Adding to the sense that anyone could win was the fact that four of the last five winners on the PGA Tour had been first-timers. Just at the time of the season when all the top players were playing most weeks, Tim Herron, Paul Goydos, Scott McCarron and Paul

Stankowski, who was the sixth alternate for the last tournament prior to the Masters in Atlanta and was a winner on the second-tier Nike Tour the week before that, had all sprung surprise victories and booked their first trips to Augusta in the process.

Nicklaus said: 'When Snead and Hogan were in their prime, you looked at five or six players to win the tournament. When I was in my prime, there were about ten players, maybe a few more. Today, you look at 30 or 40 players. But when it gets down to it on Sunday, you're going to have the top ones there. You always do. That is what makes it such a great tournament.'

With so many potential winners to choose from, a survey of golf writers' picks in the *Augusta Chronicle* produced 11 different nominations. Norman and Faldo received only one pick each. Montgomerie, Couples, Love and Daly had two each, while Phil Mickelson and Tom Lehman led the way with three each. Lehman was not a bad shout after becoming a regular contender in majors, though he would have to wait a few more months for his breakthrough win at the Open at Lytham. Mickelson was perhaps the form player of the early part of the American season, having won twice, at Tucson and Phoenix, but the 25-year-old had yet to win east of the Mississippi.

Love was the pick of a *Golf World* (US) magazine article which ruled out contenders on the basis of, for example, being an amateur (had never won the Masters); the defending champion (only happened twice); anyone older than 46 (the age at which Nicklaus won in 1986); Augusta debutants (only Fuzzy Zoeller in 1979 had won on his first appearance in modern times); and anyone who had waited longer than the 14 appearances it took Billy Casper to win in 1970. Among those dispatched were Norman (16th appearance), Strange (20th) and Kite (23rd), and with other categories applied, eventually they got down to a final four that comprised Langer, Faldo, Mickelson and Love. They gave the final nod to

Love, who turned 32 on the Saturday of the 1996 Masters, exactly matching the average age of the 59 previous Masters champions. Langer, in fact, had suffered a shoulder injury while playing volleyball in the garden with his children and had not quite recovered full fitness.

In honour of Nicklaus's win ten years earlier, when the Bear had been inspired by an infamous comment in the *Atlanta Journal-Constitution* by Tom McCollister that he was 'gone, done, doesn't have the game any more', a columnist for the *Augusta Chronicle* handicapped the 1996 Masters field in a similar style. Norman: 'When's the last time this guy made a cut anyway? Nice hat, though.' Faldo: 'Here's a little-known Masters fact for you: No player with a college-age girlfriend has ever won the tournament. At least, none that we know of.'

Faldo was in the process of getting divorced from his second wife Gill after his affair with University of Arizona student Brenna Cepelak had become public the previous autumn. He had received the full tabloid treatment, which meant he was even more wary than usual when appearing at his press conference at 9.30 a.m. on Tuesday. Dan Yates, the brother of former British Amateur champion Charlie Yates and the Augusta member who was moderating the interview, opened up in typical fashion by saying: 'Okay, Nick, if you'll say what's on your mind and then they'll have a go at you.'

'That's the problem,' Faldo responded. 'Fire away.' As a player in his prime, as opposed to once he went to the commentary box, Faldo was never exactly expansive in a Normanesque fashion with a microphone in front of him. But there were a few lines of note, including the news that the shoulder that bothered him when he missed the cut at the Players Championship was now fine. 'It was just tight for a few days and then got progressively better,' he reported. 'I feel I've been playing nicely the last couple of months and just sort of waiting for something to happen; or waiting for this week, one or the other. I'm quite happy with most of my game.'

When asked about Norman missing his last two cuts in a row, Faldo was ready with a quip. 'Write him off quick,' he said. 'I think that's the end of him, really. He's gone.'

On whether his desire was as strong as ever, Faldo said: 'Oh, yeah. My desire's always the same with the majors. Gosh, we've been thinking about them, you know, planning for this for six months since the PGA. You start thinking and working out your game plan and everything. So you're certainly conscious of the majors. They're the most important ones. That's what I'm aiming for, so I've still got the desire for them.'

On any changes to the Augusta National course: 'Everything's been really similar here for the last five or six years. It's the same set-up. The course just gets better and better. The condition is incredible.' In fact, there was one change. Since 1989 the tributary of Rae's Creek that runs in front of the 13th green had a high water level, meaning attempts at recovery shots like Curtis Strange's in the final round in 1985 were not possible. The water level had now been reduced to again expose more of the banks and rocks in the stream.

Finally, Faldo was asked whether the Masters was the severest test in golf? 'Yeah, I think so,' he said. 'It becomes the feel factor. You can't just blast in and miss a green and get up and down. You can't do that here. If you're nervous and under pressure, you've still got to hit great shots all the time. You've got to keep the ball in the right position. If you don't, you've got to have the touch to get up and down or whatever. That's where it ends up a hard test.'

The final round of the 1996 Masters was already proving a hard test for Norman. He kept getting out of position and though his short game had saved him at the 2nd hole, it had not at the 1st. But it had been his short game that had won him his last tournament, the Doral-Ryder Open just over a month earlier. He took only 101 putts for the week and got up and down whenever required but his work on and around the greens covered up some sloppy play elsewhere.

Partly this was down to a driver whose face caved in when he went out to complete the last few holes of his third round on Sunday morning. It needed replacing so his wife Laura hopped on a helicopter with a spare and flew from their home in Jupiter Island down to Miami in time for the final round. Norman also took the time between rounds to have his first session with Harmon since the previous August. 'Things tend to drift away over a period of time when you haven't seen your coach,' he said. 'There are a couple of little faults I've got back in my game.'

Overall, Norman was pleased. 'I didn't hit the ball as crisply as I'd like but winning when you are not on full song is a very positive confidence-booster.' There were even signs that the Shark's go-for-broke attitude was softening. Three ahead playing the last, he made a safe bogey rather than risk anything worse. The year before at the same tournament he had been leading by one over Faldo when he drove into the rough at Doral's 18th and then hooked a six-iron into the water to hand the title to the Englishman. It was Faldo's last win before the 1996 Masters.

The 3rd hole at Augusta is a great short par-four and one of the scariest on the course, according to Johnny Miller. It is one of the holes that has changed least over the years. While it plays at 350 yards now, it used to be recorded at 360 yards. More players now try to drive the green, or leave just a short wedge approach, but back then it was probably a long-iron followed by a short-iron for the second. Faldo hit a two-iron off the tee and a wedge to the middle of the green, 12 feet from the hole, which was cut in the neck on the left of the green. Attacking this pin position leaves little margin for error between coming up short, when the ball will roll off the shelf and all the way down the fairway, and going over the back, which is not clever either.

Just as he did at the 2nd hole, albeit with a much shorter club, Norman went over the green. But not by much. He was able to chip down to three feet and safely made his par. Faldo missed his birdie putt on the high side but tapped in for a score that was two shots better than his double bogey 24 hours earlier. So the hole was halved in pars; Norman still led by five strokes but already one of the two was beginning to look more comfortable than the other – and it wasn't the leader.

Flowering Crab Apple

Hole 4
Yards 205; Par 3

At start	Hole	1	2	3	4	5	6	7	8	9	Out	Status
	Par	4	5	4	3	4	3	4	5	4	36	
-13	G. Norman	5	4	4	4							-12
-7	N. Faldo	4	4	4	3							-8

I N *THE WAY OF THE SHARK*, Greg Norman wrote of his start to the final round of the 1996 Masters: 'Unfortunately I sensed early in the round that things weren't quite right. My hands didn't feel comfortable. My distance was a bit off. And my accuracy on the first few holes left a lot to be desired. "Boy, it's going to be a tough day," I said to my caddie, Tony Navarro. I just could not feel what I had felt over the previous three days. And the more I tried to get that feeling back, the more it went away.'

This was becoming increasingly apparent at the 4th hole, a tricky par-three that played as the most difficult hole over the course of the 1996 tournament. These days the players exit the 3rd green and turn right, up the hill into the trees as it plays a whopping 240 yards. Back then, the 4th tee was just behind the 3rd green so in a matter of moments Nick Faldo was preparing to take his tee shot. The hole plays over a valley to a two-tiered green perched on a ridge.

One bunker guards the left side of the green, another cuts into the front right of the green. The cup for the fourth round was cut on the right side of the top tier. Faldo hit a four-iron and finished on the back left of the green, 30 feet from the hole.

Norman, true to his go-for-it nature, aimed straight at the flag but his ball came up short. The shot was struck solidly but perhaps there was a touch of breeze against him, high up among the pines. Another couple of feet and he would have made the green. Instead, the ball pitched into the bank of the bunker and rolled back into the sand. It was a sickening blow. 'No one was more shocked than Norman,' reported the 1996 *Masters Annual*. 'He recoiled as if he had been shot in the chest, then bent forward, his hands on his knees. It was a moment so poignant, it would become the cover of *Sports Illustrated*.'

His bunker shot was poor. It only just came out of the bunker and left him with an 18-foot putt for a par, which came up a couple of inches shy of the hole. A bogey four. Faldo putted down to two and a half feet and stroked that in for a par; the lead was now down to four strokes for the first time since the 14th hole on Saturday.

This was Norman's 60th round in the Masters. His third consecutive bogey at the 4th hole meant that over his career at Augusta on the 3rd and 4th holes combined, he was 30 over par. In this year's tournament, he had only managed to make a par at the 4th in the opening round, on a day when the hole yielded not a single birdie. He had hit a four-iron into the bunker on the left of the green, recovered to eight feet and holed an important par putt. It was a shot saved and had helped the Shark make a steady start to what would turn into an opening 63.

In his press conference after equalling Nick Price's course record on the first day, Norman opened by saying: 'It must have been the barbecue chicken I had last night, that is all I can say, the wonderful Golf Writers barbecue. That is what set it all up.' Norman had received the 1995 male player of the year award from the Golf Writers Association of America. It was the second time he had won the award, the first being in 1986. In another lengthy question and answer session with the press, Norman did not mention any back issues, only stating in passing that his trainer had arrived that morning: 'One of those little things that help you relax and get you going.'

In *The Way of the Shark*, Norman wrote: 'On Wednesday morning, the day before the tournament began, I woke up with terrible back pain. On the driving range, I could hardly take the club back, so I cancelled my practice round. I was very frustrated. "Why now?" I asked myself. "Why now of all times?"

'Later that morning there was a knock at my door. Fred Couples, whom I'd seen on the practice range, had sent over his back therapist to help me. And help me he did, because the next morning I felt great. As a matter of fact, I made nine birdies on my way to a course-record 63 later that day.'

It was quite a transformation from the player who missed the cut in his last two events, rated his game at seven out of ten in his Tuesday press conference and had been forced to miss his last practice round on Wednesday due to back pain. 'I felt comfortable when I woke up this morning,' he said. 'I felt good. I felt like I was very relaxed and in control, and feeling like if I took that to the golf course that I'd have a good day.

'I didn't expect to go out there and shoot a 63, of course, but the way I played the first five holes basically set up the rest of my day. When I got through the 6th hole, I just said keep swinging the way you're swinging and keep the momentum going that you've built up and take advantage with the good shots that you can hit, and things happened for me on the back nine.'

Price had set the record of 63 in the third round in 1986,

beating the previous record of 64, first scored by Lloyd Mangrum in the opening round in 1940. Price started out with a bogey, then made ten birdies in the next 15 holes, including four in a row from the 10th to the 13th. He hit 16 greens in regulation and had 25 putts. This was only his second appearance in the Masters, after missing the cut on his debut two years earlier, and came after an opening 79.

It helped the Zimbabwean to his best Masters finish of fifth but he never really found the Augusta magic again. 'I knew Nick Price had the course record,' Norman said. 'Of course, when your best friend's got something, he's always going to tell you he's got it, right? But, no, I wasn't thinking about the course record at all out there.'

Norman also hit 16 greens in regulation, getting up and down from bunkers on the two occasions he did not, and had 27 putts. He had parred each of the first six holes and birdied the next three, then made six birdies in the last nine holes, coming home in 30, one outside Mark Calcavecchia's record for the back nine from 1992. He rated his performance as nine out of ten and ranked the round alongside his closing 64 to win the Open at Sandwich in 1993 and the 63 he scored at Turnberry on the way to winning the 1986 Open. This was the 18th time a 63 had been scored in a major championship but Norman was the first to achieve the feat twice, something only Vijay Singh has subsequently matched.

Although Norman had scored a 64 at Augusta in the final round in 1988, only once had he broken 70 on an opening day – a 69 on his debut in 1981. 'I come in every year consciously wanting to get off to a good start,' Norman said when asked about his slow starts in the Masters. 'It's just one of those things where I just let it flow.' Earlier in the week during the 1996 tournament, he had hit a stack of four-irons on the practice range under the eye of Butch Harmon. 'All we worked on was synchronising my lower body turn,' he said. He had been mentally practising that while fishing on his boat the previous week.

After the back scare on Wednesday, he had a good workout with his trainer the next morning, a fruitful session with Harmon on the range and was ready to go for his 2 p.m. tee time alongside the 1979 champion Fuzzy Zoeller. 'I was relaxed and everything clicked into place,' Norman said. 'I got my speed back in my body and was hitting it longer than on Tuesday, when I played with Tiger and I felt like you [referring to the hacks he was talking to and golfing hackers in general] would be out there with me. Tiger was getting it by me about 50 or 60 yards. But this morning, everything was back in sync. Literally overnight it came back. I crushed one and knew I was ready to play.'

At that time, the Masters paired players in twoballs for all four rounds, re-pairing in score order for the second round, as well as for the third and fourth rounds as is usual today. Norman and Zoeller were one of the featured pairings that would get most of the late-afternoon television coverage. It was a warm and sunny day, very pleasant, with just enough breeze to make players think, while the greens were already firming up. Norman, wearing a grey sleeveless cardigan and his black wide-brimmed hat, missed birdie chances from nine feet at the 3rd and ten feet at the 5th but the sand save at the 4th helped him post six consecutive pars, which is easier said than done. The danger of those holes was generally unappreciated by the wider viewing audience since they were rarely shown on television back then.

'I think the front nine is toughest to score well on,' Norman said. 'The hardest second shot we have is into the 5th green. The hardest par-three is the 4th hole. The hardest nine-iron shot we had for the whole day was into 3. People don't get to see those kinds of things but we're churning our guts out on those holes because if you don't get a good start, you're going to have a hard time getting into the tournament.'

Norman suddenly sparked into life by holing a ten-footer on the 7th green, then made another for his four at the 8th and a 14-footer at the 9th to turn in 33. 'When you get onto the type of roll I got onto today, it feels very comfortable. Let the reins of the horses go and let them run as fast as they want to run. That is what I did today. I wanted to get as much under par as I could. I didn't care if I got into the lead or not.'

At the 10th, Norman saved par from a bunker for the second time in the round. At the 11th, he had an 18-footer for birdie that lipped out. 'I hit a putt both Fuzzy and I couldn't believe,' Norman said. 'The ball just defied gravity when it went over the edge of the hole.' He got back on a roll at the next when he hit an eight-iron to six feet at the treacherous par-three for the first of four birdies in a row.

At the par-five 13th he found the green in two with a drive and a three-iron and two-putted from 40 feet. At the 14th, his three-wood from the tee was pulled and hit a pine tree. The ball rebounded into the fairway but left him a blind approach shot of 220 yards. He hit a four-iron which pitched 15 yards short of the green, one of the most highly contoured on the course. The ball scooted forward off a downslope, ran up the front of the green and then started taking the left-to-right break in such a manner that it finished no more than three feet from the hole. All Norman could do was listen. 'It was the gallery that told me I'd hit it close,' he said. Long before he crested the rise in the fairway and could see the green, all the spectators were standing up and applauding.

Norman was now six under for the day but he was not finished. His fourth birdie on the trot might have been an eagle at the 15th. He only needed a seven-iron for his second at the par-five and he had an 18-footer for a three. He was ready to chase after the putt but when it swerved off-line at the last minute, he ended up on his knees. 'I hit it right on the pitch mark I wanted to hit and four feet out I thought I'd made it. That is why I straightened up. I was ready to go for a walk. Then all of a sudden, it just kind of veered a little to the right.'

He two-putted at the 16th, where the pin was in a tricky spot that caught out plenty of others, and then he finished in style by making a 10-footer at the 17th and a 24-footer at the last. On the 18th green, the hole was close to where it was when Price made his 63. From a similar line, back right of the green, but from around 30 feet, Price saw his birdie putt for a 62 hit the hole and spin out back towards him. Norman's only problem with his putt came as he looked at the line and noticed a hot air balloon rising in the distance. No matter, he refocused and in the putt went.

Afterwards, he was asked: 'What does an opening round like this do for your mind-set for the rest of the week? Do you think I still have to keep attacking or...' Norman cut in with his reply: 'Well, I didn't attack today. I played the way I wanted to play. You just wake up tomorrow and keep the momentum going. You obviously know you are not going to shoot four 63s. It would be nice but it would be a very tall order to do. You don't let it get away from you and get too excited about it. I'm happy and excited but there's a long way to go.'

After Norman had talked about visualising his swing while out fishing, there was an obvious follow-up and it turned out to be the last question of the press conference. 'Greg, you've visualised the swing. How many times have you visualised putting on the green jacket?' Answer: 'I don't know. Probably a few.'

The opening day of the 60th Masters began as tradition demands, or at least as most have since 1963, with the ceremonial tee shots by a handful of honorary starters. Gene Sarazen and Byron Nelson had performed the duty since 1981 and Sam Snead joined them in 1984. The sign by the 1st tee showed not their caddie numbers but their ages: Sarazen 94, Nelson 84 and Snead 83. Sarazen was not being taken in by all the hype about 20-year-old amateur Tiger Woods. 'When I was 20,' he said, 'I won the US Open and the US PGA Championship.' At Augusta, they keep records even for the honorary starters and Sarazen had overtaken Fred McLeod as the oldest ever. He tried to stop earlier, complaining to an Augusta chairman that he had difficulty swinging the club, only to be told: 'People don't care how you swing, they just want to see you are still alive.' He would get to perform the task for three more years, while Nelson continued until 2001 and Snead until a year later.

These days another of golf's great triumvirates, the Big Three themselves, Arnold Palmer, Jack Nicklaus and Gary Player, perform the task. But back in 1996, they were all playing for real and Palmer's 74 was his best score for 12 years, which was how long it was since he had last made the cut. Player was on 73 and, on the heels of his Senior Tour victory at the Tradition, Nicklaus had a 70. His score included only 23 putts, the lowest mark of the day, but the Bear was not happy with his driving. 'It wasn't a very hard day to play golf but I didn't take advantage of the par-fives.'

It was the sort of day in golfing heaven when the roars rattled around the cathedral of pines. They all sound different, echoing back up the hill towards the clubhouse, depending on who is involved. You could feel the love for Palmer but Nicklaus always got the loudest roars. Norman recreated some noise on this afternoon, but those following Fred Couples were unusually quiet as the Players champion and pre-tournament favourite started with a 78. Couples was already 15 strokes behind and after the round his fiancée Tawnya Dodds, in reference to his generosity in offering his back therapist to the leader, remarked: 'You picked one hell of a time to make Greg Norman feel like a million bucks.'

Phil Mickelson was already building a fan club and one of the biggest cheers of the day came when he hit a six-iron to two feet at the final hole. He tapped in for a seven-under 65, another record score, the lowest ever by a left-hander in any major, beating the previous mark of 66 first scored by Bob Charles. He held the clubhouse lead until Norman posted nine under. This was only Mickelson's fourth appearance in the Masters but the patrons were already getting to know, and appreciate, his attacking style of golf and he was getting to know, and appreciate, when and how to attack Augusta.

'When I first came here,' he said, 'I felt like I should be firing at every pin. I've picked up little things over time. Now I know firing at a pin might mean being eight feet away so that I have an uphill putt.' An example of how easy it is to get out of position came at the 4th. He missed the green in the bunker on the left and although he came out to four feet it was a downhill putt. With the swiftness of the greens, he tried to dribble it in but it wandered off line for his only bogey of the round.

Like Norman, Mickelson came home in 30 with five birdies in the last six holes. He made a four at the 15th with help from a practice round the previous day when Ben Crenshaw had shown him how some putts on that green curve in the opposite direction to that in which they appear to break. 'I'm glad I helped somebody today,' said the defending champion after a 77 in which the normally supreme putter took 32 blows on the greens. Mickelson thought he was quite fortunate with his score. 'It was deceptive,' he said. 'The golf course is not playing to a seven-under round. I felt if I could shoot one, two, three under par, it was going to be a good round. I had a couple of opportunities where the ball ended up below the hole and I was able to be aggressive. It was a fortunate round.'

Norman must have been even more fortunate but there were plenty of high scores to prove conditions were hardly easy. As well as the 78 by Couples and the 77 by Crenshaw, there was a 76 for the winner of the previous major, Steve Elkington, and 75s by Tom Lehman, Corey Pavin and Woods. Tom Watson also had a 75 but had seemed on course for something better until a five-putt on the 16th green. The hole was cut in a diabolical spot, back right of the green just off a ridge and Watson twice knocked putts past the hole from the upper terrace all the way down to the front of the green.

Bob Tway and Scott Hoch scored 67s, while Lee Janzen was on 68. Alongside Nick Faldo on 69 was his compatriot, David Gilford, along with Singh, Scott Simpson and Brad Faxon. With Nicklaus on 70 were Ray Floyd, Jay Haas and Paul Azinger, who was still regaining form and consistency after being treated for lymphoma in the shoulder following his victory at the 1993 US PGA.

Frank Nobilo, who had missed a number of weeks earlier in the season with back problems, opened with a 71 having played the first two holes on his own. Peter Jacobsen, his intended playing partner, withdrew with sore ribs just before their tee time. A marker was found for Nobilo for the last 16 holes in the form of Jim Holtgrieve, the former US Mid-Amateur champion, and future Walker Cup-winning captain in 2013 at National Golf Links. Stopping by to thank Will Nicholson, chairman of Augusta's competitions committee, for some practice round tickets, Holtgrieve was asked if he had his clubs with him and fancied a game. Having retrieved them from his car, and dashed to the 3rd tee, he played the last 16 holes in two over, only one shot worse than Nobilo.

Tway's form had dipped since beating Norman at Inverness in 1986 but his confidence was finally returning. 'In pursuit of getting better, I changed a few things and got worse,' he said. The Oklahoman spent part of his growing up in Georgia and had loved the Masters ever since. It did not particularly love him, though his reward for a first appearance in five years was his best ever round of five under, helped by three birdies at Amen Corner (the picturesque part of the course that includes the 11th green, the short 12th hole and the 13th tee).

Hoch finished with three birdies in the last four holes and could have gone even lower had three successive chances on the front nine not lipped out. But he also would have been the Masters champion in 1989 had not his tiny putt for victory at the first extra hole of the playoff not lipped out, too. Instead, Faldo went on to win his first green jacket at the next hole.

For his opening round of the 1996 Masters, Faldo was paired with the 1995 Open champion John Daly. With Crenshaw and Woods in the pairing immediately in front, a lot of spectators were scurrying between the two groups trying to see which of the two big-hitters was actually the longer. At the 400-yard 17th, Woods hit a drive of 345 yards, Daly then stood up and hit one of 355 yards, though he would finish with a double bogey at the 18th for a 71. 'It was good, fine,' Faldo said of playing with the 'Wild Thing'. 'I think the Augusta crowd was very good.'

In truth, Faldo could not have cared less about the commotion around him. His 69 was his best opening score since his first Masters win. He holed from eight feet at the 3rd for the first of four birdies, hit a wedge to a foot at the 8th, got up and down at the 13th and hit a seven-iron to eight feet for a rare two at the 16th hole, where Watson had suffered his five-putt, and Player, Singh and Gilford all took four putts. Faldo's only real blemish was three-putting the 14th green. 'I had a lot of good chances,' he said, 'swung well and hit the ball where it was intended. I played nicely.'

Of the conditions, which were expected to stay dry throughout the week, Faldo said: 'It's the first time I've seen Augusta when it's dry on Monday, Tuesday and Wednesday. Normally, it's wet on the greens and the ball stops. It's the first time we've had them dry and we know what we are in for with the weather forecast. It's perfect for what they want. Just give that grass a drink, and that's all it's going to get. So the greens are going to be quick.'

Faldo added: 'If it gets firmer and firmer, you're going to have to play very safe, cagey, or whatever you want to call it. I call it smart, aggressive, defensive. You've just got to land it in the right spots and try and pick them off when you have a chance.'

After four holes of the final round on Sunday, Faldo was finding the right spots more often than not. Norman, less so.

Magnolia

Hole 5
Yards 435; Par 4

At start	Hole	1	2	3	4	5	6	7	8	9	Out	Status
	Par	4	5	4	3	4	3	4	5	4	36	
−13	G. Norman	5	4	4	4	4						−12
−7	N. Faldo	4	4	4	3	5						−7

G OLF TOURNAMENTS, particularly the major championships, are like marathons. Greg Norman sprinted clear of the field early in the 60th Masters and for two days backed up his record start. But by the time he reached the 5th hole on Sunday there were signs he was beginning to flag. It was Nick Faldo who would put in the sprint finish. 'Everyone knows the tape is at the end of the 72 holes,' said the Englishman.

Over the last four decades, scoring a 63 in a major has been some help in winning a championship, but not that much. At Oak Hill in the 2013 US PGA, Jason Dufner produced the 26th occurrence of a 63 in major championship history but became only the sixth player to go on to win. Johnny Miller was the first to do so, in the final round of the US Open at Oakmont in 1973. He started six strokes off the lead but won by one from John Schlee, by two from Tom Weiskopf and by three from Jack Nicklaus, Arnold Palmer and Gary Player. Three other players have scored a 63 in the final round of a major, but none of them ended up as the champion either.

Miller had been intent on a quick getaway from the tournament but a swift start, with four birdies at the first four holes, put him right into contention. He produced nine birdies, many from stunning approaches to only a few feet from the hole, and had only one bogey, from a three-putt at the 8th, and parred the last three holes on his way to a remarkable victory. Oakmont's fearsome greens were holding after being saturated by rain and even at the time some critics could not quite put the blond Californian's round ahead of the likes of Ben Hogan's 67 at Oakland Hills in 1951 – 'I brought this monster to its knees' – or Palmer's charging 65 at Cherry Hills in 1960 as the best round in US Open history. But the fact remains that no one has beaten his score since in any major.

Bruce Crampton, a tough Australian who took over from Peter Thomson as the country's best player, was the next to score 63, in the second round of the US PGA Championship at Firestone in 1975. An eagle, six birdies and a bogey gave him the halfway lead. 'The only thing missing from my career is a major title,' he said. But he was overhauled by Nicklaus at the weekend. Crampton finished second for the fourth and last time in the majors, but on each occasion he was second to Nicklaus. 'We all suffer from human deficiencies,' Crampton said. 'Jack just suffers from fewer of them.'

Mark Hayes produced the first 63 in the Open at Turnberry in 1977, lowering the championship record from 65, which was first scored by Henry Cotton at Sandwich in 1934. Meanwhile, the only time two 63s have been scored in the same round came on the opening day of the 1980 US Open at Baltusrol. Tom Weiskopf led the way before he was matched by Nicklaus a few moments later. Then they went their separate ways. Weiskopf added rounds of 75, 76 and 75 to finish 37th, while Nicklaus followed up with rounds of 71, 70 and 69 to beat Isao Aoki by two strokes. The Japanese player was in the form of his life and a month later he also scored a 63 in the third round of the Open at Muirfield, but to no avail as Tom Watson took the title.

As well as Miller, Nicklaus and Dufner, the other players to have scored a 63 and go on to win are Ray Floyd, at the 1982 US PGA at Southern Hills, where his record-tying round came on the first day, Norman at the 1986 Open at Turnberry and Tiger Woods at Southern Hills for the 2007 US PGA. Like Dufner, Norman and Woods both made their scores in the second round, which has seen more 63s than any other round.

Augusta National has still only seen two 63s in its history and, much to their regret, neither Nick Price in 1986 nor Norman in 1996 ended up as the winner. 'The big thing is I would trade that round for a green jacket in a heartbeat,' Price told the *Augusta Chronicle* recently. 'It's always nice to have a course record at a very nice golf course and a major championship, but in hindsight it's not something that's going to enhance my career.'

Price added: 'One of the things I'm most proud of is that I did it with a wooden driver. That's not to take anything away from Greg's 63, but I think he shot his in '96, ten years later, so technology in drivers had changed considerably. I'd like to think there would be an asterisk on mine for using medieval clubs.' Equipment improvements, better strength and fitness from the players and a more scientific approach to coaching all suggest scoring should be getting lower. And it is, as an average, but 63 still stands as a barrier or, indeed, curse.

On the other hand, courses are getting longer and tougher, especially for majors. Augusta has had two sizeable stretches in the last decade or so, while more trees and some semi-rough have also increased the degree of difficulty. Narrow fairways and serious rough of the thick and long variety is often employed liberally at the venues of the other majors in an attempt to keep scoring values in tune with the recent past.

'Majors are set up so difficult,' Dufner said at Oak Hill. 'It's just hard to shoot a 62. Even on some of the set-ups we have on tour, you don't see many guys shooting 62 or lower. There are just not that many out there. Being in a major championship, how much pressure there is playing in those, it's just a really difficult thing to do.'

'Every guy on Tour knows about 63s,' Miller told *Sports Illustrated Golf Plus*. 'There is a historical barrier there. The more you think about it, the harder it is to do.' Thinking back to his own 63, Miller added: 'It's not like I ran the table, chipped in, holed bunker shots and made 60-foot putts. It was sort of an easy 63. It can be done, is what I'm trying to say. It's just hard to get to 62 under the pressure of a major. Guys get close, maybe get to six under par through 12 holes and then sort of drop anchor.'

Dufner had a golden chance to be the first to score a 62 when he gave himself a 12-footer up the hill on the final green at Oak Hill. He did not put the most positive stroke on the putt and left it two and a half feet short, almost missing that one for the 63. There have been many chances of a 62 over the years. Steve Stricker missed a ten-footer on the last green at the end of his first round at the Atlanta Athletic Club in 2011. Woods lipped out a putt that seemed destined to go in when he made his 63 at Southern Hills in 2007. Price's putt for a 62 at Augusta in 1996 did a complete horseshoe.

No one had a better chance of a 62 than Nicklaus at Baltusrol in 1980. He had a three-footer for a birdie at the last and allowed too much break. But there were also two occasions when a player came to the last needing only a *par* to complete a 62, and instead made a bogey. Both instances were at Turnberry. Hayes drove into a bunker at the 18th and made a five in 1977 while in 1986 Norman had a 28-footer for a 61 and three-putted. Norman's Turnberry round is unique in that it contained no less than three bogeys.

Norman made his debut in the majors at Turnberry in 1977, missing the cut. It was the first time the Ayrshire course, perhaps the most scenic on the Open rota, had hosted the game's oldest championship. It was quite an introduction, hot and dry for the week and a famous climax, the 'Duel in the Sun', in which Watson beat Nicklaus by a stroke at the final hole.

When everyone returned nine years later it was very different. After a hot Monday, the rest of the week was wet, cold and windy – often all three at once – while instead of a browned and burnt-off links, the fairways were narrow and lined with thick rough thanks to a rampant spring growing season.

Norman arrived having lost the first two majors of the year after leading each with a round to play. If anything, the conditions helped to distract his thoughts from his misfortunes and left him in the same boat as everyone else. There would not be such a cacophony of moaning about the course set-up again until Carnoustie in 1999. Nicklaus said in 1986 that it would be the 'Survival Open'. On the first day, when a cold wind sprang up, Ian Woosnam was the only player to match the par of 70, and was the only player to birdie the 14th, the Welshman blasting a driver and a one-iron onto a green that most could not reach. Norman opened with a 74, which left him tied for 16th place, perfectly respectable.

The next day Norman went to the 1st tee repeating a mantra of 'blue skies and 65'. He was wrong on both counts, although at least the wind had calmed down a bit and he quickly got into his stride with birdies at the 2nd, 3rd and 4th holes. He three-putted from short of the 5th green for a bogey but eagled the 7th from 20 feet before another bogey at the 8th. Then he really set the pace. At the 10th he hit his approach to five feet, hit it to a foot on the 11th, three feet on the 14th and holed from eight feet on the 16th. By now he had picked up a sizeable gallery who were cheering him on and Norman admitted they had kept him going. When he hit a five-iron to 12 feet on the par-five 17th he thought he could get home with a 60. He two-putted there for his eighth birdie of the day and when he found the green at the last all he was thinking about was a 61.

'I really want this one, Pete,' Norman said to his caddie, Pete Bender. 'I really want a 61.' His first putt was from 28 feet and there was no way it was going to be short. He raced it far enough past to miss the one back. It meant a closing bogey and a 63, tying the Open and major records. 'I was just trying to shoot the lowest score I could,' he said. 'That's the type of person I am. I totally misjudged the speed of the putt at the last.' He added: 'I don't want people to think the score I shot today makes the course easy. It still played tough, just not brutal like yesterday.'

Even though Turnberry had produced a thrilling contest between two of the greatest golfers in the world in 1977, there were suspicions that the course was too easy to host the Open. A second score of 63 in two stagings added to the ammunition but it is never as simple as saying low scores equate to easy course. If everyone is scoring low, then, yes. But the average score on the day that Hayes made his 63 in 1977 was 74.29 and on the day Norman returned his 63 was 74.07. While Watson and Nicklaus finished at 12 under and 11 under respectively, only one other player beat par in 1977, Hubert Green on one under. He finished third and said: 'I won the other tournament.' Norman's winning score in 1986 turned out to be level par.

Back on the second day, the next best score was a 67 from Japan's Tommy Nakajima. Norman had gone from four behind the leader to two strokes in front of Yorkshire's Gordon J. Brand, with Nakajima and Faldo tying for third place, the latter having returned steady efforts of 71 and 70 in contrast to Norman's extreme yo-yoing. The Australian's performance was off in the other direction again on Saturday but then the weather had got really nasty, driving rain completing a miserable picture for the leaders late in the day. Norman hung on to the lead after a 74 but was only one ahead of Nakajima, who had a 71, and three ahead of Woosnam, after his second 70 of the week, and Brand, who had a 75.

That night, the third time in a row that he had held the lead in a major championship with 18 holes to play, Norman pondered what was to come while at dinner in the hotel. Several players wished him well but the most meaningful interaction came when Nicklaus pulled up a chair and told him: 'Greg, no one in the world wants you to win the tournament more than I do. You deserve to win.' Norman said later: 'When the greatest golfer the world has ever known tells you something like that it makes you feel very special.' Nicklaus also suggested he should be aware of the pressure of his grip during the final round. A couple of months later Norman 'thanked' Nicklaus for his advice by holing a 60-footer for an eagle at the 35th on the way to winning their semi-final of the World Match Play by one hole.

After a restless night, Norman was determined to keep himself on edge the next day, but even though Nakajima took a double bogey at the 1st and it was not long before he had a five-stroke lead, he became too tense. He hit a low snap-hook off the 7th tee and Bender, an experienced caddie whose previous bosses included none other than Nicklaus, knew he had to intervene. He got Norman to slow down, walk at the pace his caddie was setting, rather than charging off down the fairway as usual. He told a few jokes and added: 'You're the best player here and you'll win this golf tournament but you've got to take time and enjoy it. Don't rush it, don't be nervous. I'm here to help.' At the 8th, Norman hit a four-iron to eight feet and settled down.

His only miscue after that was to leak his drive at the 14th into the rough but his next with a seven-iron hit the flagstick. He was able to enjoy the walk up the 18th fairway, at least after escaping the then traditional stampede of spectators in front of the final green. With a 69 he won by five strokes from Brand, six from Woosnam and Bernhard Langer, and seven from Faldo. Seve Ballesteros was tied for eighth after a closing 64.

'Everybody knows how much I wanted to win a major,' Norman said. 'Everyone is always saying, "Come on, Greggy, you can do it," and even if you know you can, it starts to get you down. You get a monkey on your back.' Until the moment the claret jug was placed in his hands, Norman still feared the worst. 'I just knew somebody was going to walk up and say, "Gee, I'm sorry, Greg, but we can't give you this after all." I was petrified that I might have signed the card wrong or put down my nine-hole score in the box for the 9th hole.' Given his near misses in recent times it was an understandable anxiety. And given how the next two majors were snatched away from him – by Bob Tway at the US PGA the following month, by Larry Mize at Augusta the following April – it was a spooky premonition.

For the first time since before Palmer led an American resurgence at the Open in the early 1960s, there had been three non-American winners in a row, with Norman following Ballesteros and Sandy Lyle, and Faldo and Seve later extending the run to five – the US domination of the game was no longer as strong as it once was. With the world rankings having been launched in April 1986, Norman entered the Open that year third on the table behind Ballesteros and Langer.

By the end of the year, which saw him win nine times in all, including six in a row in the autumn and the European Open and World Match Play titles, Norman was the world number one. It was only ten years after he had turned professional and little more than a decade and a half after taking up the game aged 16. He had got started by caddying for his mother, Toini, who after staying up all night to watch Greg win the Open celebrated by going out and winning the women's club championship at Royal Queensland.

Norman celebrated by, among other things, buying an Aston Martin. His first Ferraris had arrived after his first victory in Britain at the 1977 Martini International. Fast cars, speedboats, riding in military jump jets, all these things went along with a fast-paced life, attacking the day from well before dawn. If he could think it, he could do it. 'It was a triumph over course and conditions,' wrote Norman Mair of Norman's victory at Turnberry, 'a triumph which owed a great deal to a refreshing and determinedly positive attitude.'

Golf had rarely seen the like before. Jim Murray, the renowned sports writer for the *Los Angeles Times*, wrote: 'If you wanted to be a golfer, this is the one you'd want to be. Like a lot of great athletes, energy just seems to radiate out of him. He lashes at the ball as if it were something he caught coming through his bedroom window at two in the morning. He's an unselfconscious puppy with a ball of yarn. He's flashy. He's got a shock of platinum hair that makes him look like Jean Harlow from a distance. When he smiles, which is a lot, his teeth light up like a keyboard. He could give Liberace lessons in glitzy.' The hair, the yellow sweater, the smile, the sun finally reappearing over Turnberry – the claret jug completed the picture perfectly.

Backing up a round as low as a 63 is not easy, which is one of the reasons so few of those who have achieved it in a major went on to win. Somehow all the magic gets used up, the feel is just not

Gravesend
DA11 0AU - 01474 535311
VAT 125 5966 51   www.wilko.com

Loctite glue gun 2x6   £7.65
Royal Mail 12 x 1st C   £7.68
        2 Items   £15.33
                            -£15.80

wilko promise

buy me / love me / keep me

or bring me back

Now for the serious stuff. Proof of purchase will be required.
All of this is in addition to your statutory rights.
All lottery products, gift cards and phone cards are excluded.

the same for the rest of the tournament. Of the 22 players who did not score their 63 in the final round, only six have broken par the next day. The average next-day score is 72.05. At Turnberry in 1986 Norman returned a 74 in the third round, although that was partly explained by miserable weather. No one has gone better than a 69 the day after a 63 and Norman was one of them at the 1996 Masters.

After his second round at Augusta, Norman was asked about the difficulty of following up on a low score such as a major record-equalling 63. Typically, he brushed the idea aside. 'I don't think there was any difficulty,' he said. 'I knew when I was headed to the golf course today with the breeze blowing the way it was, the greens were going to be firmer and quicker. I'd already factored that into my mind.

'I factored in that there were situations where you had to be more conservative. I actually thought I played better today than yesterday. I put the ball in the right place under the circumstances, except on the 11th and 12th holes. Overall, my play was solid. I don't know about the difficulty of coming back. I just kept my game going the way I had done the day before.'

So he did on Saturday as his lead built and built. But now it was Sunday and the lead was coming down. The bogey at the 4th meant his advantage was down to four strokes. There was to be some relief at the 5th hole, a sign that this could still be a day where the momentum would see-saw. Faldo, with the honour, drove to the right and then his second with a four-iron bounced through the green into a bunker. Measuring 435 yards at the time – it is one of the holes that has been stretched since – it doglegs from right to left. Norman also missed the green, almost going into the same back-left bunker but his ball stopped on the fringe and from there he got down in two with only the tiniest of tap-ins required for his par.

'There is not a pin on that green where long left is good,' Jim Furyk once said, 'especially when the hole is on that little knob front-centre. You're not going to save par from there.' Norman had managed it but he was only inches off the green. From down in the bunker, Faldo would not save his par. He came out of the sand ten feet short of the hole and missed the putt on the low side. With the Englishman's first, and what would prove his last, bogey of the day, Norman's lead was back up to five strokes.

In matchplay terms it was a hole back to the Australian but it would turn out to be his first and last of the day. Had it been straight matchplay, Faldo would have wrapped it up with six holes to spare. Norman, and all those watching who were rooting for him, might have preferred such a quick kill but, under the protocol of the four-day strokeplay marathon, he still had a sizeable lead.

Juniper

Hole 6
Yards 180; Par 3

At start	Hole	1	2	3	4	5	6	7	8	9	Out	Status
	Par	4	5	4	3	4	3	4	5	4	36	
−13	G. Norman	5	4	4	4	4	3					−12
−7	N. Faldo	4	4	4	3	5	2					−8

RATHER OMINOUSLY, the 6th tee at Augusta is perched at the top of a precipice and Greg Norman was about to throw himself off the cliff. A five-stroke lead almost a third of the way through the final round of a major championship proved not to be an effective parachute. He would lose ten strokes to Nick Faldo in the remaining 13 holes, nine of them going in the next 11, so that even by the time he got round to the 16th, all hope of winning the Masters had long gone.

At the bottom of the bank under the tee, spectators can sit and watch as balls fly way over their heads to the green. It is one of the great gathering places of golf. To the right of the 6th green is the 16th green, and farther to the right is the 15th green. Late on Masters Sunday the place is abuzz with excitement as the destiny of the green jacket unfolds. A stream, in fact an extension of the tributary of Rae's Creek, used to run in the valley between the 6th tee and the green. It was too far short of the putting surface to be in play so for a few years a pond was created instead but that was not in play either, so it was filled in and the stream buried underground. However, the area is not short of dramatic water hazards, with ponds in front of the 15th green and to the left of the 16th. Shots can be lost on those holes in dramatic fashion but the par-three 6th is a more subtle affair. It was at this hole, almost imperceptibly, that the decisive thrust against Norman was about to begin, with the first of two birdies in three holes from Faldo.

Norman, with the honour back after his opponent's bogey at the previous hole, pulled his seven-iron but for the first time in the day found the green with a full approach shot. The 6th green has a number of sections on different levels and Norman was down on the front-left section. The pin on Masters Sunday is often in the back-right quadrant, its highest point, and this is where Faldo now took aim with a seven-iron. 'I have always regarded this as one of the key shots of Augusta week,' Faldo wrote in *Life Swings*, 'because you know your game is on if you can hit this spot consistently.' He certainly did now. It was the Englishman's best shot of the day so far. It pitched just short of the hole and stopped four feet behind it. Norman made his par but Faldo holed the putt for a birdie two.

With the way the course was set up at the time, players often divided it in their minds into two sections: the first six holes, containing two devious par-threes, three tricky par-fours and only one par-five; and the remaining 12, containing all the familiar risk-and-reward holes from the back nine. 'There's a run of holes, 3, 4, 5, 6, those holes are brutal,' said Duffy Waldorf. 'The first time I came here, I had no idea how different that part of the course is than the one you see on TV.'

Brad Faxon told *Golf World* (US): 'Holes 1 through 6, you say, "Just let me make pars, please, please, please." There are just so many don'ts. Don't hit it left on the 1st green. Don't hit it left on 2. Don't leave it short on 3. The don't at 4 is, I don't know how to hit it on the green. At 5, don't hit it short. Or right. Or long. And at 6, don't hit it above the hole – not that you can usually help it.'

Even though he parred all the first six holes on Thursday, Norman played the sextet in one over, two over and one over par on the next three days. That made him four over par on the first six holes for the week. With his birdie at the 6th on Sunday, Faldo played the same 24 holes in one under par. That difference of five strokes matched the Englishman's eventual winning margin. They both played holes 7 to 18 in 11 under par for the week. Faldo the plodder matched Norman the dasher on the death-or-glory holes but made fewer mistakes on the tricky opening stretch. But this Masters was far from won or lost yet, with 12 holes still to play. With his birdie, however, Faldo had got back to within four strokes, the margin Norman had led by two evenings earlier after the second round.

Following a 63 in a major championship, no one had ever scored lower than the 69 Norman returned on Friday. The Australian's total of 132, 12 under par, was only one stroke outside the record of 131 set by Ray Floyd in 1976. Floyd, who had rounds of 66 and 65, still holds the record but in 1996 no one other than Floyd and Norman had ever scored better than 135 after two rounds of the Masters. Norman led by four from Faldo after 36 holes, one stroke short of the record halfway lead of five by Floyd and also Herman Keiser in 1946 and Jack Nicklaus in 1975.

But the one record Norman created that day which still holds good now is that it was his fifth successive Masters round in the 60s. In tying for third place in 1995, Norman had opened with a 73 but then posted three consecutive scores of 68. Now he had opened the 1996 Masters with returns of 63 and 69. That's 24 under par for 90 holes at Augusta. The first four of those rounds, and the last four, would have broken the 72-hole scoring record for the Masters of 18 under par by Tiger Woods in 1997 by three, and two, shots respectively. No further proof is required of Norman's ability to master Augusta National but it was his failure to find the right sequence in any one tournament that left him without a green jacket.

On Friday Norman was one of only seven players to break 70. He birdied the 2nd hole to get to ten under par and then had his first bogey of the tournament at the 3rd. He immediately had another at the short 4th, the first of three successive fours at the opening par-three. He failed to get up and down from the left bunker but it was his last significant mistake. He got back on track by birdieing the 8th and then completed four fours at the par-fives with birdies at the 13th and 15th holes. He finished the round in style by hitting a sand wedge to four feet at the last.

Yet the real drama of the round came at Amen Corner. Norman hit a fine eight-iron to four feet at the 11th but left the ball in the wrong spot, just above the hole. A shot struck marginally softer might have stayed below the hole, or rolled back down past the hole. 'When you looked at it, all the spike marks were ten feet below the hole and no one was above it, so you know where balls were finishing,' Norman said. The pin was cut on the front-left of the green, only four yards from the left (where the pond is) and seven yards from the front of the green. The surface slopes down to the front edge.

So Norman was left with a short putt but a devilish one. 'That was the quickest putt I've ever had in my entire life and ever will have for the rest of my golfing days,' he said. 'I took the putter back maybe half an inch. There was no tension in my fingers. There was no pressure on my putter grip. The cops would have had a hard time getting a fingerprint. I hit it and it either had to go in or I knew I was going to have a six-footer.' Six feet for the return putt might be generous, it might have been nearer eight but he sank the par putt so there was a happy ending. 'I'd like to go back there now and knock it with my finger, move it a dimple and see what would happen with the ball,' he added after his round. 'That's why we love playing here. I suppose we get situations like that that we've never gotten before in our lives.'

Not everyone was loving it and to some the testing pin positions for the second round, combined with a breezy day and greens that continued to be firm and fast, were a reaction to Norman's course record-equalling 63 the day before. 'That must have rattled their cages a bit. The pins could be in the traps by the weekend,' said Masters rookie Mark Roe. The Englishman would not find out since he missed the cut, a premature end to his tournament and his fund-raising efforts on behalf of Rainbow House, for whom he wore a sunflower in his cap. Will Nicholson, the chairman of the Augusta competitions committee, was not going to do anything other than state that the pins were 'difficult but fair' and that they had nothing to do with the 63 on Thursday. 'We get accused of that all the time,' Nicholson said. 'There are some more difficult positions but they weren't in reaction to nine under. Friday's pin positions had all been decided before the first player teed it up on Thursday.'

Roe might have benefited from the sort of insight into the greens Czech-born Alex Cejka, another making his debut at Augusta, received from Bernhard Langer during their Monday practice round. Cejka, who had won the Volvo Masters at the end of 1995, took it all on board as he safely made the cut and explained: 'He showed me some crazy chips and putts. He showed me so many it took about eight and a half hours.' Older hands were not surprised with Friday's pin positions. 'They were a little tougher, definitely,' said former US Open champion Lee Janzen. 'None of the pins we saw yesterday or today were anything new. They just used a few of the easier ones yesterday.'

Even Faldo said: 'There were a couple of racy ones. If you hit it in the wrong place, then it's scary.' That was exactly what happened to Norman on the 11th green. But the Shark was not alone. There were 31 three-putts recorded at the 11th hole in the second round, so it happened to one out of every three players. No other green saw more than nine three-putts. Having survived without three-putting for a bogey, however, Norman had to step onto the 12th tee. The day before, the treacherous par-three had played as the easiest of the short holes, and there were no balls in the water. On Friday it ranked the hardest hole on the course.

Ben Crenshaw, the defending champion, made a triple-bogey six, as did Hal Sutton, Payne Stewart and rookie Paul Goydos, who managed it without going in the water. Crenshaw went in twice. His first effort with a seven-iron was 30 yards short and left of where he was aiming, 'just the sickest looking shot,' admitted the Texan. 'That hole had the worst gusts I've seen,' Crenshaw added. In a bowl at the far end of the course, the wind swirls around the trees and leaves players pondering which club to hit to the green that sits at an angle just over Rae's Creek. Norman took a seven-iron and came up short, the ball rolling down the bank at the front of the green but stopping 14 inches above the waterline. It was the sort of moment of good fortune that helped Fred Couples to victory in the final round in 1992. 'I thought about that,' Norman said. 'I said let's do what Freddie did. He made a three, I made a three.' His chip was exquisite, and left him a tap-in for his par.

In fact, six balls out of the 18 that came up short on the 12th on Friday stopped on the bank. 'It was a little spongy there,' Norman said. 'There was a lot of water on the bank. They haven't shaved it as they did last year, they left a little long grass there. I had 159 yards from the tee and the wind was swirling. I was trying to put it over the middle bunker but the ball ballooned a little bit.

When it landed, it started trickling down but it didn't come back with any force. I knew from the practice rounds that the grass was a little longer. I wasn't concerned. Maybe a little bit but if it had gone in the water, I would have panicked. As it turned out, I think the putt on 11 was more important than what happened on 12.'

Afterwards, Norman was asked if he was looking forward to the next two days? 'Oh, I'm looking forward to it. I feel very comfortable with myself.' For the first time in his press conferences, he was asked about his back over the first two days. 'My back is fine,' he said. 'It hurt a little yesterday.' Asked if he had had treatment, he said: 'I have treatment every day. Freddie [Couples] had been working with a guy named Tom Boers from Columbus, Georgia. I've seen Tom a couple of times.

'Freddie's back and my back are very similar, and this guy is good with what he does. When he first came here, I went to see him just to make sure I wasn't out of alignment. I was stiff Monday, Tuesday and Wednesday and Tom basically helped it out and loosened it up a little bit. And now I have my guy, Pete, who always works with me when he's in town to make sure everything stays in place. You know, you just protect it and make sure nothing gets out of line.

'I've got a pretty good feel going now and if I wake up stiff, you've got somebody there who can help me get unstiff. I like to say stiff in the right parts, not the wrong parts.'

Norman was also asked if he was surprised at doubling his lead from two to four strokes. 'No, not really. It's a nice feeling. Faldo played good today. Phil [Mickelson] struggled a little today, but he kept it together coming in. There's a lot of scores up there from the guys who have got the capability to shoot the low scores.

All I do is shoot the best I can. And if it's good enough at the end of the week to win, I'm a happy camper.'

Norman finished the day at 12 under par. Faldo was at eight under and David Frost and Phil Mickelson were at six under. With the leaders teeing off last in the second round, as was the custom at the time in the Masters, Mickelson had teed off in the last group alongside Norman. The left-hander bogeyed the first two holes and so dropped out of his overnight second place with a 73. As on Thursday, however, there was a dramatic birdie at the 18th, this time with a miracle recovery from the trees.

Janzen and Bob Tway were at five under after rounds of 71 and 72 respectively. Like everyone, Janzen was asked about trying to catch the runaway leader. 'He's the best player in the world and he's going to be tough to catch,' he said. 'No one's invincible. I know he wants to win this badly. The good news is that everyone else wants to win it badly, too. It's quite a challenge. I think I'll have to play the best 36 holes of golf I've ever played.'

At four under were Scott McCarron, Vijay Singh and Scott Hoch and at three under were Corey Pavin and Ian Woosnam. Pavin had the best round of the day with a 66 that included an inward half of 32. In the first round the 1995 US Open champion had bogeyed four holes in a row from the 2nd hole to be four over after only five holes of the tournament. He had played the next 31 holes in seven under. From 60th place after round one, he was now tied for tenth. He said he was inspired by Curtis Strange in 1985, who led during the final round after opening with an 80. 'I had nowhere to go but up,' Pavin said. 'I like where I'm at, considering yesterday. If it doesn't rain at all, we could very likely have single digits winning this tournament. I would not be surprised to see that happen.' As it turned out, only one player finished better than single digits under par.

After Pavin's 66, the next best score was the 67 of Faldo. Then came the 68s of Frost, despite a double bogey six at the 10th hole, and Couples, while there were 69s for Norman, Woosnam and Steve Stricker. Couples had teed off at 8.36 in the morning after his opening 78. It was an hour he was not accustomed to playing at during Masters week. A fan favourite even before his victory in 1992, he would usually be selected for a later tee time on Thursday and would then be faring well enough in the tournament for the remainder of the week to be teeing off nearer, or after, lunch than breakfast. 'First time in a while I've teed off before noon,' Couples said. 'The greens were really smooth. It was a lot of fun.'

His four-under round, including a double bogey at the 12th where he found the water, meant Couples made the cut, as he did for 23 years in a row between 1983 and 2007. That streak tied the record by Gary Player whose span was from 1959 to 1972. But what people were actually talking about was a rumoured altercation between Couples and Woosnam on the practice range before Thursday's round. It was all denied, of course, with Woosnam calling it 'rubbish'. Couples said: 'I don't know how I could get in a shoving match, maybe with some spectators but not with Woosie. He's so easy-going and happy-go-lucky. I don't know where that came from.'

Some suggestions were made. Woosnam said there might have been some 'f-words' flying around over some confusion with starting times for the par-three contest, while Couples said that he did have a playful shouting match with Davis Love's wife Robin, a friend of long standing, and perhaps 'someone was mistaking Woosie for Robin Love?' Unlikely.

After going out in 37 in the second round, Woosnam was another to come home in 32. The 1991 champion and former world number one, all five-foot-four of him, was asked: 'People have said your hunger's not there, but you showed today it's still there, isn't it?' He replied: 'Absolutely. I want a green jacket that fits me.' 'What, your jacket doesn't fit?' 'I'm just kidding. It does fit.' It is not always possible to tell when Woosie is joking. He was not when he was asked about Norman storming away with the tournament, giving short shrift: 'Norman's not won until the 72nd hole.' What, he was further asked, was a realistic gap at the halfway stage to still win? 'Six or seven shots. Anything can happen on those scores.'

How far back was too far back? Certainly, those on a 145 total, 13 strokes behind Norman, were too far back. John Daly, the reigning Open champion, said after rounds of 71 and 74: 'Greg has the potential to run away with it. I don't see anyone catching him the way the course is.' Jack Nicklaus was two shots better at one under par after rounds of 70 and 73 and admitted he was 'not in a great position'. Inevitably, the six-time champion was still asked if he could win? 'I'm in a better position right now than I was in 1986,' came the reply. In 1986 he was tied for 17th place at one over par but only six shots behind Seve Ballesteros. This time he was tied for 16th at one under par but 11 strokes behind Norman – and at 56 he was ten years older than when he became the oldest ever winner of the Masters.

Nicklaus had at least made the cut, unlike Player and Arnold Palmer, who both had rounds of 76. Tom Watson had a 72 to miss by one after bogeying three of the last four holes. It ended his streak of made-cuts at the Masters at 21, two short of the record. The cut fell at two-over-par 146, only one stroke higher than what remains the lowest cut-score seen in the Masters. Brad Faxon holed a 15-footer on the 18th green to save par and knock out those at three over.

Until the recent change to the top 50 and ties (and anyone

within ten strokes of the lead) making the weekend in the Masters, the long-time tradition was for the leading 44 players and ties, plus anyone within ten strokes of the leader, to qualify. The ten-shot rule did not apply, as there were only 15 other players within ten of Norman's lead, and there were exactly 44 qualifiers for the weekend. Among those who just made it thanks to a birdie at the last hole were Ballesteros, despite his poor recent form, Colin Montgomerie, one of the favourites at the start of the week, and joint course record-holder Nick Price.

David Gilford missed the cut by following his opening 69 with a 78. Sandy Lyle, the 1988 champion, missed out on five over and others not to qualify included Strange, Stewart and Ian Baker-Finch. It was a 22nd consecutive missed cut on the PGA Tour for the engaging Australian who triumphed at the 1991 Open Championship at Royal Birkdale but is now more familiar as a commentator. Swing changes and playing through injuries had ravaged Baker-Finch's game, especially his driving, and on this occasion a hooked drive into the trees at the 13th hole cost a quadruple-bogey nine and he finished at 13 over par.

Tiger Woods, unlike on his debut in 1995, missed the cut with twin rounds of 75. He was one of those to three-putt at the 11th, where his second putt was longer than his first, and he was one of those to find the water at the 12th. The 20-year-old Stanford student was not yet a professional but his post-round summary was of the seeking-the-positives variety that would become famil-iar throughout his career. 'The score didn't show it but I played better this year than I did last year,' Woods said. 'I was a bit more comfortable, I knew what to expect this year.'

He had been lauded by Nicklaus and Palmer earlier in the week as a future multiple winner of the Masters and despite the early departure, his six competitive rounds as an amateur over the 1995 and 1996 tournaments clearly held him in good stead.

'It's like Jack Nicklaus told me, you have to be patient here,' he said. 'Jack said he missed the cut his first year and had eight three-putts. It took him five years to win it.' Woods was not so patient. He returned in 1997 to win the Masters on his third appearance and his first as a professional (and in record-breaking fashion).

As he left Augusta in 1996, he had to get back to college. 'I've got an economics paper due Wednesday and I haven't even started,' he explained. In contrast, Gordon Sherry was met by his mother Anne behind the 18th green with the words: 'Welcome to your professional career.' Sherry against Woods was meant to be the big amateur battle of the week. In 1995 'Big G', as the six-foot-eight-inch golfer from Kilmarnock was known, had finished fourth at the Scottish Open, had a hole-in-one in practice alongside Nicklaus and Watson at the Open at St Andrews, won the Amateur Championship and starred in Great Britain and Ireland's Walker Cup victory over Woods and the Americans at Royal Porthcawl.

Like Woods, Sherry missed the cut with scores of 78 and 77, playing alongside Couples for both days. 'It's been a good experience,' the Scot said, 'although my first impression would be to say it's been the worst experience I've ever had on a golf course.' Not to worry, it seemed certain that there would be plenty more Woods-Sherry contests.

Except there weren't. At Augusta, Sherry was already feeling the effects of as-yet-undiagnosed glandular fever. He had to miss his proposed pro debut at the Italian Open and his career never got going. The next big thing that can't miss did just that. While Woods was acquiring a green jacket in April 1997, Sherry was still awaiting the result of a blood test that would give him the all-clear on his illness.

As the defending champion, Crenshaw had to stay around even though he missed the cut. He would be required to present the green jacket to the new champion at the close of play on Sunday. 'I'm going to stay right here and be an interested bystander,' said the Texan. The last defending champion to miss the cut was Lyle in 1989, while Nicklaus (1967), Tommy Aaron (1974) and Ballesteros in 1981 and 1984 had all suffered the same fate. It would happen to Faldo in 1997, his only weekend duties being to present Woods with his first green jacket.

But in Friday's second round of the 60th Masters, Faldo had some catching up to do. He teed off three groups before the final pairing of Norman and Mickelson, six shots behind the leader. That became seven when he bogeyed the 1st hole. He got that shot back at the par-five 2nd and did not drop another. He hit a wedge to six feet on the 7th and holed a downhill 20-footer at the 10th. He got up-and-down for a par on the 11th and admitted he got lucky when he was able to play the 12th when it was 'flat calm'.

A blocked drive into the trees at the 13th initially gave him thoughts of playing his second shot down the 14th fairway (over on the right, coming back in the opposite direction), but the crowd was too big to move. Instead, he snap-hooked a five-iron back to the 13th fairway and got up-and-down for a four. He was over the back of the 15th but got down for a four there as well. As his pairing with Faxon had fallen behind the players in front, they had been observed by a rules official from the 12th hole. On the 14th, Faldo received a bad time for taking too long over a shot, which only meant a warning. Faldo, like Langer and others, might be meticulous in the extreme but were too professional to have another bad time and risk a shot penalty. 'Miraculously, by the time we got to 15, we were waiting for the group in front... so tell me more,' Faldo queried afterwards.

At the last he hit a wedge to 12 feet and closed with his sixth birdie of the round. With rounds of 69 and 67, Faldo was at eight under par and lying second, four behind Norman and two clear of third place. 'I'm obviously very pleased because Greg was way ahead and going along nicely,' he said. 'I've really taken every chance I was given today. I was pleased about the scrambling I did; 13 and 15 were great. That was a very good round of golf for me.'

Not since 1994 had Faldo been near the top of the leaderboard at a major and not since 1993 had he been quite so in the thick of it. 'It's nice to be in contention again in a major,' he said. 'That's what it's about. That's what we play for.'

He added: 'Who knows what will happen with four strokes? You just keep going, playing the best you can. It looks like Greg's in control of everything the way he's going, so you've got to do the same thing.' For the first time in a major championship since the third round of the 1990 Open Championship, the next day Faldo and Norman would be playing together. A former world number one and the current world number one. 'Like I said, I'm going to play my own game,' Faldo reiterated as his press conference drew to a close. 'I'll worry about little old me first.'

Pampas

Hole 7
Yards 360; Par 4

At start	Hole	1	2	3	4	5	6	7	8	9	Out	Status
	Par	4	5	4	3	4	3	4	5	4	36	
−13	G. Norman	5	4	4	4	4	3	4				−12
−7	N. Faldo	4	4	4	3	5	2	4				−8

TIM GLOVER wrote in *The Independent* on Saturday 13 April 1996: 'When Bobby Jones, the moving spirit behind Augusta National, first set eyes on Jack Nicklaus he remarked that he played a game with which he was not familiar. There were many here echoing similar sentiments about Greg Norman following his blazing start in the 60th Masters but yesterday a familiar figure moved into his slipstream. This afternoon Norman will not only have to contend with the course but with Nick Faldo. We know that the Australian can cope with Augusta National but it is by no means clear that he can handle the Englishman with the same degree of confidence.'

By the 7th hole of the final round, with Norman still four strokes in front, it was not clear to what degree of confidence the leader could resist the challenger. Back on Friday evening, Norman was asked indirectly about the challenge of playing with Faldo in the third round but the answer did not contain the name of his great rival. 'How much attention do you pay, Greg, to the names on the board and who's coming at you? Do you know about the different people and what their make-up is?'

Norman answered: 'Well, I don't think it's the names. The

guys that are on the leaderboard now are playing good golf, irrespective of who they are. You've got guys who have won many major championships up there. You expect to see that name-wise, but you don't pay attention to it because you've got to do the job yourself.'

He was later asked specifically about playing with Faldo. On Thursday he had played with Fuzzy Zoeller and on Friday he had played with Phil Mickelson. 'Irrespective of who you play with, you play your own game. Whoever I play with I'll enjoy playing with over the weekend. I like Fuzzy. I like Phil. I'll enjoy playing with Nick tomorrow. We're all out there playing our own game and trying to win.'

Faldo had said the same just moments before: 'I'll worry about little old me first.' But when Faldo played his own game, and Norman played his own game, and they did that together, history suggested Faldo played his game better. The last time they had been paired together in a major championship had been in the third round of the 1990 Open at St Andrews. The scores that day were Faldo 67 and Norman 76.

Faldo did not always get the better of Norman. In their early days on the European Tour, they were part of an ensemble cast along with the likes of Sandy Lyle and Bernhard Langer, and although the main attraction was Seve Ballesteros, Norman, with his shock of blond hair and attacking game, was not far behind. Between 1980 and 1986, Norman and Ballesteros between them divided up the World Match Play Championship at Wentworth. Norman won three times in 1980, 1983 and 1986, and Ballesteros the other four times (he went on to equal Gary Player's record of five victories before Ernie Els broke that mark with seven titles). The

36-hole matches over the West Course, often played in glorious autumnal sunshine, produced some thrilling head-to-head battles and the event was considered one of the highlights of the year, a fitting finale to the British season. Norman and Faldo met there twice, with the Australian winning both times.

On his debut in 1980, Norman was seeded into the quarter-finals so his first match was against Faldo. It was cold and wet and at lunch he was four down after the first 18 holes. He got two holes back at the turn in the afternoon and a mistake from Faldo at the last meant the match went to extra holes. A birdie at the 16th gave Norman victory at the 38th hole. It was pretty dark by then but the Aussie had claimed a classic come-from-behind win and two days later, although taken all the way by Lyle, he hung on for a one-hole victory in the final.

Norman and Ballesteros only butted heads twice in the World Match Play and never in a final. The honours were shared but the Australian won a particularly thrilling match when they met in the semi-finals in 1983. Ballesteros made the crucial error at the 35th before the last hole was halved in birdies to give Norman a one-hole win. In the final he faced Faldo, who was enjoying his best ever season with five titles on the European Tour, including a run of three in a row. The match was tight, all square at lunch before Norman pulled away to go two up at the 9th in the afternoon. Birdies at the 11th and the 16th gave him a 4 and 2 victory.

Faldo would go on to win the title twice, in 1989 and 1992. By then he had revamped his swing with David Leadbetter and become hardened under the pressure of major championship victories. Consequently, his duels with Norman went up a notch in the 1990s when they were the best two players in the world. Norman still held the top spot when they met at the Australian Masters at Huntingdale in February 1990. Faldo was only just starting out on what would be an historic season but both he and

Norman scored rounds of 68 and 67 to share the halfway lead. They played together over the last 36 holes, with Faldo's 68 on day three giving him a two-shot lead over Norman after 54 holes.

Norman fell four behind when he had a double bogey at the 6th in the final round but on one of his favourite courses, the home star knew he had to get extremely aggressive and he bounced back with an eagle at the next hole. He added four birdies in the remaining 11 holes for a 68 and ended up winning by two from Faldo, who fell back into a tie for second place with Mike Clayton and John Morse. 'It was a great struggle, I enjoyed it every step of the way,' Norman said. 'You get someone as tough as Nick and he gives you no quarter. That's great because it means you have to make it happen yourself. It's the best way of winning.'

Faldo, still considered a par-machine since winning the 1987 Open at Muirfield with 18 of them on the final day, had shown he was also perfectly capable of producing birdies, with 20 of them on one of Melbourne's classic sandbelt courses. He reflected: 'I used to be able to win by playing conservatively but not any more. There are just too many good players around these days.' It was an important victory for Norman, his sixth in the Australian Masters, which awards a gold jacket for the winner, but Faldo was not too distressed. 'I'll be over it in half an hour,' he said. 'Say a few rude words and it's all out of the system.'

Only a few months later and the contrasting twosome met again at St Andrews. By now Faldo was in the ascendancy. He had successfully defended the title at the Masters and only just missed out on the playoff at the US Open in which Hale Irwin beat Mike Donald. Arriving at the home of golf he was in a confident mood. Norman regularly went into a tournament expecting to contend at the end of the week. Faldo rarely did, but this occasion was an exception. 'From the moment I arrived in the auld grey toun, I knew that, given the form I was in, I had but one man to beat – Greg Norman,' Faldo wrote in *Life Swings*. 'At the Monday night dinner for past champions, which is only held at St Andrews, the first person I bumped into outside the clubhouse was the Great White Shark. We shook hands and I stared him in the eyes like Muhammad Ali used to do in the middle of the ring, as if to say, "Let's shake hands and come out fighting."'

Norman had suffered a couple of shattering defeats on the PGA Tour that spring, to the last-gasp hole-outs of Robert Gamez and David Frost, and he had missed the cut at the Masters. But he finished fifth at the US Open at Medinah and now got off to his best start at the Open, a six-under 66 without a dropped shot. Faldo had gone along steadily but bogeyed the 17th and saw from the scoreboard at the final hole that he was three behind leaders Norman and Michael Allen. A two-wood off the last tee came up 40 yards short and left of the green and he then played the most delightful pitch-and-run with an eight-iron which ran through the Valley of Sin, over a ridge and onto the green and into the hole for an eagle two. Even playing partner Scott Hoch, whom Faldo beat in a playoff at the 1989 Masters and whose unflattering opinion of the Englishman had been spiced up in some of the newspaper preview stories, muttered: 'Good shot.'

Norman again scored a 66 the next day. He had a couple of bogeys this time but still had six birdies, including four in a row from the 7th. Faldo was playing three groups behind so their paths crossed at the Loop, where the holes turn back on each other at the far end of the course. While Faldo lined up a putt on the 8th, Norman, playing the 10th, was holing for birdie on the other side of the shared green. Norman continued his surge by holing a full sand-wedge shot for an eagle at the 14th, somewhat ironically given his playing companions were Gamez and Bob Tway, both men to have caused Norman pain with ridiculous hole-outs.

Norman topped the leaderboard at 12 under par but Faldo matched him with a second round of 65. He did not drop a shot, not even at the fearsome 17th; he had gone out in 32 and added birdies at the 10th, 15th and 16th holes. They shared the same 132 mark of Henry Cotton's then 36-hole Open record and they were four ahead of the field. That Friday at St Andrews gets overlooked as one of the great days of Open action. 'Throughout the day the bulging grandstands and the human chain of spectators lining the fairways back to the ancient clubhouse had been humming with the excited buzz of record scores, record low cut mark and the prospect of a duel that even Turnberry 1977 couldn't live up to,' wrote Daniel Davies in *Golf Illustrated Weekly*.

But this was no Jack Nicklaus-Tom Watson affair, whose 36-hole head-to-head at Turnberry 13 years earlier had ended with a single stroke between them. The deflation for all, bar Faldo, was overwhelming. 'There was a whiff of cordite in the air,' Faldo wrote in *Life Swings*. 'Our duel had become a gunfight and I have never felt so determined to be the last man standing.' It showed at the 1st hole on Saturday. Faldo and Norman's putts were on the same line, Faldo from 18 feet, Norman about three feet inside him. Faldo holed, Norman missed.

'I lost my rhythm with my putter,' Norman said. 'I had a makeable one at the 2nd and hit it too hard through the break. The next one I hit too soft. So now I'm second-guessing myself and it gets worse and worse.' The Australian three-putted at the 2nd and although he made two birdies in three holes from the 4th, a bogey at the 9th meant a two-shot swing when Faldo picked up his third birdie of the day. Faldo was three ahead and went four clear with a 15-foot birdie at the 11th.

Norman, whose fine play over the first two days had been built on an element of caution, went back to his default setting and started attacking. It did him no good, finding sand off the tee that led to bogeys at the 12th and 13th holes. Faldo had all the answers, even escaping from a gorse bush for a par at the 12th, and he hit his approach at the last to two feet to end with a 67 and a new 54-hole Open record of 199. Norman came home in 40 for a 76, the third worst score of the day.

'Saturday, July 21, will be remembered as the day Nick Faldo undressed Greg Norman in front of 45,000 fans and millions more on TV and left him with a new nickname: Crocodile Gerbil,' wrote Dan Jenkins in *Golf Digest*. 'Simultaneously, it was both an astounding sight and a pitiful sight. One man confident, dominant, executing his shots with a studied perfection; the other trying to figure out which end of the club to take a grip on.'

Norman rallied for a 69 the next day and finished joint sixth. David Miller wrote in *The Times*: 'Greg Norman is a man tormented by two conflicting five-letter words: money and glory. He has all he could ever want of the former, but still yearns for the latter.' Faldo hit his approach to three feet at the 1st for an opening birdie, which was the perfect settler. After 12 holes, Payne Stewart got within two shots of him but then drove into one of the Coffins bunkers at the 13th and dropped a shot. Faldo's bogey at the 4th was the first time he had been in a bunker all week and was the only dropped shot that did not come at the 17th. His only three-putts came at the Road Hole, as well, but originated from off the putting surface as Faldo's plan was to stay as far away from danger as possible, even if it meant deliberately missing the green. He finished off his victory with a 71 for a then record score of 18 under – improved to 19 under by Tiger Woods ten years later – with Stewart and Mark McNulty five strokes back.

Jenkins compared Faldo's play that week to that of his hero, Ben Hogan. No praise could be higher. 'Not since the days of Hogan had a player so mastered a golf course and a field of competitors as Faldo did at St Andrews,' he wrote. 'It was time for Faldo to win a major the way he did. His prior British Open (1987) and his two Masters victories the last two years had something unsettling about them; he had sort of picked them up off the floor after others had lost their grip. But this time, he just Hoganed the hell out of everybody, and you had to remind yourself that this is what he's been doing for the past four years.'

The Sony Rankings still had Norman at the top of their list. But everyone knew Faldo, with his fourth major title, was now the best player around. The Shark might have been bruised but he was not conceding anything. 'If I admit he was the No 1 guy, it would be admitting that he's better than me,' he said. 'I don't think that ever. He's a great player but he can be beaten.' In recent times, when they had played in the same tournament, each man had won three – but in Faldo's case they were all majors.

This was Faldo's first experience of leading from the front in the last round of a major. He had led by five and won by five, but it had not been comfortable. 'My stomach was churning before the last round started,' he explained. 'I had to force my lunch down. With a five-shot lead, everybody expected me to win. If I had lost, it would have been a real blow-out.

'I settled down when I hit a good tee shot and a good second shot to birdie the 1st hole. I wasn't trying to be defensive at all – I just wanted to try and hit the right-shaped shot all the way round.' Not just 'one shot at a time' but the 'right-shaped shot'. Not just any shot between thoughts of lifting the Open trophy but a constant immersion in the detail. Finally, walking up the famous 18th fairway of the Old Course, and for the only time in his career, he was able to truly enjoy a stroll to major victory. 'It's nice to have my baby back,' he said on receiving the claret jug.

Faldo had also found a worthy accomplice in his pursuit of history. Fanny Sunesson had only started caddieing for the Englishman that season and they had won two of their first three majors together. She had quickly proven herself under the greatest pressure. Diligent in the extreme at scouting the turf underfoot each week and each championship day, her 22-year-old eyes helped Faldo, 33, with the lines on the greens. She also knew how to keep her man focused and relaxed at the right times.

Of the final round, when Stewart was getting close to the lead, Sunesson told Norman Dabell for his book *Winning the Open*: 'I had to keep myself calm and I remember thinking that I must keep Nick calm as well. He was obviously tense, well aware that he had someone running as hot as he could to try and catch him. I tried to take his mind off the tournament a bit. Nick's great for chat, he tells some great jokes all the time, but this was the last day. My turn. I felt I had to relax him a bit so I talked about dogs, wallpaper, how many bedrooms he was going to have in his new house, anything I could think of. At the end, it was unbelievable. The crowd was shouting my name and Nick just turned round and said, "Enjoy this moment." '

Another classic Faldo-Norman clash took place at the Johnnie Walker World Championship at Tryall in Jamaica in December 1992. It was the week before Christmas and Faldo was looking for his sixth win of the year. Even the world rankings had him as the No 1 by now. 'It was a strange week,' wrote Guy Yocom in *Golf World* (US), 'one in which all the other 27 players in the field seemed afflicted by Jamaicaitis, that drowsy, near-hypnotic state brought on by exposure to relentless sunshine, tropical flora and fauna, endless cocktail parties, hammering reggae music, sauna-like warmth and overhead fans. Faldo, somehow, never caught the bug. He was... well, he was Faldo, grinding intensely from start to finish.'

In the third round Faldo scored a 65 and led by five but Norman got himself in the final pairing with his old rival. On a course where missing the fairway was inadvisable with the penal rough but highly likely owing to the strong sea breezes, Faldo missed only one green in the final round which cost a bogey at the 14th. Since Norman had collected his sixth birdie of the day at the same hole, the Australian had gone from five behind to one ahead. At the 18th, Norman hit a nine-iron from a fairway bunker to just over three feet, giving himself a putt for a 62 and a winner's cheque of $550,000 (one of the highest around at the time). Faldo, however, had not given up. He was still grinding. He had a 15-footer for a birdie and, telling himself to 'let the big muscles do the work', he holed it for a 68.

Norman still had his putt for the win but with a strong right-to-left grain as well as contours breaking in the same direction. Inevitably, almost, Norman's putt ran over the left edge of the cup and stayed out. It meant a 63 (a course record) and a playoff, which Faldo won when Norman bogeyed the 18th at the next time of asking. 'It's been a great year and I wanted to finish on a great note,' Faldo said. 'Everybody wanted a bit of drama and, kind person that I am, I gave it to them. But I aged about ten years in the process.'

Norman thought he had produced quite enough drama. 'I thought I played effing great,' he said. 'I may not have won but I came away with a lot more than that. I feel like I'm 21 again. The dedication I've put into my game has paid off.' For Norman it was confirmation that his slump of the previous year was lifting and he was working along the right lines with new coach Butch Harmon. The following summer he won his second Open at Sandwich and was well on the way to being the game's biggest beast again.

Faldo noticed something about Norman's game in this period: 'The putting helps a lot. He has always been a strong, confident player but now he is finishing it off by holing the putts. You reward yourself by finishing it off and that is why he is such a tough man to beat.' And why he was the one being hunted again on the final day of the 1996 Masters.

With live television coverage just now starting as the final pair played the 7th hole, a graphic was flashed on the screen showing the four players to have won the Masters 'wire-to-wire' – by leading after every round. Craig Wood was the first to do it in 1941, followed by Arnold Palmer in 1960, Jack Nicklaus in 1972 and Ray Floyd in 1976. Norman was in position to become the fifth player to achieve the feat. But his lead was now only four and a chance to extend it again could not come quick enough. Unlike the leader's pre-shot routine which, Faldo pointed out in *Life Swings*, was getting slower and slower after Faldo's birdie at the 6th. 'Visibly reeling from that latest blow, Greg began taking longer and longer over every shot, his seeming need to constantly regrip increasing.'

Pampas, the 7th hole at Augusta National, has been lengthened considerably in recent years but at 360 yards in 1996 it required only a mid-iron off the tee followed by a wedge approach, but with bunkers surrounding the raised green, it needed to be an accurate approach. Faldo put his to 18 feet but it was downhill and quick so two putts for par was his best outcome. Norman put his approach to eight feet, right of the hole, a golden opportunity to collect only his second birdie of the day. But the putt never looked like going in.

'Several pivotal moments punctuated this round, but that missed putt at number 7 was one of the most important,' reported the *Masters Annual*. 'Although Norman was still four strokes clear, the missed opportunity seemed to change his tenor. The shots he played on the next two holes seemed to betray an impatience, an anxious need to put the tournament on ice before Faldo could apply any more heat.'

Was Norman losing his putting touch, as he had in the third round of the 1990 Open at St Andrews, just when he needed it most? Apart from a couple of holes early in the third round at Augusta, his putting had been secure, in contrast to Faldo's iffy spell on the back nine. Norman had been asked about his short putting at his press conference on Saturday night. 'It doesn't matter what the tournament is, you've got to make those four and five-footers,' he said. 'Short putting is very important, especially on a day like today where you hit a lot of good shots that don't end up the way you think they will. You have to have your full artillery working for you.'

Does it have an effect on your playing partner, he was asked? 'Oh God, I don't know. I didn't go up to Nick and say, "Hey, Nick, how are my four and five-footers?" I don't think he pays attention to my game and I don't pay attention to his game. You have to keep your mind focused on your own job.'

Oh, they notice. They just don't want to talk about the other guy too much. Certainly not Faldo on Saturday evening when he was asked: 'Greg's damage control on 12, where it could have really been a disaster, would you look back on that as Norman winning this tournament there?' Faldo: 'I don't really know because I don't know what he's been up to for the first 36 holes.

That's really a question for him to answer. Who knows what's in store tomorrow?' Later, Faldo was asked how it was playing with Norman: 'Good. Did you make a note of that? I need to go and practise.'

In contrast to the final round, when they did not converse between the 1st tee and the 18th green, there were a few pleasantries exchanged during their round on Saturday and even the odd joke. Compared to his reluctance to mention Faldo by name the night before, having got through one round with his nemesis on Saturday allowed Norman to open up a tad more. 'Anytime you play with Faldo, it's great,' he said. 'I think the top players enjoy playing with top players. We enjoy each other's company and each other's ability to play the game. I think we've had a good rivalry since '76, '77, I would say. We hope there's plenty more to come.'

Yellow Jasmine

Hole 8
Yards 535; Par 5

At start		Hole	1	2	3	4	5	6	7	8	9	Out	Status
		Par	4	5	4	3	4	3	4	5	4	36	
-13	G. Norman		5	4	4	4	4	3	4	5			-12
-7	N. Faldo		4	4	4	3	5	2	4	4			-9

W HEN PEOPLE think of Greg Norman and the final round of the 1996 Masters, they think of his downfall setting in at the 9th hole. Look at the scorecard and that is where his destructive run of over-par figures begins. But in terms of destructive shot-making, it actually began a hole earlier. He arrived at the 8th hole having missed that birdie chance on the previous green and perhaps ruing the lost opportunity to get his round back on track. How often does a missed chance lead to a mistake? That is what happened to the Australian on the long, uphill par-five.

Norman had outdriven Faldo, naturally, and seen his opponent lay up with a two-iron second shot that got to the top of the hill, around 50 yards short of the green. He was in the middle of the fairway and had a three-wood in his hands. 'Don't overcook it,' Dave Marr murmured on the BBC television commentary. Norman overcooked it. He took a slash and a half and hooked the ball into the trees on the left. Moments before, in the pairing ahead, Phil Mickelson had taken four to get down from a similar spot. Instead of taking advantage of his power, Norman had put himself in trouble.

At first, it looked as if Faldo would not capitalise on the

error. He had 55 yards for his third shot and hit a little pitch with a wedge. The hole was cut on the front of the green but Faldo's shot only just crept onto the putting surface and he turned away after his follow-through in a momentary show of frustration.

Norman, however, was blocked from taking a direct route to the flag by two pines 30 yards in front of him. He was forced to play to the right of them, keeping his pitch low under a branch, and the ball stopped just short of the green. From there, his chip was exquisite and he tapped in for a five. It was not a dropped shot, nor was it a birdie. While Faldo was over his putt, some spectators moving away towards the 9th tee caught the attention of Fanny Sunesson. 'Stand still, please,' came the piercing instruction. Faldo backed off his putt briefly but stepped back to the ball completely unperturbed. The putt was 20 feet long and broke slightly from the left. It went in.

Faldo's was the 16th, and last, birdie made that day at the 8th hole, which ranked as the 16th hardest both for the round and the tournament as a whole. Today, the tee at the 8th has been pushed back to 570 yards, making it a three-shot hole for most. Although it has always been shorter than the 2nd hole, it runs up the hill that the 2nd descends so it plays as the longest par-five on the course. Even so, Faldo, who was never the longest of hitters, birdied the hole three of the four days (making a par on Friday).

Norman had birdied the hole on each of the first three days. His failure to do so in the final round compounded the lost chance from the previous hole. Back-to-back birdies at such a crucial part of the round would have demoralised his opponent and meant a still-commanding lead of five strokes. Instead, Faldo was gaining in both ground and confidence. Norman's lead was down to three strokes for the first time since the 9th hole of the third round. Exactly half of his overnight advantage had disappeared.

On Saturday, Norman had gone six strokes clear after extending his lead by two shots for the second day running. It had been the most difficult day of the week. The wind got up, gusting up to 25 mph at times, and there was the threat of a thunderstorm. The skies got dark as the leaders got towards the turn – Norman and Faldo had teed off at 2.09 p.m. – but the electrical activity stayed away and there were only a few sprinkles of rain, nothing to take the fire out of the greens. There were only nine scores under par and only two of those were under 70. The 69s of Duffy Waldorf and rookie David Duval propelled them up the leaderboard. Having recovered from a bout of flu earlier in the week, Duval had got himself up to ninth, alongside Frank Nobilo and others. Scott Hoch and John Huston were on three under in seventh place, while Waldorf had jumped into a tie for fourth with David Frost and Scott McCarron. The trio were two behind Phil Mickelson, who on six under trailed Faldo by one and Norman by seven.

Mickelson, only 25 but contending in the Masters for the second year running, had an uncharacteristic round of 72. He did not birdie any of the par-fives, had only two birdies, both from a foot with a six-iron at the 10th and a wedge at the 17th, and two bogeys. There were some adventures along the way. At the 2nd he was in the trees on the right and was forced to play right-handed, turning round his left-handed four-iron to hit with the back of it, and hooked the ball out only to find the trees on the left. From there he punched down in front of the green, chipped on and made his par. Then at the 9th, he was behind a tree on the left of the fairway and took a driver, hit down on the ball with an open face to produce a huge slice and knocked it to 12 feet. You cannot take your eyes off him for a second.

In his interview afterwards, someone got right to the point. 'Phil, is Greg catchable?' Mickelson volleyed back: 'Well, I don't know. What do you think?' Keeping the rally going, the questioner replied: 'Well, with his history, and you guys aren't going to lay down tomorrow...'

'You know, I think that anything's possible, so I don't want to rule out the improbable,' Mickelson said. 'But as well as he is playing... and when he does make a mistake, he's recovered. Look at 12. He knocks it in the water, gets up and down for a bogey, birdies the next hole, where that could have been disastrous. It just seems like he's not going to make any mistakes. For any of us to catch him, it's going to take 63 or 64. I don't know if that's possible on this golf course right now.'

Just being at the Masters was a blessing for Waldorf after he underwent an operation for torn cartilage in his left knee on 14 February, returning to the tour just a month later. Waldorf favoured colourful outfits and shirts that looked like they had been drawn in by hand. They hadn't but his hat featured many signatures of friends from back home and even fellow players, while his golf balls all had patterns drawn on them by his wife, Vicky. The tradition started four years earlier when one of his children got hold of some of his tournament ammunition and doodled away. The sun and smiles often feature but this week Vicky had added some green jackets and other Augusta-related markings. 'To remind me I'm at Augusta, in case I forget,' Waldorf laughed. So used to it had he become that the only thing he found distracting was a completely white ball.

Clearly enjoying himself, Waldorf had a different take to almost everyone else on the day's scoring potential. 'To me it seemed a little easier,' he said. 'I think without the sun, it seemed some of the greens were not quite as fast or as hard, with it not being so hot. But there were some very hard pins and the wind was tough. I didn't give myself a lot of putts above the hole. When I did have an uphill putt, I made a good putt at it. I played with Davis [Love] and he played very well but he had more downhill putts than I did.'

All eyes, however, were on the Faldo-Norman pairing, the last of the day. In recent times, it has become common for the world's leading players to be paired on a regular basis. Woods and Rory McIlroy got to know each other exceedingly well on the course in 2012 and 2013. But two decades ago it was comparatively rare. You had to wait for two of the big fish to catch the same tee time at the weekend. If it was on the big stage, say at Augusta National in the first major of the year, so much the better.

Bill Fields wrote in his third-round report for *Golf World* (US): 'It was the kind of pairing that spectators want to see and reporters want to write about. And lurking someplace in their inner selves – perhaps behind a pre-shot routine – even today's golfers themselves savour the prospect, so seldom do the game's top-of-the-line performers compare their skills so intimately. It is the closest thing pro golf has to a prize fight, and in the third round of the 1996 Masters Tournament, Greg Norman and Nick Faldo were thrust into the ring. The only problem for Norman, who reigns as the game's best player, and Faldo, who was the best a couple of blinks ago, was that the Augusta National course took off its gloves and entered the fray, punching with vigour.'

'It's a four-letter word called wind,' Norman said when asked about the conditions. 'It was a lot tougher, blowing 23-24 miles an hour out there. There were situations where you had to hit when there was a lull so it was difficult to judge. There were long shots, and the wind's holding you down or pushing you up, where you are hitting to a very small spot, it chews you up.' Faldo agreed that the pin positions were especially difficult. 'They sure were,' he said. 'There were some beauts – three paces on 3; three paces on 4; on the top of the hill on 5; three paces on 6. I mean, it's not exactly a lot of room, is it?'

Faldo added: 'The blustery wind is the tough bit. You can hit a perfect shot, get a little gust, and it doesn't come off quite right.' Norman found that out on the short 12th but otherwise it was a very solid round from the Shark. Forgotten were the two missed cuts in his last two tournaments. He was playing like the world number one who had already won three times that year. Faldo, on the other hand, had an off day. His game had been generally good but perhaps he lacked the confidence that comes with winning – his last victory having been 13 months earlier. In recent weeks there had always been one round that tripped him up: an opening 77 at the Honda Classic, a closing 73 at Bay Hill and the second-round 75 at the Players Championship. In the third round at Augusta, he hit only nine greens in regulation and made only six pars.

Faldo began brightly enough by hitting the green at the 2nd with a four-iron and two-putting for a four. With Norman only making a par, after missing from five feet for his birdie, the lead was down to three. But at the fiendish 3rd hole, Faldo suffered a double bogey. With the hole located at the front left of the green, he caught his wedge approach shot heavy and came up short. 'That was a bad swing on that one,' Faldo admitted. His chip up the bank in front of the green rolled back to his feet and another chip and two putts were required to complete the six.

Norman, in the meantime, had hit a nine-iron to 18 feet but had to wait so long for Faldo to play up that he ended up three-putting for a bogey five. There was only one shot lost in the end for Faldo but he flew the green at the 4th with a three-iron and failed to get up and down so that was a bogey four, although Norman three-putted from 45 feet to also drop a shot. At the 3rd, thinking his first putt was uphill, Norman had blasted his birdie try eight feet past, so inexorably at the 4th he ended up five feet short. 'From there on I had pretty good speed with my putts,' he said. 'The difficult part of putting today was judging the last two feet of break because the wind was going to roll the ball a little more than you anticipated.' Norman was back to ten under par, Faldo was six under: the gap was still four.

By the turn, it was down to three, Faldo making an 18-foot putt at the 9th. On the back nine, however, Norman drew away again. At the 10th, Faldo, trying to hit a low seven-iron onto the raised green, pushed his approach and dropped a shot. Then came the 12th. Norman went with an eight-iron but caught a gust of wind and saw his ball land in Rae's Creek, the water he had been lucky to avoid the previous day. He had made a fine up-and-down for a par on the Friday, and this time he again stayed calm, making a 'good' bogey. Giving himself the yardage he wanted with the drop, he hit a sand wedge from 81 yards to ten feet and holed the putt for a four.

Faldo had selected a seven-iron for his tee shot at the 155-yard hole but the wind had died down slightly when he came to hit and he went through the green. Instead of taking advantage of the Australian's visit to the drink, the Englishman now had the more difficult second shot. He was on a downslope, with pine needles and seed pods behind the ball, playing over a small depression to an upslope, after which the green runs down towards the water Norman had just visited. 'That sounds pretty tough to me. And it's Augusta,' Faldo said later in trying to convey the high tariff of the shot. He got it to around the same distance for par as Norman had for bogey but, still miffed at having let go a chance of closing the gap with a tee shot on the green, he missed the putt.

Norman said: 'When I hit the tee shot and it ended up in the water, I never got mad because I hit the shot solid. It would have been a different story if I had hit a bad shot. Then it would have been, "why did you make a stupid mistake like that?" But I put a good swing on it. It obviously got caught up in the wind. So you just take your medicine from there and make your four. When you do that type of stuff, it makes you feel good because you know you never hit a bad shot. You walk off with a bogey but it could have been worse.'

Asked why he selected the yardage he did for his third shot, Norman answered: 'Because I've probably hit 50,000 golf balls from 81 yards and I know how to hit 81-yard shots. That's the type of shot where you know you want to be certain to put a lot of juice on the ball. That green is very, very firm. That's the reason I put it at that distance because it was a good three-quarter sand wedge shot.' Alas, the following day when faced with a similar recovery, it did not work out quite so well.

Norman was asked if he had had a little luck during the round, such as at the 12th hole, to keep his lead intact. 'I don't think that is luck,' he said. 'I see that as the way the game is played. Luck is when you get a bounce off a tree and come back on the fairway [as he did at the 14th in the first round] or what happened at 12 yesterday [when his ball stayed on the bank]. That was a bit of luck.'

After a 'half' in bogeys at the 12th, both men completed Amen Corner with birdies at the par-five 13th. It might well have been a half in eagles as both hit big drives round the corner and then mid-irons close to the flag. Norman missed from ten feet, Faldo from eight feet – another chance lost, he felt. Another went at the 14th. Norman chipped and putted for a par from the back edge but Faldo had a ten-footer for birdie which slipped by. Yet again, at the 15th, it was Faldo who seemed to be in a good position. Norman pulled his drive and had to lay up with a four-iron back to the fairway. Faldo hit a fine drive and then a four-iron onto the green but 60 feet right of the hole. While Norman got up and down with a pitch shot and putt from six feet for a birdie four, Faldo three-putted, missing again from inside ten feet.

The 15th had already seen plenty of drama in this third round as Jack Nicklaus eagled the hole, chipping in from beyond the bunker to the right of the green. Seve Ballesteros had a fright when his chip from behind the green ran down the bank into the pond at the front. He did not like that pond, having deposited a four-iron shot there when he lost to Nicklaus in 1986 and now, as he peered into the water to see if his ball was playable, a fish jumped out of the water and made him jump even higher. Colin Montgomerie, meanwhile, was not enjoying himself at all. One of the pre-tournament favourites, the Scot hit his third shot over the green, left his chip short on the fringe (fearing the fate of Ballesteros's chip from earlier) and then four-putted for a triple-bogey eight. 'This is the most frustrating place I've ever played,' he wailed as he fell back to five over after three rounds.

At the short 16th, Faldo pushed a nine-iron into the bunker short-right of the green. He later ranked it as his worst shot of the week. It cost him a bogey as his par putt lipped out. Norman had hit a nine-iron to six feet and made the putt for a birdie so he had gained three shots in two holes. He was now seven ahead of Faldo.

Coming into the week, Faldo had been most confident with his putting and until this series of miscues it had served him well. Even with them, he was only a hair behind Corey Pavin at the top of the putting statistics for the first three rounds. 'Play wasn't bad,' Faldo said as he summed up his round. 'I could have saved the day by making some of those putts on 12, 13, 14, 15, 16. I missed all of them, the longest being eight to ten feet.'

It was, in fact, at the next two holes that he saved the day as his putting came good. At the 17th, he hit a wedge to six feet and made that for his sixth birdie of the day. It not only reduced his arrears to six strokes but took him back to seven under par and one ahead of Mickelson in third place. Had he remained at six under, he would have shared second place with the left-hander. But because Mickelson had been playing ahead of him in the third round, under the 'first-in, last-out' rule, it would have been Mickelson playing with Norman in the final round. And how different might history have been?

Of course, Faldo still had to par the last and to do so he faced yet another ten-footer. It was the sort of overcast day where dusk closes in early but there was still enough light around. At the time, it is likely not many people watching realised the importance of Faldo's putt. A lead of six shots or seven, surely Norman had enough of a cushion either way?

But Faldo recognised how important it was. It wasn't that he thought if he could play alongside Norman on the final day he *would* win. But, at least, he *could* win. Or, at the very least, apply some pressure in a way that would not be possible if he were not in Norman's eyeline the next day. Other players might have thought the opposite, that getting out ahead of Norman, away from the intensity of the final pairing, and posting a target that the Australian would have to chase would give them their best hope of causing an upset. Not Faldo. He wanted to be alongside Norman for another 18 holes. He made his par.

Norman's third successive sub-par score, a 71 that felt even better given the conditions, put him at 13 under par on a total of 203. Only two players had ever been lower at the same stage of the Masters, Ray Floyd on 201 in 1976 and Nicklaus on 202 in 1965. More pertinently, the day's battle with Faldo had been won, the Englishman had not been at his best and returned a 73 to be seven under par. To be fair to Norman, he was the last person to concede his conquest was in the bag. Faldo, hanging on for grim death as only he can, was admitting nothing.

After the round, with daylight fading fast, Faldo had little inclination for a lengthy debrief in the interview room. 'I'm a long way back,' he said. 'But, you know, anything is possible. It's all to gain and nothing to lose tomorrow. Just go out and play, and if it comes off, well, it will put a lot of pressure on him.' Asked if he had a target score in mind for the next day, he said: 'To shoot something good. Who knows? You shoot 66, 65, it could be something around there. It's got to get me in the right direction.' There was only one direction he was heading in at that moment – the range before the light totally went. 'I need to go and practise, guys.'

Norman, who parred the last two holes, also wanted to practise after his round and ended up on the putting green well after darkness had fully descended. But first there was another long session in the interview room. He went through his round and tackled everything thrown at him from grim reminders of his past defeats to predicting the future, or at least the next 24 hours. Overall, he was happy with his 71. 'That's the equivalent of shooting in the 60s, I suppose. There wasn't a lot of give in the golf course. I'm sure there's not going to be a lot of give tomorrow, either.'

'Do you feel as in control of the tournament as the leaderboard would indicate?' he was asked. 'The best way for me to answer that is I feel good within myself forgetting the golf tournament. That's the only way I can approach it, in a very good philosophical sense in my mind. I've got another day to go and there's 18 tough holes to play.'

'Greg, is there an urge to be maybe a little more cautious tomorrow?' 'I'm just going out there as if nobody's got a lead. We're all at the same mark tomorrow, as far as I'm concerned, when we tee off. I'm just going to play the necessary shot I see to play at the time.'

'Since you have a six-shot lead, why approach it like everybody's tied?' 'That's the way I approach it every day. Everybody's even and if you beat the guys in your mind when you're even with them, then you know you're going to beat them.'

'Greg, how excited are you right now?' 'I feel pretty good. Yeah, I've a lot to do, so there's no point in getting excited now.'

'Greg, if you win tomorrow, are you going to look back over the last couple of days as being the difference in the tournament?' 'Ask me that tomorrow.'

'Is it fair to say you're anticipating this round of golf more than any others you've played knowing the history of the Masters?' 'Sure. Irrespective of what happens, I'm going to enjoy every step I take. I've got a chance to win the Masters. I've been there before. There's no better feeling than having a chance to win a major championship.'

Carolina Cherry

Hole 9
Yards 435; Par 4

At start	Hole	1	2	3	4	5	6	7	8	9	Out	Status
	Par	4	5	4	3	4	3	4	5	4	36	
−13	G. Norman	5	4	4	4	4	3	4	5	5	38	−11
−7	N. Faldo	4	4	4	3	5	2	4	4	4	34	−9

D ON'T CALL Greg Norman a 'choker'. Someone tried it once. Understandably, Norman was less than chuffed. Well, perhaps more than once. It comes with the territory when you have put yourself into contention on the biggest stages so often and ended up not winning so many of them. But golf being such a mannerly game, the word 'choke' is not generally bandied around. Professional golfers are naturally sensitive to the accusation, particularly when, as Bobby Jones pointed out, the 'six inches between the ears' have such a vital impact on the difference between success and failure.

As Colin Montgomerie knows all too well, being a foreigner who is purported to be one of the best players in the game (and therefore a threat), but who manages not to win the biggest titles in America, is considered fair game for those who are inclined to verbal antagonism. The trick is never to let it show. At the 1991 Masters, Tom Watson told Ian Woosnam, as the Welshman was on his way to victory, that the old pros' method of dealing with hecklers was to turn round, touch the peak of your cap politely and say simply: 'Fuck you very much.' Monty was unable to master the art of never letting it show and, in the mind's eye, is still to this day standing on the 71st green at Congressional waiting for the gallery at the 1997 US Open to quieten down.

New York galleries are hardly shy and retiring and Norman suffered plenty of abuse as he tied with, and then lost a play-off to, Fuzzy Zoeller at the 1984 US Open at Winged Foot. Two years later at Shinnecock Hills, just months after losing the 1986 Masters to Jack Nicklaus, Norman was again in contention at the US Open. Leading by three at the turn in the third round, he dropped a shot at the 10th and then had a double bogey at the 13th. Now Lee Trevino, his playing partner, was level with the Australian. On the 14th fairway, Norman and Trevino were waiting for the group ahead to leave the green, when a spectator shouted: 'Are you choking, Norman? Are you choking just like at the Masters?'

Norman, who was not far from the right-hand edge of the fairway, standing with his arms crossed staring at the green, slowly turned his head to the right and looked into the crowd. Tight-lipped but seemingly more amused than irritated, Norman soon turned back and, as the green cleared, got on with playing his shot. Instead of marching after his ball, however, Norman walked into the crowd, wagging his finger in the face of one particular man and remonstrating: 'Look, if you want to say something to me, say it in the car park afterwards when I can do something about it.'

It was an extraordinary outburst which Norman immediately regretted, but having got the anger out of his system he soon settled down and held a one-stroke lead overnight. The following day he fell down the leaderboard and said he felt 'flat'.

A few years later, Norman and Steve Elkington, along with their pro-am partners from a charity event hosted by Peter Jacobsen in Portland, Oregon, were having a drink in a bar when four men in their twenties entered, recognised one of the group and started up with taunts such as: 'You're a choker, Norman.' The group were swift to leave but the hecklers followed them out and threw beer bottles at their car before getting in their own car and blocking the exit from the car park.

The police had been called and were swiftly on the scene. Establishing the story, the police asked Norman and his party if they wanted to press charges but mindful of not wanting to create any negative publicity for Jacobsen's tournament, they offered the idiots the choice between apologising or a night in jail. They apologised.

There were countless references in print to Norman choking throughout his career, not least in the days following the 1996 Masters. His collapse was labelled by the *Sydney Morning Herald* as 'one of the greatest chokes in sporting history' and when Emirates Team New Zealand lost the 2013 America's Cup to Oracle Team USA after leading 8-1 with eight races left, it was another excuse to put Norman into a list of sporting chokes. Later in 1996 Norman told *Golf World*: 'A lot of nonsense is talked about "choking". To me it means not being able to pull the club back, it means struggling to breathe. Of course, there are nerves when you are just a few holes away from a major title. Then it is very difficult. It's like when you are a kid and you don't want to walk into a dark room because you are not sure what is in there or if you can handle it.'

When it came to knowing if one can handle winning a major, Faldo was pretty certain about it but for Norman there were always doubts. Faldo seemed to be marching towards the light, Norman back into the dark that he feared as a child. Only in his chosen sporting arena could a frailty be so publicly exposed. It is not a great epitaph when you feature in the tail-end summation of a Malcolm Gladwell essay in the *New Yorker*, published in August 2000, entitled 'The Art of Failure – Why some people choke and others panic'.

Describing the circumstances on the 9th hole of the final round of the 1996 Masters, Gladwell wrote: 'Norman was next. He stood over the ball. "The one thing you guard against here is short," the announcer said, stating the obvious. Norman swung and then froze, his club in mid-air, following the ball in flight. It was short. Norman watched, stone-faced, as the ball rolled thirty yards back down the hill, and with that error something inside of him broke.'

For the first three days, the 'most striking aspect of Norman's performance was his composure', wrote Lauren St John in her 1998 biography of Norman. 'He was as tranquil as a Zen student trimming a bonsai tree.' But watching the final round on television, Australian golfer Wayne Grady noticed a difference in Norman, still leading by three but with his lead cut in half, saying: 'You could see in his face then that he was in trouble.'

Faldo had regained the honour and drove off first. The 9th hole scoots downhill and turns from right to left as the terrain in the landing area slopes from left to right. At the bottom of the valley is a spectator crosswalk and then the hole juts severely uphill to a green seemingly perched up in the heavens. Faldo's drive finished on the right side of the fairway still just on the downslope. Norman, as usual, knocked his drive past Faldo's and found a more level lie, just short of the crosswalk. Faldo only had a wedge shot to the green from 112 yards but, with his lie, found it difficult to impart enough backspin on the ball. His approach scooted through to the back of the green.

The 9th green has upper and lower plateaus, providing all the necessary pin positions for the week, but also a third section at the front which is merely the start of the precipice that then becomes the steep decline back down the fairway. The hole on this Masters Sunday was cut on the left of the middle tier but only just over the 'false front' to the green. Norman always got extreme backspin with his short irons and now, from his level lie 98 yards from the green, he needed to hit his wedge shot to the back of the middle tier so that it recoiled towards the hole but without going past it.

Instead, he pitched the ball hole high. There was a momentary pause as the backspin kicked in and the ball gained purchase on one of the most slippery Augusta greens. Then it was rolling back down the green and the fairway, on and on for what must have felt like eternity to the Australian. Both players, their caddies, all the spectators and all those watching on television knew this was a cardinal error. 'I just mis-hit it,' Norman admitted.

Norman now faced a chip from 30 yards short of the green that had a high tariff. He played it well, and the ball almost hit the flagstick, but it rolled on eight feet past. Faldo, meanwhile, had a putt of around 35 feet which had to go down from one tier to another. It would have been easy to rush it past the hole and then face the same fate as Norman, except having taken a stroke more, but he judged it perfectly; the ball even touched the right lip before gently stopping a foot away. He raised his hand to the tip of an imaginary cap and tapped in for a safe par. Norman's par putt swung violently from right to left, too early to hold the right line, and finished well left of the hole. He tapped in for his third bogey of the day and an outward 38, two over par. Faldo was out in 34, two under par, and the lead had now gone from six to just two strokes.

Bruce Edwards, who caddied for Tom Watson for many years but also had a spell with Norman, told St John: 'The reason Nick Faldo is such a wonderful player is because he doesn't really care about being in there three feet from the hole. He's going to put it in there where he's not going to make bogey. He won the British

Open with 18 pars which, God bless him, is how you play the game. The 9th hole at the Masters was a typical example. He didn't care that he was 35 feet by. He'll take his four. "Go ahead and make your mistake. Oh, you just did."'

Choke, such an ugly word but perhaps appropriately so for a such a painful act – it is often harrowing to watch, let alone experience. In golf, the classic chokes come when a player is on the verge of victory but misses a tiny putt, such as Scott Hoch at the 1989 Masters or I.K. Kim at the 2012 Kraft Nabisco Championship, the first women's major of the season. These are momentary aberrations – along with shots heading into water or the crowd on many a finishing hole. Norman was guilty of those mishaps in his time but the 1996 Masters was more of a full-length meltdown. It just was not his day.

According to Gladwell in 'The Art of Failure', panic and choking are opposites. 'Choking is about thinking too much. Panic is about thinking too little. Choking is about loss of instinct. Panic is reversion to instinct.' Novice pilots and scuba divers can get into trouble when a lack of experience means they have too few instincts to fall back on. Experienced performers get into trouble when they stop acting on instinct and start second-guessing themselves. Choking occurs under pressure, when trying to live up to expectations, when the big prize is on the line. 'Choking is a central part of the drama of athletic competition,' Gladwell wrote, 'because the spectators have to be there – and the ability to overcome the pressure of the spectators is part of what it means to be a champion.'

To Nick Price, it is ridiculous to call his friend Norman a choker because he won countless tournaments throughout his career: 'Guys who are good players but won only two tournaments their whole careers, something stops them playing well under pressure, and whether that's guts or that they're afraid of success... those guys are the chokers.' Norman never seemed afraid of success or playing in front of crowds, though, he later admitted, at the start of his professional career he went 'from being an introvert, a shy guy, to a guy thrust into the world, and I had to adapt very quickly and teach myself to change'.

Golf, like other sports, operates at different levels, even in the professional game where there is a commercial necessity to suggest there is a big event on every week. Charles Price wrote in *A Golf Story*, a chronicle of Bobby Jones and the history of the Masters: 'Tournament golf is to ordinary golf what walking a tightrope is to walking along the ground. You have to watch your step. But in tournament golf, relatively speaking, the rope is only six feet off the ground. In championship golf, they raise the rope to 60 feet. Golfers who at six feet off the ground could do handstands, pirouettes, and back flips, now find that they can't even walk across it. National championship golf – to go as high in golf as you can go – is when they throw the net away. What's more, you are playing under the glare of the spotlight, the whole world waiting breathlessly to see what mistakes you might make.'

Jones walked that tightrope better than anyone else but each of the big events he competed in, most of which he won, took their toll. There were only so many times he could put himself through the mental torture and he retired after winning the Grand Slam – the Open and Amateur championships of America and Britain – in 1930. He was only 28. He went on to found both Augusta National and the Masters, first played for in 1934. It started as a gathering of Jones's friends, who happened to be the best golfers in the world, but soon became one of the most important titles in the game.

On the final day of the Masters, in line with the other major championships, the tightrope is at its highest and tautest – and there's no net. Precision is everything. After his round, Norman identified a catalogue of shots that weren't quite right, including those into the first four holes, and into the 9th, which was six feet shy. 'This is a very precise golf course and when you're trying to play precise golf, you've got that fine line about where you can land it. It's easy for me to sit here and say I hit good shots into those holes and got screwed, but I hit good shots and the results weren't what I wanted. Now, if I'd hit them two feet further, maybe it'd be different. But that didn't happen. We can all sit back and second-guess about why I didn't hit it two feet harder.'

Rather than talking about choking, sports psychologist John Crampton, the nephew of Bruce, wrote in *golfmed.net* magazine in 2006 that performers slide up and down a scale between 'competitor' at one end and 'victim' at the other. 'Competitors are able to remain in control of their thinking, tension levels, technique and their game plan during key competitive opportunities. A "competitive opportunity" is a chance to improve your score, position in the field or potential to perform in the event. Victims have trouble converting opportunities; competitors convert a realistic share.'

Faldo was all competitor on that final day; Norman had been as well for most of the week but for a crucial four-hole stretch, from the 9th to the 12th, he was a victim. The article continued: 'He got found out in a small number of shot-making situations that were probably a combination of shot selection, shot execution, and emotional control errors. The many offhand and poorly informed comments criticising Greg that have circulated since the tournament have really not added anything to our understanding of what being an effective competitor is about.

'Any analysis of a competitive performance (good or bad) must consider the environment and the statistical realities of the event. Augusta National is brutal on players who make mistakes. Norman's string of mistakes and their consequences proved just how little difference there is between 68 and 78. Without the approach on 9, the chip on 10, a putt on 11 and a full shot on 12, Norman would have waltzed home. Obviously, he played those shots, and has to live with the consequences.'

Over the first nine holes of the final round, Norman had only hit the green in regulation three times (and one of those was at a reachable par-five). It was actually impressive he was only two over par for the day. Compared to 1995, when he topped the PGA Tour money list and had the best stroke average, Norman hit three per cent fewer greens over the whole season, ranking him 149th rather than 82nd. So something was up with his iron-play all year. Is it choking if there is a technical flaw which happens to show up at an inconvenient time? Of course, there did not seem to be any technical issues for the first three days. 'During the last day at Augusta, Greg's clubface got more closed and across the line,' Hank Haney, later Tiger Woods's coach, told *Golf Digest*. 'He always shows that tendency under pressure. I just don't see Nick Faldo doing that in the last round of a major. His swing is so fundamentally correct. And Greg's isn't.'

David Leadbetter, who was Faldo's coach and ironically the man Norman turned to later in 1996, said: 'He gets the club a little bit too far around him going back, which creates an in-to-out downswing path. Those two factors combine to make him sweep the ball away even with short irons. It's always been the weak point of his game. That's why he doesn't hit them solidly. That and he swings very hard. With Greg it's full-out attack.'

For Peter Thomson, the five-time Open champion and Australia's pre-eminent golfer before Norman, that was the problem. He told St John: 'He has a faith in strength, whereas the real golfer is the opposite. The reason Hogan took about 45 waggles before he ever hit a shot was to get the lightest possible grip. Greg was trying to hang on tighter and tighter in the mistaken belief that that would get him where he wanted to go. That was his downfall. He was trying to crush the club. It's a wonder the shaft didn't buckle.'

Thomson added: 'He's never lost because he's been afraid, which is what choking is about. That's absolutely untrue. But he had a faith in, I think, the wrong things, like hanging on too tight and using strength.'

A measured definition of choking is provided by sports psychologist Dr Bob Rotella in *Golf is Not a Game of Perfect*. The man who helped Padraig Harrington and Darren Clarke to Open titles wrote: 'A golfer chokes when he lets anger, doubt, fear or some other extraneous factor distract him before a shot. Distracted, the golfer then fails to do one or more of the things he normally does. He fails to follow his routine, particularly his mental routine. He forgets his game plan. He fails to accept his shots. Quite often under pressure, a distracting doubt or fear turns on the conscious mind. The golfer stops trusting his swing. He starts going through a checklist of errors to avoid. He gets tight and careful. When he's tight and careful, his body must work against gravity, rhythm and flow. His muscles get spastic, his feet get stiff, and he loses his natural grace and tempo. He hits a bad shot, relative to his ability. That's all that choking really is.' That's all!

Norman had noticeably slowed down his routine standing over the ball. He had tried to swing himself off his feet on the second shot at the 8th. He said afterwards: 'I never felt tight on the golf course but I felt I lost my rhythm.' One of the bullet points that Rotella provided at an HSBC seminar before the 2013 Open Championship summarised much of the above as: 'Be in a state of mind where process is more important than outcome.' Norman had lost a repeatable process and was wondering about the outcome of his shots, not his dwindling lead.

'As the thing starts to get away from you,' he told Jaime Diaz in a 2011 *Golf Digest* interview, perhaps the best analysis of that fateful afternoon, 'I wasn't paying attention to the shots disappearing [on the leaderboard]. I was paying attention more to, "Oh my God, I'm not hitting the ball the distance I want. Why am I doing that? Am I tight?" so I'd be thinking about my grip pressure or if my shoulder was tense. So with my perfectionist nature, with ten holes to go at Augusta, I'm trying to go through a checklist of problems I might be servicing, instead of trying to just... aaahhhhh... calming yourself down. I should have softened my mind. "You know you're playing great, there's nothing wrong with your swing, you're in position, just soften it." Instead, I had to know why, why, why. I got fixated on that, and I redlined in my decision-making.'

Norman was not a choker in the pejorative sense of the word but he could get out of rhythm, lose tempo, forget his game plan, and start second-guessing himself with the best of them.

Interviewed by *Today's Golfer* in 1997, sports psychologist Dennis Vardy said: 'One of the things that happened was that Norman was probably putting too much pressure on himself. It strikes me he is a very self-conscious individual, the sort of guy who likes people to like him, and that he felt he would let all these people down if he failed to win. This may be his weakness.' On the plane home to Florida that night, Norman hugged his friends and family and said: 'I'm sorry I let you all down today.' Later he spent a long time on the beach with his wife, Laura, churning it all over in his mind.

Vardy added: 'Some people perceive him as a great loser but that's because he gets himself into position to win so often. The more opportunities a man has for success, then the more, relatively, he will fail. It's nonsense to even talk about nerve or lack of it.'

Bill Elliott wrote in *Golf World* in September 1996: 'Winning most certainly is not everything, no matter what the tabloids scream each day. Not trying is a sporting sin, not succeeding is merely human. The thing I most like about Greg Norman is that he will never stop trying. This, I insist, is the mark of a truly exceptional champion as well as a balanced human being.'

A lot of people realised they liked Norman quite a lot after the worst of his Masters disasters. Not, perhaps, while he was dropping five strokes in four holes, going bogey, bogey, bogey, double bogey from the 9th to the 12th, but for how he handled himself in defeat, fronting up at another lengthy press conference at close of play. It was almost as if it was Norman's job to cheer everyone else up after a distressing day all round. 'It made riveting yet strangely painful theatre, rather like watching a cat play with a mouse before the kill,' wrote John Huggan in *Golf Digest*, 'although Norman made himself a whole slew of fans with his admirable display of sportsmanship in the immediate aftermath of what must have been a traumatic experience.'

Norman played in the Heritage Classic at Hilton Head the following week and there, on the course and on his boat *Aussie Rules* moored in the harbour in the evenings, he found players going out of their way to commiserate and say how much they admired the way he had conducted himself at Augusta. Jealousy of Norman was not unknown on the PGA Tour. Only a few weeks earlier, Brad Faxon had told *Sports Illustrated*: 'He's got that great look, the black clothes, the black hat, the blond hair. And players say, "Yeah, he's got all that money, so it's easy to go at every flag." But it's going at every flag that made him the money in the first place! All the helicopters and jets – that pisses guys off, too. They think he's big-timing 'em. But if he didn't buy the helicopters and the jets, they'd call him cheap.' Suddenly, Norman found he had rather more friends on tour than he had previously thought.

And then there were the messages that flooded in from all over the world. Former President George Bush wrote: 'You did more for the game of golf in defeat than you have done in victory. You deserved the victory, but in losing you showed us all something great about character. I know it hurt, but you are and always will be a winner, a true champion.'

From Scott and Sally Hoch: 'Been there, done that! We know what you are going through. Greg, keep your chin up. You will wear that green jacket one day.'

Jackson Stephens, the chairman of Augusta National, wrote: 'It takes a person with a great deal of equanimity to be the same on the three days you led the tournament and on the fourth day when you didn't. Your conduct and attitude will serve to improve not only your image but also reflect admirably on the game of golf.'

Most of the messages were in a similar vein, whether coming from those within golf or just members of the public. Norman found the messages from children particularly moving. David Tiffenberg, from St Petersburg, Florida, wrote: 'My name is David and I am ten years old. I have been playing golf since I was four years old. I hate, hate, hate to lose, but if I won every tournament I would quit golf tomorrow. We can't always have our heart's desire, but failing can make us stronger. You are the best golfer in the whole world. Be happy and know that there are a million kids like me who love and respect you.'

Inevitably, at Hilton Head, there was a heckler who, on the 18th tee on the Saturday, shouted: 'Why'd you choke last week? You cost me a lot of money.' Tony Navarro, Norman's caddie, wrestled the man to the ground. The spectator told a marshal:

'You saw that, didn't you? That's assault and battery, I'm going to sue Greg Norman.' The marshal replied: 'All I saw was a drunk redneck being obnoxious to a golfer.' The man was led away by police and charged with disorderly conduct.

'Perhaps something good did come from the whole experience,' Norman wrote in *The Way of the Shark*. 'I never would have thought I could reach out and touch people by *losing* a golf tournament. It was extraordinary. At a time when I might have been driven to a low point in my life, I was uplifted by the warmth of the thousands of people, most of whom I didn't even know. All of the good wishes, the kind words, the hugs, the renewed friendships – it was all like a shining light coming out of the darkness. And that light caused me to see life in a different way. It made me realise that there is goodness in all people.'

And, by the end of the day, he had also changed his opinion of his great rival, Nick Faldo.

Camellia

Hole 10
Yards 485; Par 4

At start	Hole	10	11	12	13	14	15	16	17	18	In	Status
	Par	4	4	3	5	4	5	3	4	4	36	
-13	G. Norman	5										-10
-7	N. Faldo	4										-9

NICK FALDO stood on the 10th tee at the 60th Masters trailing Greg Norman by two strokes. But as the players walked from the 9th green, past the back of the 18th green, and arrived at the start of the back nine, it was hard to tell who was leading. Had they started level and a two-shot margin opened up, that might have felt something substantial. This was far from the case. It was Norman who had set out with the notion that the two would start the day level and on that basis, he was already four shots down. In London, Ladbrokes were now offering each player at 5-6. But as Norman wrote in *The Way of the Shark*: 'Then everything started to cave in. And I do mean everything. I couldn't hit a shot to save my life. At the same time, Nick played extremely well.'

Faldo lives for just this sort of situation. 'It's a perverted sort of thing,' he told *Golf World* in 1991. 'You like to put yourself under the pressure of the majors to see just how much you can take, and at times you surprise yourself with how you actually feel and how well you are coping.' Ten years later, he told the same magazine: 'That's what it was all about – playing the game with that feeling inside your stomach. In that situation you have to say to yourself: "This is why you practised so hard, this is the final test." Somehow you find a way of enjoying it when you are under the cosh.'

It might have been hard to tell, but Faldo was enjoying himself this Sunday at Augusta. Norman less so, and Faldo knew it. Ever since the 2nd tee, Faldo had noticed Norman becoming more fidgety over the ball, taking longer than usual. The regripping got worse and while Faldo, famously, rarely talked to opponents during a vital round – any round, some of them would say, although that was not entirely true – he was a master at the dialogue of body language.

He wrote in *Life Swings*: 'For my part, I made a conscious effort to stand taller, walk more purposefully, to show no reaction whatsoever to any wayward shot. That is all you can do in golf. You cannot physically beat up the other guy and I would never dream of trying to psyche someone out with a patronising remark or throwaway line. But with my stride, my bearing, my expression, I wanted to remind my opponent, "Hey, I don't know about you, but I'm all right, mate."'

If Faldo was putting on an act, it was all part of the sportsperson's craft. 'I've long suspected that the best players are often the best actors,' wrote Ed Smith, the England cricketer turned author, for *ESPNcricinfo* in 2013. 'They are able to project an aura of confidence even when times are hard. This confidence trick is only partly about fooling the opposition. More importantly, it is also about fooling yourself. Mental strength, Steve Waugh once told me, is about behaving the same way in everything you do at the crease, no matter how badly you are playing. The strongest competitors are better equipped at superimposing a better alternative reality that replaces the facts as everyone else perceives them. Hope, optimism, belief – call it what you will. Perhaps it is simply the ability to conjure the feeling of afternoon sunshine on your face while striding into the teeth of a winter gale.'

Starting the day six strokes behind, and having battled his way through a winter gale in recent times, Faldo was displaying a confidence he probably did not feel. He had not won a major for almost four years, had barely contended at a major in the last two years and in the last 12 months his second marriage had fallen apart while his relationship with American college student Brenna Cepelak had titillated the newspapers back home. However, at the conclusion of the 1995 Ryder Cup at Oak Hill, during which he had not been at his best, Faldo had played a vital role in Europe's victory, withstanding immense pressure over the last few holes to beat Curtis Strange. Of the vital wedge shot to the last, his third on the par-four, he said: 'Knees went, first time that had happened. It took me to my max.'

His form early in 1996 was good but nothing special. His goal at the start of the Masters was simply to have a good week. Asked at the end of the week about his form of the last two seasons, during which he had dropped from first to 11th on the world rankings, and his Ryder Cup singles the previous autumn, he said: 'The game just wasn't as consistent. One of the things I felt was weak was eight-iron, nine-iron and in. You've got to get back to those shots and get them around the hole all the time. I simply didn't play as well, swing as well. There's a fine line in this game between shooting 68s and in the 70s.

'To play at the Ryder Cup and have it partly on my shoulder for a short time was absolutely nerve-racking. That was the biggest pressure I'd played under for a couple of years. It was a good booster. But here, you've got to survive for four hours out there. My mouth was sore. I was having to swig water at nearly every shot.'

They say the Masters doesn't start until the back nine on Sunday. It is one of the most familiar clichés in the golfing lexicon, right up there with 'never up, never in'. Television partly explains this. The Masters was first shown on CBS in America in 1956, with colour being added ten years later to better appreciate the Augusta scenery. At first, only the last few holes were televised. More holes were added over time but it was not until the mid 1970s that the entire back nine could be broadcast.

And although coverage was available from all 18 holes from 1984 onwards, it somehow became the norm to only show the leaders on the back nine – perhaps preceded by the last couple of holes on the front nine – even though it had become standard to show the whole of the leaders' final rounds at the US Open since 1977. It took until 2002 for the Masters to follow suit. Old habits die hard, however, for many of the local patrons, as spectators at Augusta National are known. If they do not have positions secured on the back nine, many will watch the leaders through the turn and then flood out of the grounds to watch the rest on television.

By 1996, there was plenty of discussion in golf magazines and newspapers about extending the three-hour window for television coverage on the final day. Once again, it was brought up at the pre-tournament press conference given by the Augusta National chairman, Jackson Stephens. The previous year Stephens had promised to look into it. The answer: no change. 'It's been studied and the answer is that we'll just stick with what we do.' Emphasising that the three-hour broadcast was only interrupted by 12 minutes of commercials, Stephens added of the prospect of any additional airtime: 'Until we can be sure of the same quality of television presentation, I just don't think that it deserves further consideration.' Another year, Stephens was asked if he watched the Super Bowl and replied, in his mighty slow, southern drawl: 'Fourth quarter.'

Apart from a close finish to a Ryder Cup, the last couple of hours of Masters Sunday are the best golf television there is. But, as 1996 showed, plenty can happen on the front nine that is also essential viewing. Norman could have been out of sight, but instead, another classic afternoon of drama was in store.

It is the course itself, and in particular the sequence of holes on the back nine, that dictates the drama. The front nine plays marginally harder but things tend to happen very quickly after the turn. Historically, the 10th rates as the hardest hole on the course. The 11th is the second hardest and the 12th is the joint-third most difficult. While the third-round leaders, playing last of all, are confronting this stretch of beasts, those playing ahead have reached happier hunting grounds. Two of the next three holes, the reachable par-fives 13 and 15, rank as the two easiest on the course and while the 16th is no pushover, it has seen almost double the number of holes-in-one as the other three par-threes put together.

With this concertina effect, there are certain to be multiple changes on the leaderboard, as players drop shots over the stretch from 10 to 12 and recover them from 13 to 16. But with water in play at the 11th, 12th, 13th, 15th and 16th, disaster can await anyone so eagles and birdies sit side-by-side with bogeys, double bogeys and worse. Players have won the Masters by charging home in as little as 30 shots – witness Gary Player in 1978 and Jack Nicklaus in 1986 – and after stumbling back to the clubhouse in 40 – Player, again, in 1961, and Craig Stadler in 1982.

'It is remarkable how rapidly the Masters is transformed from breathtaking sporting pageant among the glories of a Georgian spring into a savage challenge of a player's ability and an assault on his composure ruthless enough to leave a scar on his soul,' wrote Peter Corrigan in his preview of the 60th Masters in the *Independent on Sunday*. 'The battle for the famous green jacket doesn't really begin until the final nine holes and by then Augusta National has shed the trappings of paradise and takes on the character of a snake-infested swamp.'

But someone always makes a run and in 1996 it was Frank Nobilo. The Kiwi is the descendant of Italian pirates who made their merry way around their homeland and into the Balkans before decamping for New Zealand. Nobilo, 35, was a regular winner on the European Tour and since 1989 had sported a piratical beard, claiming that whenever he shaved it off he did not play as well. Though bothered by back problems, he had a fine swing and enjoyed playing on courses you could describe as 'tough but fair'. He had been in the top ten at the last two US Opens and he had a simple answer to questions from the American media about why he was suddenly playing better in the majors – because now he was getting to play in them.

This was his second Masters and, having started the day tied for ninth, he birdied four holes in a row from the 8th. After a particularly fine approach at the 11th, he overshot the green at the short 12th but was on the fringe and elected to putt. He struck the putt far too hard and missed the one back. After his bogey there, he drove into the trees on the right at the 13th, and had to lay up, but holed from more than 20 feet for his fifth birdie in six holes. Nobilo was now five under for the tournament and sharing second place with Phil Mickelson. The left-hander had birdied the 6th to get to seven under, briefly level with Faldo and five behind Norman, but his hoped-for charge never materialised after he bogeyed the next two holes. There was little else to distract from the Faldo-Norman show.

Overall in the 77 Masters up to 2013, 49 of those leading with nine holes to play went on to win, while 37 lost (some inevitably as there can be co-leaders out on the course but not co-winners). Lee Westwood got himself into the lead on the 10th tee in 1999 and then out of it pretty quickly, finishing in a tie for sixth. 'I felt sick,' he recalled. 'I feel nervous like anyone else, but that's as nervous as I've ever felt. I didn't handle that situation as well as I'd have liked to. That's the first time I had ever experienced a lead in a major championship, so it's bound to come as a bit of a shock.'

Norman twice failed to hold on to the lead with nine holes to play at Augusta, as did the last three 63-hole leaders, at time of writing. In 2013 Angel Cabrera went on to lose in a playoff to Adam Scott; the year before Louis Oosthuizen, out in front thanks to his albatross at the 2nd hole, lost in a playoff to Bubba Watson; and in 2011 Rory McIlroy just lost it totally. The young Northern Irishman had led for three days and despite an outward 37 still had his nose in front until his tee shot at the 10th. His drive finished between the Peek Cabin and the Berckmans Cabin – the latter named after the Belgian baron who founded the Fruitland Nurseries on the site in the 1850s – after hooking his drive into one of the 150-year-old pines and getting a horrid bounce backwards and farther left.

Never before had the CBS cameras had to focus their lenses on that area of the course and when they finally picked him out, the long-distance and unsteady pictures only added to the sense that we were intruding on a very private grief. McIlroy hacked his way to a triple-bogey seven, before three-putting the 11th for a bogey, four-putting the 12th for a double bogey and then pulling his drive at the 13th into the tributary of Rae's Creek that runs up the left-hand side of the fairway. He slumped over his driver, close to tears. It was a desolate image that might have become a defining one. But it turned out this was the moment the boy became a man. After an 80 he braved the media and said: 'I just unravelled. It was a character-building day, put it that way.' And two months later he won the US Open by eight strokes.

The only cabin a golfer in the Masters wants to end up in is the Butler Cabin, where the green jacket ceremony is performed for television. But since McIlroy's miscue from the 10th tee, the cabins to the left of that fairway have become one of the visitor attractions for patrons, especially those on practice days for whom it might be their only time on the grounds. Another new spot that draws a crowd is way down the hill from the same tee, deep in the trees on the right. This is where Watson ended up when his left-handed drive failed to cut back to the fairway. In the perfect illustration of his self-proclaimed 'Bubba golf' – 'If I have a swing, I have a shot' – he then hit a miraculous recovery that took a right-hand turn halfway through its flight and ended up on the green. 'As soon as I saw it, it just set up for a perfect draw, well, hook,' Watson said. 'It was only about 15 feet off the ground until it got under the tree and then it started rising, and hooked about 40 yards. Pretty easy.'

For any visitor to the Masters, whether newcomer or veteran, the first few steps onto the course, almost automatically, tend to be down the 10th before going on to catch the familiar vista of Amen Corner that opens up halfway down the 11th fairway. It is a magical walk. When the club opened in 1933, and for the first Masters the following year, this was how a round of golf at Augusta National started as well.

Dr Alister MacKenzie, the famous Scottish architect who designed the course with help from its founder Bobby Jones, originally intended the holes to play as they are numbered today. But just before the opening he and Jones reversed the nines, deciding that what now stands as the front nine was a far superior challenge. However, given that the National is only open in the winter, closing in the harsh southern summer, frost delays were a problem in the dell where Amen Corner sits. By starting on what is now familiar as the front nine, play could get underway earlier and by the time golfers got round to the 11th and 12th the winter sun had made them playable again.

Switching back was a fortunate move for the tournament as it has provided the opportunity for so much drama over the closing stages. But it was soon clear that the 10th hole could be improved. Originally the green sat at the bottom of the descent off the tee, near where the large, sprawling and tentacled bunker lies in the fairway seemingly not in play. It used to be a green-side trap. Moving the green farther back and up an incline made for a stronger hole and also avoided the flooding problems that plagued the original green. The old bunker in the fairway was once reached by a huge drive by Tom Weiskopf and today it is probably in range for the monster hitters – Watson's drive into the trees was roughly level with the sand – but the hole requires a hard right-to-left shot to take advantage of the tilt of the fairway and the combination of modern driver head and ball are not conducive to shaping such a shot so players tend to hit a draw (or a fade for the lefties) with a three-wood.

When the defending champion at the 60th Masters was asked for his decisive hole at Augusta, Ben Crenshaw nominated the 10th: 'Because it gets you in the mood for the back nine.' He might say that, given he holed an outrageous putt from nearly 70 feet on the 10th green on the way to his first Masters victory in 1984. 'It was absolutely off the charts,' he said. 'After it went in, I began to think it might be my day.'

Norman's history at the hole was not as encouraging. In 1981, his first Masters, he was just off the lead when he hooked into the trees at the 10th and took a double bogey six. Five years later, he had a four-putt on the 10th green for another six on the Friday. On the Sunday, which he had started at the top of the leader-board, he was still in a share of the lead when he took another six at the 10th. His drive hit a tree on the left and he had a long way to go for his second, which he hit short and crooked. He then chipped from behind a pine over the green into a bunker and took three to get down from there. Up by the clubhouse, his wife Laura sighed: 'Not the 10th again.'

It was the year, of course, of Nicklaus's last golden afternoon at the Masters and the scene at the 10th was beautifully described by Peter Higgs, the *Mail on Sunday* golf correspondent who, having a day at leisure with his next deadline almost a week away, had walked the first nine holes with Sandy Lyle, who happened to be playing with Nicklaus. Although tempted to return to the cool of the media centre to watch the rest of the action on television, he made a surprising decision to stay on the course. 'There seemed little point in trudging out into the countryside to stay with two players who were simply making up the field. But for some reason I did,' Higgs wrote in an essay in the sporting anthology *Moments of Greatness, Touches of Class*.

'The 10th is a wonderful long downhill par-four, which slopes up again to a green shaded by towering pine trees and decorated with dogwood and azaleas. It provided me with a lasting image of the day. I walked down the hill alone as my colleagues had hurried away to meet approaching deadlines or had given up this pair as a lost cause. By the time I reached the green, I had to stretch to see Nicklaus hole a 20-foot putt to go four under par. I remember being singularly unimpressed and having a feeling of contempt for the Americans all around me who were whooping and hollering and shouting: "Go get 'em, Jack", and "Way to go, Jack."

'As I stood there impassively I knew that this man could not possibly win. His fans were making fools of themselves.' But they weren't and he could. Higgs walked all 18 holes and saw all 65 shots that day played by the six-time champion and 18-time major winner.

Back to Norman and his adventures at the 10th: when he finished third behind Crenshaw in 1995 the Shark chipped in for a birdie here in the final round and afterwards boldly announced: 'Anybody who writes that the 10th is my nemesis, I'll wring their neck.'

In 1996 he parred the hole for the first three days. But it got him again on the Sunday. Faldo had the honour and his drive found the middle of the fairway. Norman hit a three-wood and came up some yards short of the Englishman. Norman's approach was pulled, though it just stopped on top of a mound on the fringe to the left of the green rather than rolling down the bank towards the gallery. Faldo now stood over his second shot and Dave Marr on the BBC said: 'This is not a man you want to be giving this much room to, by the way. He is a cold player when he plays and it is beautiful to watch how he takes apart a golf course.' His nine-iron did not flirt with the left side of the green where the pin was but found the centre of the green, 18 to 20 feet short and right of the hole.

Norman then hit a stiff-wristed chip that came off far too hot and ran on ten feet past the hole. Asked later about his worst couple of mistakes, he would say: 'If I had my second shot into 9, I'd have that again and just hit it six feet harder. And probably my chip at 10.' Australian golfer and commentator Jack Newton noted to *Golf Digest* the comparison with the third hole of the four-hole playoff for the 1989 Open at Royal Troon, which Norman lost to Mark Calcavecchia. 'Greg birdied the first two holes of the playoff,' Newton said. 'Then it got to the 17th hole and he hits it just off the back edge. He could have putted it, hit it with a seven-iron, anything. Instead, he tries to hit a fancy, spinning chip. Seven years later he tried the same fancy chip at the 10th hole in the final round at Augusta. He still wants to play the low-percentage shot he'd play in the first round, and that isn't the way to win majors.'

Faldo's birdie putt came up just a few inches short and, momentarily forgetting not to show any emotion, he turned away muttering to himself. But after he had walked up and tapped in for another comfortable, priceless par, the mask of inscrutability was back in place. Norman spent a long time standing over his putt with his left arm dangling freely, trying to ease away the tension, before regripping the putter with both hands. The par-save attempt was a poor one, the ball always on the low side. It was his second bogey in a row but the third hole in a row, and the fourth in five, where Faldo had gained a stroke. The lead was now only one shot.

Lauren St John, of the *Sunday Times*, saw Norman's manager Frank Williams 'rushing numbly down the hill in the sultry heat, panicking about Laura', Norman's wife. 'She's a wreck,' Williams said. That evening Faldo was asked when he sensed Norman was really in trouble. 'I thought 10,' he said. 'It was down to a shot. He missed his chip shot, and I felt then we were getting tight.' He added: 'Once I realised that Greg was in trouble, then I was just getting harder. Not harder on myself, just doing everything a little bit better. I mean, the pressure was immense.'

Between 1970 and 1995, 20 times out of 26 the leader with nine holes to play went on to win the Masters. The two most recent times that had not been the case were in 1990 (Ray Floyd) and 1989 (Scott Hoch). On both occasions the eventual winner was Faldo.

White Dogwood

Hole 11
Yards 455; Par 4

At start	Hole	10	11	12	13	14	15	16	17	18	In	Status
	Par	4	4	3	5	4	5	3	4	4	36	
−13	G. Norman	5	5									−9
−7	N. Faldo	4	4									−9

NICK FALDO's favourite golf course would be a composite including features such as the coastline at Pebble Beach, the pines of Augusta and the atmosphere of St Andrews. At the 2013 Open Championship, where Faldo was tempted out of retirement to play in his first event for three years, he added: 'But then you have to think of memorability and I've got a pretty special place right here, the 18th green at Muirfield.' Faldo won the Open at St Andrews in 1990 at a canter. But for his two victories at Muirfield in 1987 and 1992 he was racing flat-out until the tape, only confirming possession of the claret jug on the 18th green. No wonder it is one of his favourite places in golf.

Another is the 11th hole at Augusta National.

For his first two Masters wins, in 1989 and 1990, Faldo found 72 holes were not enough. Each time he was forced into a sudden-death playoff and it took two extra holes to prevail. By the time he did so, he was standing on the 11th green, far from the clubhouse, in the gloaming and, on at least one occasion, in the rain. His hallelujah moments came in Amen Corner. The 11th green was also the exact spot of Larry Mize's outrageous chip at the 1987 Masters.

If Augusta only ever became a scene of recurring nightmares for Greg Norman, it was always a dreamland to Faldo, from the moment when colour television first brought the sights and sounds of the golfing funfair to a 13-year-old watching late into the night over the weekend of Easter 1971. 'Even though the game and the great players were completely unknown to me, Jack Nicklaus made a clear impression on me,' Faldo wrote in his 1994 book *Faldo – In Search of Perfection*. Tony Jacklin's Open victory of two years earlier had clearly passed him by. But now Nicklaus 'drew my attention like a magnet', even though the Golden Bear did not win, finishing joint second with Johnny Miller, two behind Charles Coody.

'I was struck that weekend,' Faldo went on, 'by the same things that hit everyone who experiences Augusta for the first time: the tall, dark pines, the green grass and the colourful golfers. What most impressed me, however, was the sound. Not the whooping of the crowds – though that is thrilling the first time – but the very sound of the club on ball and the rush of air as the ball set off. I suppose the closeness and height of the trees exaggerates the sound, but I was very aware of that wonderful swoosh – the hit and the ball's launch are really all one noise. When I took up the game, one of the things I was seeking was to recreate that unique sound. It was a long time – a year or so – before I hit one properly and heard it again.'

That was doubtless on the practice range at Welwyn Garden City Golf Club, in Hertfordshire, where the teenager virtually took up residence, swiftly making a dent in the 10,000 hours of purposeful practice that is the basic requirement for expertise, according to popular recent theories. Swimming, athletics and cycling never had the hold on the youngster that golf did and in 1973 Faldo and his father, George, set off for Troon and his first visit to the Open. Sleeping at a campsite at night, the not-quite

16-year-old spent the long hours of daylight watching as much golf as he could find, being particularly impressed by watching Tom Weiskopf 'pinging' iron shots on the range while wearing only regular shoes, without any grip. 'That's impressive, he's going to win,' Faldo-the-future-television-analyst said to himself and he was right.

Three years later and Faldo was playing in the Open. He made his debut in the Masters in 1979 although after that he did not return to Augusta until 1983. That season he went on to win five times on the European Tour and claimed the Harry Vardon Trophy as the leading money winner. His success, which up until then also included three PGA Championships in four years from 1978, was helped by his putting, which could be brilliant but streaky and inconsistent. Tall and handsome, his swing was upright, flowing and graceful. 'In those days he had a long over-swing, a tremendous, willowy hip slide, a typically young man's action which propelled the ball enormous distances, not always in the desired direction,' wrote Peter Dobereiner.

A tendency to break down under the greatest pressure became apparent, however. At Birkdale in the 1983 Open, he led briefly during the final round but crashed to a 73 to finish five behind Tom Watson. At the 1984 Masters, he was in contention on the last day but went out in 40 and a 76 left him eight behind Ben Crenshaw. 'By halfway through Sunday's final round, the greens could have been written in hieroglyphics such was the difficulty I was experiencing in reading them, while the fairways, previously so accommodating, suddenly appeared narrower than a ten pin bowling alley,' Faldo wrote in *Life Swings*.

It was late in 1984, at Sun City, in South Africa, that Faldo met a man making his way as an instructor, David Leadbetter. Faldo admits to a fascination with taking things apart to see how they work – one of the things he found most enjoyable about cycling was getting a new bike, taking it apart and putting it back together again – and he had always taken the same approach to his swing. In Leadbetter he found someone on a similar wavelength. They started working together properly in 1985 and for 18 months remodelled every part of Faldo's swing – backswing, downswing, follow-through and everything in between. 'What gave me encouragement,' Faldo said, 'that I was on the right track was that suddenly I could hit a shot or a series of shots that were better than anything before. I'd hit a drive with real penetration or some iron shots which went where they should go. They were the stepping stones, the little boosts that kept me going.'

His form in tournaments naturally suffered at first. In 1987, he did not qualify for the Masters but happened to be going through Atlanta Airport, on his way to Hattiesburg, Mississippi, when he bumped into a bunch of European players and officials, and representatives of Her Majesty's Press, who were in transit to Augusta. 'The golfing world was assembling for the Masters and I was heading for a tumbleweed town in the woods somewhere,' Faldo wrote in *Life Swings*. 'I felt grievously humiliated.'

Instead of heading to the first major of the year, Faldo was entered into the Deposit Guaranty Classic, along with everyone else who had not qualified for Augusta. Still, it was a turning point, with four consecutive rounds of 67 leaving him second to David Ogrin. He returned to Europe to win the Spanish Open, and then that summer he claimed the Open for the first time at Muirfield. 'I had finally proved to myself that I had been right all along to go back to the beginning and start again,' he said. 'I had now achieved more with the new version than I ever could have done with the old.'

The following April, Faldo was back at Augusta and finished tied for 30th in the 1988 Masters. After his round he went up on to the balcony of the clubhouse to watch the closing stages of Sandy Lyle's victory alongside the BBC's Steve Rider. Lyle, with his effortless power and easy grace, seemed to be ahead of Faldo at every stage of their careers. Lyle won the Open first, in 1985, and now that Faldo had a claret jug, Lyle had added a green jacket. Mind you, if you were European and a golfer and swinging a club in the 1980s or 1990s, you weren't anyone if you didn't have a green jacket.

Between 1980 and 1999, Europeans won 11 out of the 20 Masters contested (in contrast to no triumphs at the US Open and the US PGA during the same span). Seve Ballesteros led the way in 1980 and 1983, Bernhard Langer followed in 1985 and 1993, while José María Olazábal was another double winner in 1994 and 1999. For four years in a row the winner of the Masters was British: Lyle in 1988, Faldo in 1989 and 1990 and Ian Woosnam in 1991. It was an unprecedented run of success, yet no European has won at Augusta in the new millennium. And although seven Open Championships were claimed in 14 years from 1979 to 1992, it is really at Augusta that the dominance of this group of players had to be acknowledged by the world.

Since the days of Harry Vardon and the Great Triumvirate had ended, all the leading players had been American, with the notable exceptions of the likes of Henry Cotton, Bobby Locke, Peter Thomson and Gary Player. But suddenly, a new generation of European stars all arrived at once, and brought along with them the likes of Norman and Nick Price for good measure. Ballesteros was born in April 1957, Faldo in July 1957, Langer in August 1957, Lyle in February 1958 and Woosnam in March 1958. They were Europe's 'Big Five'. Olazábal came along later, born in 1966, but from the moment he made his debut in the 1987 Ryder Cup as Seve's protégé, he was put on a par with the others.

Ryder Cup victories from 1985 onwards showed that the balance of power was shifting (Europeans joined the competition in 1979 to help Great Britain and Ireland, who had not beaten the Americans since 1957). But it was quite another thing to storm the great citadel of American golf, Augusta National, founded by the immortal Bobby Jones, quite so breathtakingly. How did it happen?

One theory Faldo subscribed to was that although Augusta might have become spiritually the home of American golf, the test on offer was quite different from that at other major venues in the States, or on the week-to-week PGA Tour. 'It's so different from everywhere else anyone plays, we all have to adapt,' he said. Europeans, it was felt, were at an advantage because instead of getting used to the same conditions every week, they had to adapt wherever they travelled, be it from the British seaside across to continental Europe or travelling around the world to Africa, Australia, perhaps Japan or South America as well as in the States. While the modern European Tour travels all over the globe virtually every week of the year, back then it stayed in Europe and was only open for business between April and October. To get ahead, Europe's best had to travel the world.

Faldo had left the confines of Welwyn Garden City when he grasped the need to challenge himself to an even greater degree. In his mind, he turned a relatively featureless north London parkland course into a major-championship worthy test by imagining water hazards and out of bounds features. Still, his first trips to the States were an eye-opener. 'When I first came to America,' he said, 'water scared me because you didn't see it as much in Europe. For a while, you really had to get over that. In Europe, you could miss a green by 30 to 40 yards and if you were a good chipper you could still get up and down. But in the States, plonk, you are in the water, you are dropping out and taking a double bogey when you are just two yards off the side of the green. It came as a real shock.'

Augusta National has its share of treacherous water hazards but in comparison to courses such as Oakmont and Winged Foot and other typical venues for the US Open or the US PGA Championship, there was not the thick rough just off the fairways and greens. There still isn't, although a bordering 'second cut' was introduced in 1999 that is as pristine as most courses' fairways. Someone like Ballesteros was constrained at the other US majors, with his off-line driving severely punished and his exquisite short game neutralised by long grass just off the greens. At Augusta, he was able to give full expression to his skills.

'The best players win on the fairest courses and Augusta National is, of all the courses used for majors in America, the fairest – by a considerable distance,' wrote David Davies in *Golf Weekly* just before the 1992 Masters. 'Augusta National feels no need to defend itself by growing debilitating rough. All the course asks you to do is to drive into the right place in order to have the easiest second shot. A bad drive is its own penalty, for it will make that second shot exceedingly difficult. Should you miss the green, the difficulty in making par is imposed by the speed, and the gradient, of the greens. Thus Augusta removes the element of chance attendant in golf, while the other two US majors enhance that element, and emphasize it.

'The best players will flourish where their skills are allowed to be expressed, and it is arguable that all the European winners of the Masters, with the possible exception of Ballesteros in 1980, were, at the time, one of the top-three players in the world. Given a course on which they could express their talents, it is perhaps not so surprising that they have won so frequently.'

It is a tribute to the genius of the design by Jones and MacKenzie that Augusta has always churned out quality champions. It is also the secret to why the tournament has become so popular with players and fans alike. For the first few decades of the Masters, the best players were all American, then they were suddenly European. Michael McDonnell, in *Golf World*'s Masters preview for 1992, also pointed out: 'Perhaps the most important factor in this run of victories has been the domino effect of success itself. More exactly, it is the *if-he-can-so-can-I* attitude which not only prompts each rival into action but also reduces the awe in which previously he held the grand title that his mate has now won.'

Ballesteros was the one who showed the rest it was possible. Price told *Golf Digest*: 'A lot of us who would win majors – me, Greg, Faldo, Sandy, Langer – were the same age, but Seve was our benchmark. He won four majors before any of us won any and he had immense charisma.'

'Seve was golf's Cirque du Soleil,' Faldo said upon the Spaniard's retirement in 2007, singling out the final round of the 1988 Open, when Ballesteros beat both Faldo and Price, as the greatest he had seen. 'The passion, artistry, skill, drama, that was Seve. It was the swashbuckling way he played. He hit it and chased after it and hit it again, but no two follow-throughs were ever the same. You just had to stand back and admire it. We had great respect for each other.'

Ballesteros loved nothing more than beating Americans at golf, and he also loved it when the likes of Lyle and Faldo followed suit. A mark of his greatness was not just his own achievements but what he made possible for others. 'I led them all,' the Spaniard said, 'winning the Masters, winning the Open, winning the Ryder

Cup, winning in America. If anybody asked me what my biggest achievement is, I always say that I am very proud that I was the first to do all those things.'

When Player made his great back-nine charge in 1978, Ballesteros was playing alongside the South African. On the 13th hole, Player told him: 'Seve, these people don't think I can win. You watch. I'll show them.' It was exactly the attitude the Spaniard would adopt and two years later, having already won his first Open at Lytham, Ballesteros went into the final round leading by seven strokes. What would Norman, 16 years on, have given for a start that included three birdies in the first five holes? Seve was ten ahead at the turn but such is the back nine at Augusta that moments later it was a very different situation. He bogeyed the 10th, then found the water at the 12th for a double bogey and was wet again at the 13th which cost a bogey six. Meanwhile Jack Newton had made three birdies and was now only three strokes behind. Soon, Gibby Gilbert was only two adrift but Ballesteros pulled himself together and eventually won by four.

Player, the three-time champion, was the only other overseas player to have won the Masters. Now Seve was the first European winner and, at 23, the youngest ever champion (and would remain so until the 21-year-old Tiger Woods won in 1997). He repeated the feat three years later, again winning by four strokes after starting the final round birdie-eagle-par-birdie.

More Masters titles should have followed for Ballesteros but he missed out due to the four-iron into the pond at the 15th in 1986 and his exit at the first playoff hole in 1987. Instead, it was Langer who was the next European to don the green jacket on Easter Sunday in 1985 – teamed with his red trousers the German said it made him look like a Christmas tree.

Lyle had played alongside Nicklaus on the magical afternoon in 1986 when the Bear won his sixth Masters. Two years later Lyle led after 54 holes and despite leading the US money list and having won the previous week at the Greater Greensboro Open, he admitted in his autobiography *To the Fairway Born*: 'With dawn came the same sheer gut-wrenching panic I used to feel as a child while sitting in the dentist's waiting room contemplating the pain to come and fully aware that it might be even more intense than my worst imaginings.'

He added: 'The difference between sporting triumph and disaster, always a very, very thin line, is even more slender at Augusta.' At the 18th hole, Lyle drove into a bunker but he just had enough clearance from the high lip to hit a seven-iron that flew majestically over the flagstick and then trickled back down from the top tier of the green ever closer to the hole. He made the putt to beat Mark Calcavecchia by a stroke, and the Scot became only the fourth player at the time to have won the Masters with a birdie at the last, following Art Wall (1959), Arnold Palmer (1960) and Player (1978). Mark O'Meara and Phil Mickelson have managed it since, in 1998 and 2004.

Lyle helped Faldo into a green jacket in 1989, and Faldo did the same for Woosnam in 1991, after the Welshman had holed a vital par putt at the last to beat Olazábal by a stroke. After Langer won for a second time in 1993, this time coordinating his outfit with a yellow shirt, Olazábal won the first of his two jackets in 1994 by two strokes from Tom Lehman. Ballesteros had left a note for his countryman before the final round: 'Be patient. You know exactly how to play this course. Allow the others to become nervous. You are the best player in the world.'

When Seve said something like that, you listened up. Coincidentally, at the Champions Dinner before the 1999 Masters, Player had Olazábal up against a wall reminding him of what a great golfer he was. Player is another who must be believed and victory duly followed. Faldo never needed anyone else to give him such a pep talk. What Seve told Olazábal was what Faldo always told himself.

It took until Faldo's sixth appearance at Augusta in 1989, ten years after his debut, to get comfortable with the course. Lee Trevino was making his 18th appearance and still did not like the course – the six-time major winner was never better than tenth in the Masters – but he took the lead by one over Faldo on the first day and the pair were tied at the halfway stage. It was the only time when the Englishman topped the leaderboard after one of the first three rounds of the Masters. Faldo actually led by three at the turn on Friday but as the weather got ever colder and wetter, his form shrivelled. Six under for the first 27 holes, he was eight over for the next 27. A third-round of 77 was completed on Sunday morning after returning to the course and playing the last five holes in two over par.

He was now five behind Crenshaw and spent the short break between rounds trying out a new putter on the practice green and working on a tip he had received from fellow tour player Mike Hulbert a week earlier: left hand back, right hand through. It worked. He holed from 25 feet on the 1st green and produced the round of the day with a seven-under 65. He was still three behind with four to play but birdied the par-five 15th, the 16th, holing a slick 15-foot downhiller with enormous break, and the 17th, where he popped one in from 35 feet up the slope. It gave the Englishman the clubhouse lead at five under and then he had to wait as others finished behind him. Ballesteros went in the pond at the 16th and took a double bogey while Scott Hoch, who had been leading by one, bogeyed the 17th and finished level with Faldo. Norman and Crenshaw both had the chance to birdie the last to win but ended up with bogeys so it was just the twosome of Hoch and Faldo in the playoff.

At the 10th, Faldo found a greenside bunker while Hoch's approach finished 30 feet from the hole. Faldo came out to eight feet and then Hoch putted up to two feet. Rather than finish off, he elected to mark and let Faldo putt. The Englishman missed so he registered a bogey. Hoch now had his short putt for the victory but to the shock of everyone but Faldo he missed on the left and had to hole the one back from five feet to continue the playoff. It was his first three-putt of the week. 'I never thought I was out of it, even when Scott had his two-footer,' Faldo said at the time. 'I know what was going through his mind. He's got to make that to win the Masters. That doesn't make it easy. This one was a battle of emotions.'

Hoch never did win the Masters, or any other majors, and was inevitably asked to look back on his miss when he stepped into the interview room after the first round seven years later. 'Oh, it's something that I wish wouldn't happen,' he said. 'It haunts you, guys and ladies. I look back on it two ways – that was probably one of my finest moments in golf and one of my worst all at the same time. I know I did everything that I wanted to do on the 10th hole to make that putt. I felt good about it, I thought I put a good stroke on it, I just must have lined it up left.'

Many consider that Hoch handed Faldo his first Masters title and had the American missed his bogey putt, they would be right. But Faldo certainly did not want to win that way and by going to the 11th hole he got a chance to do something exceptional to seal the victory. In what was almost pitch dark, and with rain that had been falling for some time, Faldo, playing the 25th hole of a long day, had 209 yards for his second shot with the wind off the right and he hit what he considered to be the best three-iron of his life on to the green.

Hoch, visibly shaken, missed the green on the right and did not pull off a Larry Mize chip-in. Faldo had a 25-footer for a three and probably only needed two putts for the win. He asked his caddie, Andy Prodger, for a line but all he got by way of reply was: 'It's all a bit of a blur to me, guv, you had better do this one on your own.' So he did. 'The putt came off perfect and then dived into the cup. That was the ultimate feeling,' he said.

A look of disbelief came onto his face as he raised his arms above his head, putter in his left hand, the fingers of his right hand spread wide, eyes skywards, mouth agape. It remains one of his favourite images from the game. 'What was so sweet was the way my kids copied it,' he told *Golf International*. 'I can remember Natalie showing me her golf swing and she finished it with her arms raised over her head, like I did. She was just 18 months old, and that was part of the swing, as far as she could see. It was what daddy did.'

A year later Faldo found himself in remarkably similar circumstances as he became the only player other than Nicklaus (1965–66) to defend the title successfully. Woods (2001–02) has managed the feat since. Faldo was playing with Nicklaus in the final round, which, thanks to a 66 on the third day, he started three behind Ray Floyd. He was four behind with six to play but then came his charge with birdies at the 13th, 15th and 16th holes, the last of those having been dreamt about by both Faldo and his new caddie Fanny Sunesson the night before. A 69 left Faldo at ten under par and after Floyd three-putted the 17th he also finished on the same mark.

In the playoff at the 10th, Faldo was in the same greenside bunker as the previous year. This time he came out to four feet. Floyd was a far different proposition to Hoch. A four-time major winner, he had claimed the Masters title in a runaway procession in 1976. Although he was now 47, he had another Ryder Cup in him as a player, having been the US captain in 1989, but in his prime he would have simply stared his 15-foot birdie putt into the hole. Instead he came up short and Faldo holed out for the half. After their tee shots at the 11th, Floyd nipped into a Portaloo and seemed to have to rush to catch up to play his approach first, Faldo having hit the longer drive. In contrast to his fine approach at the previous hole, Floyd now yanked his second shot into the pond on the left of the green.

'Bloody hell, what's he done,' Faldo thought. The Englishman now only had to avoid a similar mistake and hit a 'half eight-iron' 20 feet below the hole. Two putts were good enough for a successful defence. This was the fifth sudden-death playoff in Masters history and the fourth to end on the 11th green (and the last – now the playoff holes are the 18th and the 10th, on a loop if required).

Traditionally the previous year's winner hands the green jacket to the new champion. Had Faldo lost, he would not only have had to graciously shake hands with his conqueror on the green but patiently hang around for the presentation ceremony in Butler Cabin – incentive enough not to 'let go of the jacket'. Instead, the club chairman, Hord Hardin, did the honours for Faldo although secretly the double-winner would have liked Nicklaus to have per-formed the task. Like the man who had inspired him to take up the game in the first place, Faldo was now the dominant player and he almost won three majors in a row, just missing a playoff for the US Open by a stroke before claiming the Open at the home of golf. Only Woods in 2005 has matched the feat of winning at Augusta National and on the Old Course at St Andrews in the same year.

Faldo could not win the 1996 Masters at the 11th hole, as he had his two previous titles, but he could take another step towards victory. Norman, having lost a Masters here in grievous fashion in 1987, seemed more than a step closer to again losing what he coveted most.

Before the trees were added to pinch in the right side of the fairway in 2004, the landing area for the drive seemed wide open. But Faldo would aim for a groove that ran down the centre of the fairway. With a mid or short iron, there was no need to obey Ben Hogan's maxim that the second shot should be played to deliberately miss the green on the right. Hogan was talking when it was routine to face a long-iron or even a fairway-wood shot for the approach and the pond on the left, added in 1950, was to be avoided at all costs. Hogan would say that if he was on the green you knew he had 'missed' his shot. With the hole now extended back to 505 yards, 50 yards longer than in 1996, and in cool conditions, certain players still need to head right of the green and rely on a chip-and-putt.

But on that hot Sunday afternoon with the course running as fast as it ever has, Faldo, the first to play his approach, just needed a wedge. The hole was cut only four paces from the pond on the left of the green but Faldo went right for it. His ball came up just over 15 feet short of the hole but he had an uphill putt. Norman then hit his best approach since the 7th and finished pin-high right, just under 15 feet away. Faldo putted up just past the hole and marked, a tap-in only required for his four. Norman's problem was that his putt was downhill on one of the fastest greens on the course. He had found that out on Friday when he raced a short birdie putt well past the hole.

This time he did not race the putt but after it touched the right-hand side of the cup, the high side, the ball just kept on dribbling away from the hole. His par putt was almost three feet and this time it lipped out on the low side. A bogey five, his third in a row. Faldo tapped in and for the fourth hole in a row he had gained a stroke. In fact, he had gained six shots in 11 holes and Norman's advantage had been wiped out. For the first time since early on Thursday he was not leading on his own. 'This is where golf, pedestrian game that it is, can be so cruel,' said Peter Alliss as the television cameras focused on Norman. 'What demons are flying though his brain at the moment?'

Golden Bell

Hole 12
Yards 155; Par 3

At start	Hole	10	11	12	13	14	15	16	17	18	In	Status
	Par	4	4	3	5	4	5	3	4	4	36	
-13	G. Norman	5	5	5								-7
-7	N. Faldo	4	4	3								-9

ALL-SQUARE with seven holes to play, this was not a sudden-death playoff for the 60th Masters but it was a classic matchplay confrontation. Or, it would have been if there was not the feeling that a death had, in fact, already taken place. Amen Corner is usually abuzz on Masters Sunday but now there was silence. 'People were streaming back up the hill at the 11th,' recalled golf writer Patricia Davies. 'They could not watch any more.'

As Nick Faldo tapped in for his par on the 11th green, leaving him tied for the lead on nine under par, Greg Norman was already marching towards the 12th tee. Those in the gallery who had staked out their spots close to the tee were not moving yet and some had words of encouragement for the Australian. 'Hang in there, Greg' and 'Let's go, Shark' they shouted. But it was Faldo with the honour so Norman had to wait.

On this devilish par-three, having the honour is not always to be recommended. But now Faldo embraced the opportunity to put Norman under further pressure. His seven-iron found the heart of the green, 15 feet from the hole. The pin was on the right of the green, as it usually is on the last day of the Masters, that portion being angled slightly farther away. It is a sucker pin and plenty have gone for it and come up short in Rae's Creek. Faldo had aimed left of the flag, over the front bunker, the ball landing between that and the two bunkers at the back.

'It was like good old matchplay,' Faldo said. 'I got to go first and that was a breathtaking shot to hit across there. I hit a great shot and it went right where I wanted it to go. He had to hit it perfect.'

He did not. Norman's tee shot set off right at the flag. It looked like a high-tariff shot that was not struck with sufficient precision. In fact, he was never aiming at the flag, it was just badly hit. 'I pushed it,' he said. 'I wasn't trying to hit it at the flag. I pushed it probably 18 feet to the right and didn't hit it hard enough to carry it all the way on that line. I was just trying to put it on the middle-right of the green and I pushed it.'

The ball did not carry all the way onto the green but landed on the top of the bank in front of the putting surface. Down it rolled and the ripples as it entered the water soon fanned out. In the gallery behind the tee, Norman's wife Laura and daughter Morgan-Leigh hugged each other in mutual shock. There were a few shouts but the excitement was gone. 'It was unlike any Masters I've ever seen,' one regular attendee told Steve Eubanks in *Augusta*, his history of the Masters. 'The sounds were different. It was like a funeral out there. Nobody said anything. We were all just stunned.'

Back up at the top of the hill, far from Amen Corner, Nick Price, Norman's great friend, marched out of the clubhouse and said: 'This is upsetting. It hurts to watch. It's making me feel sick.' He was not the only one.

Amen Corner is the name given to the part of the course that includes the approach to the 11th hole, the short 12th and the tee shot at the 13th. Right about now for Norman it was more like, 'Oh, man, corner'. The official label was bestowed by the great American golf writer Herb Warren Wind in 1958. He opened his report for *Sports Illustrated*: 'On the afternoon before the start of the recent Masters golf tournament, a wonderfully evocative ceremony took place at the farthest reach of the Augusta National course – down in the Amen Corner where Rae's Creek intersects the 13th fairway near the tee...' Wind had got the phrase from the title of a song recorded by a Chicago jazz band led by Milton (Mezz) Messrow entitled *Shouting in the Amen Corner*. Whatever had taken place down there on the day before the tournament, it was the drama of the events at the 12th on the Sunday that helped Arnold Palmer to his first Masters title.

Jack Nicklaus says Augusta's 12th hole is the most dangerous in golf. The kidney-shaped green is extremely shallow, seemingly too wide for its depth. Rae's Creek runs in front of the green, waiting to catch tee shots that are not struck properly or weakly pushed, as well as little pitch shots from the drop zone and, if the initial shot has gone over the green into one of the bunkers or up onto the bank behind, recovery attempts that come out far too strongly. The biggest problem with the tee shot is gauging the strength of the wind, and its direction since the breeze swirls manically in this corner of the course, trapped between the pines behind the green and those behind the tee. There have been three holes-in-one here, most recently by Curtis Strange in 1988, but also a 13 by Tom Weiskopf in 1980.

Golden Bell is one of the most familiar holes in all of golf and Augusta National one of the most familiar courses thanks to its exposure year after year, the Masters being the only one of the four major championships to be played at the same venue. The First Annual Augusta National Invitation Tournament, as the event was initially known before co-founder Clifford Roberts persuaded

Bobby Jones that everyone else knew it simply as 'The Masters', was played in 1934; the 77th version took place in 2013. Of the other major venues, the Old Course at St Andrews has hosted the Open 28 times up to 2010, while Prestwick, the birthplace of championship golf, has been stuck on 24 Opens since 1925.

The Old Course has become familiar to many who have not even stepped foot there thanks to regular television coverage not just of the Open but, since 1985, the Alfred Dunhill Cup and the same sponsor's Links Championship. But St Andrews is all about being there, experiencing the spirituality of the place, and does not look at its best on the television screen. Even when actually there, it can take some time to get to know, as Jones discovered when he failed to complete his first Open there in 1921. But he came to love the place, winning there in 1927 and setting his Grand Slam in motion with victory in the Amateur Championship in 1930.

Augusta National tends to be love at first sight, though, whether on screen or in reality. Thanks to high definition and three-dimensional television, which bring out the gradients in a way regular 2D pictures can't quite capture, the expectations are pretty high for the first-time visitor but they are always surpassed. It was the same for Jones when he first saw the old nursery site in the early 1930s. 'It seemed that it had been lying there for years just waiting for someone to lay a golf course on it,' Jones said. Dr Alister MacKenzie, responsible for such gems as Royal Melbourne and Cypress Point and, like Jones, a fan of St Andrews, set out the initial routing, with Jones hitting thousands of shots during the construction phase to get the course just right.

The genius of the design was to offer a course that was enjoyable to play for any standard of golfer, that would not embarrass regular members and guests but, under tournament conditions, would test the finest players to the limit. 'Our overall aim,' Jones wrote in *Golf is My Game*, 'has been to provide a golf course of considerable natural beauty, relatively easy for the average golfer to play and at the same time testing for the expert player striving to better par figures. We hope to make bogeys easy if frankly sought, pars readily obtainable by standard good play and birdies, except on the par-fives, dearly bought.'

In contrast to many of the courses built in the early 20th century in America, with narrow fairways and thick, deep rough, where a 'shot poorly played should be a shot irrevocably lost', in the words of William Fownes, whose father Henry created Oakmont, Augusta National offered open fairways and little in the way of rough. Hazards such as water and sand were minimal but strategically positioned to allow higher handicappers to tack around them but to challenge the better players going for a big shot such as trying to hit a par-five in two. Again, the contouring on the greens and mounds surrounding them tax those unwilling to accept the medicine they deserve for getting out of position. There was a route for everyone, even out of the trees, but always a well-positioned shot was rewarded with an easier next one.

'MacKenzie and Jones both felt that Oakmont and other adamantly punitive courses rewarded straight, conservative shooting at the expense of the games more thrilling elements,' David Owen wrote in *The Making of the Masters*. 'A good golf course, they believed, is one that consistently supplies situations in which superior players can demonstrate their superiority. Houdini thrilled his audiences by escaping, not by being trapped.' Golfing escapologists Arnold Palmer, Seve Ballesteros and Phil Mickelson, with nine green jackets among them, were thankful to be allowed to show off their thrilling skills to such good effect but each might have won more often if they had not got into trouble quite so much.

British golf writer Leonard Crawley, a fine amateur golfer as well as the correspondent for the *Daily Telegraph*, played the course for the first time in 1947 and noted the St Andrews influence but added: 'They have not copied one single hole on those maddeningly difficult and infinitely fascinating links, but they built 18 great holes, every one of which is perfectly fair and provides a problem. It seems to me that each one demands that a player shall firstly and foremostly use his brains and not merely his physical and, in these days, mechanical ability to hit a target from a particular range. It restores the ideas of some of the old original golf links which furnished the world with those great players upon whose methods and tremendous skill the modern game is now based.'

Since Jones retired after his Grand Slam in 1930, no one has used his golfing brain to better effect than Nicklaus, who holds the record of six Masters victories with four runner-up finishes to boot. 'Augusta is one of the toughest golf courses as far as the mental challenge,' Nicklaus said. 'You have to think on each and every shot you hit. There are dangerous shots all over the course. I never felt there was a place you could relax at Augusta.'

But it was a moment of luck that really propelled the Masters and Augusta into the limelight when the 1935 champion Gene Sarazen hit the 'shot heard around the world', a four-wood second shot at the 15th that went into the hole for an albatross. Instantly the shot, the course and the tournament found a place in the game's folklore and it is has been building on it ever since. Wrote Owen: 'The double eagle [as an albatross is known in America] is more than just a notable moment in Masters history; it is woven into the fabric of the course.

'Every important shot is played against a backdrop that consists of every other important shot, all the way back to 1934. Every key drive, approach, chip and putt is footnoted and cross-referenced across decades of championship play. Every swing – good or bad – has a context. The history of the tournament is so vivid in the minds of the competitors and spectators that it almost has a physical reality on the course.'

After players have failed to emulate Sarazen at the 15th, they have to walk over a bridge that is now named after him to get to the green. The bridge over Rae's Creek to the 12th green is named after Ben Hogan for his then tournament record score of 274 in 1953, while the bridge back across the stream from the 13th tee is named after Byron Nelson, who picked up six strokes on leader Ralph Guldahl by scoring a birdie and an eagle at the 12th and 13th in 1937. And if your ball refuses to stay up on the bank above Rae's Creek at the 12th, then you are just not destined to win as Fred Couples was in 1992, when moist and slightly longer than usual grass on that bank saved the American in the final round.

But it is not just the good stuff that gets remembered at Augusta. Weiskopf is not the only player to have a 13 on the course; Tommy Nakajima did likewise at the 13th hole in 1978. 'Augusta is easy until you start doing things wrong – and it's easy to start doing things wrong,' said Tom Watson. 'Each wrong decision or wrong shot can multiply on you; it can spiral on you. It exposes every weakness. It exposes your doubts. I've seen it happen and it's happened to me. Augusta has a singular ability to make you feel helpless.'

At Augusta, a player has to contend with his own past disasters and everyone else's demons as well. This is exaggerated for the generation of golfers who grew up with ever-greater television coverage of the tournament. Players fear making a mistake because the consequences of doing so are seared into their memories. So on the 12th tee, as the wind swirls and swirls, players stand motionless, one hand on the head of a club that still rests in the bag, as if auditioning for the role of *The Thinker* by Rodin.

As Jones himself wrote: 'When a player is familiar with a course, as each hole is played, it is natural for him to conjure up in his mind visions of the way in which he has encountered trouble before on that hole. There is then a part of his concentration taken up with something he ought not to do, and that is so much taken away from the ability to play the stroke correctly. This is nothing but fear – dread of what may happen to the shot about to be played.'

'There is an element to Augusta that has a scare factor to it,' Faldo said. 'You know where you can't miss the ball. All the chip shots are tough. You have to loft the ball perfectly onto the green and you've got to release it and let it run perfectly. If you get either one of them fractionally wrong, it makes a massive difference. So that is always in the back of your mind. The great thing about Augusta is that the more you bail out, the harder it gets. You have to stay what I call "defensively aggressive". You've got to be able to hit the ball as close as you dare to the ultimate spot. You have to control your fear to hit the shots you have to hit.'

A great dichotomy about the Masters is that players have to get to know the course – only three golfers have won on their debut – in order to understand all the subtleties of the design, but that also brings experience of what not to do. The course forces players to think, but the trick is not to think about the bad stuff. Under pressure, however, that becomes harder to do and the pressure increases as the week goes on. 'Every day, every minute, the greens become a little more difficult to read and the fairways become narrower,' said veteran US tour player Frank Beard.

He added: 'It is hard to spar with history and tradition. You have to be able to keep it out in front of you like it's a punching bag and you punch at it. I could never quite get the right perspective the way Nicklaus could. I don't think I ever felt like I was worthy enough to win a Masters. I dreamt of it, but I don't think I ever saw myself in the winner's circle. When we went to Augusta, Nicklaus became someone different. He was worthy. He was a champion.'

Sports psychologist Dr Bob Rotella told golf writer Dave Shedloski: 'This is probably the one tournament – because of what Augusta is, what it represents – where guys go into it with so much desire to win that it almost overwhelms them psychologically. They make one mistake and they take it way too seriously. They try to get their games too perfect, and they try too hard. Then there's an intimidation factor of stepping onto this very important golf course, this historic place where you better dress right and act right and talk right, and it gets you out of your comfort zone. They have so much respect for the place that they don't want to mess up in any way. Throw all that into the mix of wanting to do great there, combined with getting into the history books – all of that comes to bear and might be more important than the golf course itself.'

After the second round of the 1996 Masters, Faldo was asked for his strategy on playing the 12th hole. 'Well, I try to breathe in and out,' he said. On the same day, Corey Pavin was asked what it was about the hole that 'seems to be driving everybody up the wall'. He replied: 'Isn't that like a standard question every year?'

Pavin added: 'The green is very shallow. I would say at most the depth from front left to back left is 15 yards and in the middle from front edge to back edge it is probably ten feet.' The moderator for the interview, Augusta member Dan Yates, confirmed those figures before Pavin continued. 'Also, it's a very flat green. So a shot that you hit in there, it's hard to hold it because it is not hitting into any slope. That makes it difficult. And anything that trickles over the green, there's a slope behind the green, so it will go away from you.

'And there's the creek. It's a shot you want to cut. The way the wind is blowing today, it's right to left in your face and if you miss your shot a little bit, it's going to get hung up in the wind and come up short. If you go left, it's going to go long. You have to be precise with it. And when the wind's blowing, it's hard to be that precise.'

In *Life Swings*, Faldo wrote of the hole: 'Standing on the tee, you have to make a decision on exactly where you want to land the ball; you cannot afford to pick a club then change your mind or you will have to start the thought process all over again. Given the brutish angle of the 12th green, if you intend to go for the heart of the target area then suddenly think, "No, I'll go left," you will have too much club, but if you decide to go right, you will come up short. It is one of the subtlest holes in world golf.'

In 1990 in the final round, Faldo went into the back left bunker and had a plugged lie. He got his second shot just over the lip and kept it from going into the creek but he still had to make a 15-footer up a slope from just off the green to save his par. It was an important moment in the round, allowing him to charge to the top of the leaderboard over the last six holes and get into a playoff. He was playing that day with Nicklaus. They had not exchanged a word until that point. Faldo said: 'Thank God we don't have to play that hole every week.' Nicklaus replied: 'Hell, I've been playing it for the last 35 years.' Faldo, cheekily: 'That's older than me, Jack.' No further response from Nicklaus.

Six years later, Nicklaus was playing the final round well ahead of the leaders. In the group just ahead of him, Fred Funk had hit his tee shot at the 12th over the green into the bunker back left. As Funk prepared to play his next shot he discovered a two-foot-long snake in the sand. He looked towards a rules official for some help but was told to play on. It is well known that Nicklaus does not like snakes. Before their playoff for the US Open at Merion in 1970, Lee Trevino produced a rubber snake from his bag and threw it across the tee, frightening the life out of the Bear. Nicklaus now hit his tee shot at the 12th into the same bunker with the snake in it and, as he walked towards the green, rules officials from both the 11th and 12th greens managed to persuade the snake to disappear into the woods behind the green.

Faldo had pars at the hole on the first two days and then dropped a shot in the third round when he went over the green. On the first day, no balls at all went in the water. On the Friday, the 12th was the hardest hole on the course. It all depends on the pin position and the wind. Norman birdied the hole on Thursday and did a Fred Couples on the Friday when his ball stayed up on the bank and he chipped close to save par. On Saturday he found the water and then dropped in a position that gave him a third shot from around 80 yards and he managed to get up and down for a bogey four.

On Sunday, just when he needed something positive to go in his favour, Norman had found the water again. Once more he dropped in a position to give himself a shot from around 80 yards as he had the previous day. He hit a good third shot, but not the great one he needed, leaving himself a 12-footer for bogey. Faldo putted first from 15 feet for a birdie and stroked it a foot past the hole, a confident putt that only just missed on the left, and he then tapped in for his par. Norman, again taking an age over the ball, never got the ball running at the hole. It finished just short and below the hole and he tapped in for a double bogey five.

Extraordinarily, Norman had taken a five at each of the last five holes: par, bogey, bogey, bogey, double bogey. Over those five holes Faldo had made up six strokes with nothing more than a birdie at the 8th followed by four pars. He had gone from four behind to two ahead. Had it indeed been matchplay that afternoon they would have now shaken hands on a 7 and 6 victory to Faldo. Eight strokes had been exchanged in 12 holes and now Norman trailed for the first time since early on Thursday.

Faldo, still at nine under par, led by two from Norman at seven under, with Frank Nobilo and Phil Mickelson at five under par after 15 and 13 holes respectively. After a bogey at the 12th, Mickelson birdied the 13th from the pine straw right of the fairway, not quite the stunner he hit 14 years later from an even trickier spot but another sign of his willingness to go for broke. At four under par were Duffy Waldorf and Scott Hoch, while Davis Love had the clubhouse lead on three under.

Until then, the largest lead lost at the Masters was the five-stroke advantage Ed Snead relinquished in 1979. The 34-year-old three-time tour winner was five ahead of Watson and Craig Stadler with a round to play and was still three ahead with three to play. But he bogeyed each of the 16th, the 17th and the 18th, where he missed a three-footer for the victory. He shot a 76 and ended up in a playoff with Watson and Zoeller. All three parred the 10th hole but Zoeller won with a birdie at the 11th. This was the only time Snead contended at Augusta, and afterwards he only won once more in his career.

For Norman, his latest collapse had become a long-drawn-out, gut-wrenching affair. By now he was six over par for the day and in danger of not breaking 80. 'I just told myself it's not over,' he said. 'I was two back and I said you can finish with straight birdies. A good run to the barn is what I said to myself in my head. I never gave up belief that I could win the tournament. But Nick played great golf the last six holes. Very, very solid.'

Was Norman still thinking straight? To his credit, a couple of birdies did arrive in the next few holes but it was Faldo's summation of the situation that hit the mark. He said that night: 'It's excessive pressure. It's the highest degree of accuracy of any golf course. It's the most strategic-thinking golf course in the world. You know what it's like, how they set it up. As the week goes on and the screws get tighter, it's a very tough golf course. That's what makes it tough.'

What Faldo said to his caddie Fanny Sunesson as they walked back to the 13th tee was: 'Bloody hell, now it's mine to lose.'

Azalea

Hole 13
Yards 485; Par 5

At start	Hole	10	11	12	13	14	15	16	17	18	In	Status
	Par	4	4	3	5	4	5	3	4	4	36	
-13	G. Norman	5	5	5	4							-8
-7	N. Faldo	4	4	3	4							-10

A S HE PREPARED to tee off at the 13th hole, Nick Faldo looked anything but machine-like. He was a whirl of motion, or at least of slow and soft movements, not fidgety exactly, just loose. He took his glove out of his pocket, rubbed his nose, put the glove on his left hand and took his driver out of the bag. He placed his ball on a tee in the ground and took two steps back, wiped his left hand down the left side of his shirt, then stretched each arm in the air one after the other.

He took two practice swings, the first just the backswing and the downswing, arriving back at the address position, then a complete swing all the way to the top of the follow-through. Then he took another step back and briefly rested the grip of his driver on his thigh while he spread the fingers of each hand. As he walked forward towards the tee markers and his ball, he transferred the club from his left hand to his right, then back to his left hand. He placed the clubhead behind the ball and gave it a waggle. Then he spread his feet into his stance. Backwards and forwards he shifted his weight from one foot to the other.

And then he hit the ball. The process took almost exactly a minute and at no point was he completely still, at no point could tension be allowed to creep into his body. Faldo was now leading the 60th Masters by two strokes from Greg Norman. He did not actually hit the best of drives at this always-critical par-five. It finished just on the edge of the fairway up by the copse of trees on the right, but not in them. Not ideal but fine in the circumstances. This is how Faldo had learnt to feel the pressure and still be able to cope. Faldo the golfer was no robot.

Yet he often was labelled a machine after having parred all 18 holes to win the Open Championship at Muirfield in 1987. Further proof seemed evident in the mechanical way he had spent two years completely dismantling his swing and putting it back together again.

Sports science was in its infancy in Faldo's heyday but he was at the forefront of it. He was prepared to work tirelessly with his coach, David Leadbetter, to understand which bits of his action worked and which did not and needed upgrading (pretty much all was in the latter category). But he was also aware of the need to attend to fitness, nutrition and psychology, although the last he only admitted years later when it had become fashionable rather than a reason to be laughed off the fairways. The week before the 1996 Masters his eyes underwent electrical stimulation massage from American eye specialist Craig Farnsworth, so it was no surprise to him that he was near the top of the putting statistics for the week.

What Faldo never lost sight of, however, was the passion needed to endure and ultimately conquer. All the vital preparation was only a prelude to hitting the right shot at the moment it mattered most. On the 18th hole at Muirfield in 1987, he had 190 yards to the green and thought about hitting a soft four-iron, as the yardage suggested and logic demanded, and instead, taking into account the adrenalin of the situation, went for a hard five-iron.

This is no machine talking: 'You can't imagine what it is like to try and play in those conditions. It's like those heart-stopping moments when you think you're going to be involved in a car crash. You go all hot and cold. It's such an important moment and yet it's over in seconds. I had to hit the shot and I didn't know if I could – but I knew it had to be done. Then, suddenly, there it was flying straight at the green and all I could think was, "Cor, look at that."'

He probably should have hit the four-iron since his approach finished on the front of the green, 40 feet from the hole. He putted up pin-high but five feet wide of the cup. He knew he had to hole the putt to win his first major championship. And he did. But he was not the champion until Paul Azinger, the overnight leader playing in the pairing behind Faldo, had bogeyed the 18th hole. The American had led by three strokes at the turn but came home in four over, bogeying the 17th hole as well as the last. Not for the last time, Faldo had won by avoiding mistakes when others could not do so.

In *Beyond the Fairways*, David Davies wrote of Faldo's 18 successive pars that: 'It led to him being labelled "machine-like" and "boring", yet nothing could have been further from the truth. Some of Faldo's pars were as exciting as any eagle, given the strain of the occasion. At the 8th, he was in a bunker some 30 yards from the green and hit it to four feet, to save his four. His huge sigh of relief was echoed later when he described that moment as crucial.'

'I was trying to make birdies,' Faldo told *Golf World* in 2002. 'Everyone makes a big thing of the 18 straight pars, and it used to irritate me a bit when people said I was boring because I churned out all those pars. If it had been four bogeys and four birdies, they would have described it as extraordinarily exciting. I was trying to birdie every hole, but I was nervous. I hadn't won a major before, the weather was like pea soup all week, and I wasn't putting great.'

It did not help that Faldo went into a 'cocoon', as he described it. He found a switch to shut everyone and everything else out, but that meant in terms of watchability he was some way behind the charisma of Seve Ballesteros, the showmanship of Norman, the casual effortlessness of Sandy Lyle, the pugnacity of Ian Woosnam. Even the Teutonic efficiency of Bernhard Langer had its own charm. But there always seemed to be a barrier between Faldo and his fans. 'Walking down the 14th,' Faldo wrote in *Life Swings* of the 1987 final round, 'everything became a blur; I could no longer hear the encouraging voices in the gallery, I was no longer aware of my surroundings, I was cocooned in a little world of my own. I could see my shoes and each footstep, but beyond that, nothing. In modern parlance, I was "in the zone".'

The better Faldo became, winning more by making fewer mistakes, the worse it got. By 1990 he was the most dominant player in the world but Peter Dobereiner, in a tongue-in-cheek column for *Golf Digest* that year, pointed out there was a conflict between his twin ambitions to win every major – he had won the Masters and the Open at St Andrews that year as well as just missing out on a playoff at the US Open – and inspiring people to fall in love with the game. 'My advice,' Dobereiner wrote, 'is that you perfect your recovery shots. Then, once you have the situation well under control, you can enjoy yourself by devising private challenges. "What if I were to pull-hook a drive onto that tiny island in the middle of the lake and then blast a three-wood over the trees onto the green?" That sort of thing. That would do a world of good both for you and your golf. After all, nobody loves a machine and nobody would want to take up a game that a machine can play better than a human.'

Hopefully, we are a long way off the time when a machine can play golf better than a human but perhaps we found out when Tiger Woods was at his peak in 2000–01 that making the game look too easy, or too much of a foregone conclusion, makes it more difficult to hold people's attention. There is the man in heaven in *A History of the World in 10½ Chapters*, by Julian Barnes, who takes up golf, starts getting better, but eventually gives up the game when he goes round the celestial course in only 18 strokes. It is the earthly, human element of players overcoming adversity that makes golf interesting.

Faldo demonstrated this at Muirfield in 1992, when he almost threw away a third Open crown. He had played sublime golf all week, almost faultless, especially during a second round of 64. 'It was a unique feel,' he said. 'I felt comfortable over everything, whatever club was in my hand. I have been trying to lessen my perfectionist tendencies. I learned this winter not to be hard on myself and realise you could hit bad shots. I am not worried about the clinically perfect round of golf. I enjoyed today because on every shot I set myself a target and nearly always got it.' The last day however was a different story. Faldo started with a four-stroke lead, but after 14 holes he had not made a birdie, which would have been reminiscent of five years earlier had he not had four bogeys. John Cook, playing ahead of Faldo, birdied the 15th and 16th holes to take the lead by two. Fortunately, it was at times like this that Faldo became inspired. At the 15th, he told himself: 'I have to forget about the whole week and play the best four holes of my life.'

He then hit a 'half five-iron' approach, a low runner that used the various contours of the green to such effect that the ball finished three feet from the hole. 'It was a shot we were working on all week in the breeze,' he said. This is the sort of creative shot, yet played under the maximum strain, that the constant 'fine-tuning with Lead' was all about. 'Everyone says Nick is so technical but he is far from a robot,' Leadbetter said. He is so feel-orientated. He has an uncanny ability to control his irons, which is all natural feel. He is very creative, very sensory, very artistic.'

At the 17th Faldo hit a four-iron to 20 feet and two-putted for another birdie, while Cook had only got a par moments earlier. Then the American bogeyed the last. 'I was alive, I was dead, I was alive again, then I was pretty much dead,' was how Cook summed up his day. For Faldo it was the reverse. Once more he needed a par at Muirfield's fearsome 18th to join only James Braid as a two-time Open champion at the course. This time he hit a three-iron from 196 yards to 25 feet and took the two putts he had in hand. Afterwards he was a wreck, in no fit state to give a winner's speech – lowlights included thanking the press from the 'heart of my bottom' and trying to sing *My Way*; he regretted the latter but not the former.

'It's the enormity of it all,' he gasped in the interview room. 'The pressure was so great. Thank God that putt on 18 was only one foot. I might not have been able to manage more. That it turned around was unbelievable. I had this horrible feeling of what it would have meant to have had a four-shot lead and to end up losing. It would have needed a very big plaster to patch it up. It went from almost a disaster to the absolute ultimate.'

Like this third Open victory, Faldo's third Masters triumph was another story of disaster and the 'absolute ultimate'. Few people knew how big a plaster Norman would need but Faldo was one of them after his Muirfield experience. Now he was playing the perfect round while Norman was self-destructing. But Faldo had managed to turn it around then, so he had to expect the Shark to attempt to do the same, however much onlookers thought the die was cast.

There were some things that Faldo and Norman had in common, as well as having been ranked the number one player in the world. They both took up the game late, at least by modern standards: Faldo was just short of his 14th birthday, Norman was 16. They were both inspired by Jack Nicklaus. And they both admitted to being perfectionists. It was how they dealt with the last that may point a clue as to why one ended up with six major titles and the other only two – 'only', as if it was not a considerable achievement in itself.

In a *Sports Illustrated* profile that was published on the eve of the 1996 Masters, Rick Reilly wrote of Norman: 'The biggest problem with a compass that's always fixed on Perfect is that golf is the most imperfect game. There are too many variables: wind, funny hops, golf gods who might think being handsome, cool and ridiculously talented is enough; majors we'll dole out to somebody else. The greatest golfers did not think Perfect. Walter Hagen used to count on missing seven shots every round. If he missed only six, he broke out the champagne.'

Reilly quoted Bruce Edwards, who caddied for Norman as well as Tom Watson, as saying: 'Greg has that tremendous ability to have six or seven straight birdies but then he'll get pissed off with a bad bounce or a bad result. I expected Greg to react like true champions react. If Watson hits a bad shot, he'll watch and take it and say, "That's my punishment."'

'Hell, that's not fair,' was Norman's response to the *Sports Illustrated* piece. But in 2011 he told *Golf Digest*: 'It's funny about pressure, because people often assume I didn't welcome it. In those situations, I usually felt... I liked it for some stupid reason. But obviously the recipe wasn't quite right. I've analysed it, big time, and I see more now. Because I've opened myself up to the realisation that I wasn't perfect, even though for so long I tried to be perfect and was sort of blinded by fear of failure to admit flaws. I still became the number one player in the world for other reasons, but I did some things wrong.'

This was a realisation that Faldo made during his career, not after it. 'He's done a wonderful job of changing his game over the years, not just his physical game but his mental game,' Norman said when the pair met in a *Shell Wonderful World of Golf* contest on the Old Course at Sunningdale in 1994. 'As one of his peers, who has the utmost respect for him, he's got that ability to lock in and be very tenacious.'

Norman won the exhibition with a 66 to a 67 but it was only close because the Australian dropped a couple of shots at the last two holes. Most days of the week, you would prefer to cross many fairways to catch a glimpse of Norman or Ballesteros, Lyle or Woosnam, Fred Couples or even John Daly. But on Sunday afternoons, with a big prize on the line, Faldo was riveting in his own way. 'One look at him in competition,' wrote Jaime Diaz in *Golf World* (US) in 1993, 'peering down another perfectly shaped iron shot, his eyes narrowed and his mouth grimaced, it is evident he is playing for more than money, more even than being the best of his time. Faldo is playing for the little cups, as he calls them. For History.

'It is a higher narrower path, and a sense of mission is palpable in Faldo. For all the criticism of the monotony in his game, this passion has made him a dramatic golfer, one whose intense sense of the moment lifts him to the occasion. How else has Faldo been able to win twice at Augusta National GC? On a course that rewards risk-takers, long hitters and supernal putters, Faldo has transcended himself.'

Faldo won six times at the two majors that are all about flair (the Masters, and the Open on the links of the British seaside) and never at the two majors that, in theory, reward monotony. It was not for want of trying. At the US Open he lost a playoff to Curtis Strange at Oak Hill in 1988 and just missed out on a playoff at Medinah in 1990 before finishing fourth at Pebble Beach two years later. His best result at the US PGA was joint second behind Nick Price at Bellerive in 1992, while he just missed the Azinger-Norman playoff a year later and was twice fourth.

Perhaps he was unlucky not to have picked up one of those championships but many thought Faldo lucky to have won as many majors as he did, when so often other people's mistakes proved crucial to the outcome. Azinger bogeyed the last two holes at Muirfield the first time and Cook bogeyed the last the second time; Scott Hoch missed a tiny putt in the playoff at Augusta in 1989 and Ray Floyd dumped his approach in the water at the 11th a year later. Faldo invokes the Nicklaus line that other players 'knew that I could finish but didn't know if they could or not. Of course, they didn't know I wasn't sure but as long as they think it, you have an edge.'

Faldo's version: 'It amuses me when fellow professionals say, "Faldo was lucky because he was given a couple of majors." I mean, how many do you think Jack won because he was in the right place at the right time, when someone else can't handle it? That's not being given it. Everyone has their own pressure threshold. Some people can't handle it on the 1st tee; others crack after 71 holes. That's all part of the test.'

'As a golfer, you put your head down and you go shoot a score,' Faldo said after the second round of the 1996 Masters. 'I'm in charge of my score and I can't influence anybody or anyone else, so the rest of it is history.'

History suggests that Faldo could influence the outcome even when he was trailing – as he was by five, three and six going into the final rounds of his three Masters wins, by three with nine to play at Muirfield in 1987 and by two with four to play five years later. 'I guess I didn't do too badly with my hair on fire,' he said. 'Trailing isn't really such a bad thing – as long as you have some holes left. You can see what's going on, you have maybe a little less pressure on you. Leading the Masters, gosh, it's almost too much because of all that it means. Behind, you can pace yourself a bit more and breathe.'

But now Faldo was leading the Masters and had driven to the right edge of the fairway. Norman, not exactly able to breathe freely, was still hoping to put some pressure on with two par-fives coming over the next three holes. But he pushed his drive through the first copse of pines on the right almost to the spectator rope line. His ball was lying on the pine straw, making ideal contact less than certain. Norman being Norman, his plan was still to smash the ball on the green and make something happen.

His caddie, Tony Navarro, did not like the play from such a scabby lie. The pin was tucked on the right side of the green, near where the tributary of Rae's Creek which runs across the front of the green turns up the right-hand side. Norman had 213 yards to the front of the green and was thinking about hitting a two-iron but it was fraught with disaster. As if he had not suffered enough already. 'We can make four the other way,' Navarro said, meaning his boss should consider laying up, pitching on and giving himself a putt for the birdie.

'I wanted to go for the green,' Norman explained that evening. 'I wanted to knock a two-iron onto the green and put some pressure on him. I thought that would be a really gutsy play from where I was but Tony talked me out of it.' Even when he was holding a short-iron club with which to lay up, Norman was still wrestling with himself. Navarro told him: 'Make sure you want to do it.' Norman shot back: 'I want to do the other one.' But after about three minutes, he finally did hit the lay-up shot down the fairway.

Leadbetter, Faldo's coach, later observed: 'His caddie had to drag the two-iron out of Greg's hands before he played the lay-up shot. He wanted to go for it. If Faldo is six shots ahead – and his own game is normally 60 per cent conservative and 40 per cent aggressive – Nick would raise that ratio to 80-20. So he's maybe a little more flexible.'

Faldo now had a decision to make as well. And he took even longer about it than Norman. He had 228 yards to the hole and initially thought of the five-wood he had put in the bag that week for just such a situation. But as he put the clubhead behind the ball, something was wrong. Although the fairway slopes from right to left, so his feet were below the ball, the ball was actually sitting on a slight depression that made it a downhill lie. 'It wasn't looking right,' he said. He backed off and then stood over the ball before backing off again, this time to a number of catcalls from the gallery. 'Too much angle,' he muttered. Having got himself into the lead, the last thing Faldo wanted to do was give his beleaguered opponent any encouragement by making a mistake.

'Now it's all mine to lose,' he said. 'Now I'd be very upset if I lost the tournament. It's as simple as that. I just wanted to play sensibly and not make a mistake and I managed to do that. I hit all the shots where I intended to hit them.'

Although the shot did not suit a five-wood, Faldo's ball was still lying well enough to take a two-iron to it. 'I thought about whether I should lay up but it was such a good lie. So I said if I want to go for it, it's a two-iron shot. It was 206 to the front, so that's fine. And I knew if I mis-hit the two-iron, I'd hit it left, where I could get up and down.' Finally, Faldo was ready and stroked the ball onto the green, the shot of the day and the week. 'I just buttoned it,' he said. 'I hit a great shot and it went right where I wanted it to go. That crispy iron shot was the best shot I hit all week.'

His ball was safely in the heart of the green, around 30 feet from the hole. In a strange reversal of the expected pattern, Faldo had ripped a long-iron shot onto the green and Norman had laid up. Faldo, being 'defensively aggressive', had delivered the blow that Norman could not. 'With the pendulum having swung in my direction, I knew one fantastic shot would send out even more forcibly the "I'm alright" message,' Faldo wrote in *Life Swings*. 'The visualisation complete, I executed one of the very best shots of my life, the ball soaring as if laser-guided into the heart of the green.'

Norman wedged his third shot to 12 feet and, after Faldo had lagged his extravagantly curving eagle putt down to the hole, he holed the putt to resounding cheers from the nearby grandstand. He had made four but perhaps not in the emphatic manner he had initially intended. Still, there are no descriptions on the scorecard, only figures, and he had avoided putting down a sixth successive five. It was only his second birdie of the day and his fourth in a row at the par-five. Moments later Faldo tapped in for his fourth successive four at the hole and he was now ten under par, still two ahead of Norman. A possible counterthrust had been parried.

Up in the television tower at the 13th hole was Ken Venturi. The main analyst for CBS, he would call the leaders through the par-five finale to Amen Corner and then hightail it back up the hill to the tower at the 18th for the conclusion of the tournament. No one knew what Norman was going through better than Venturi. In 1956, the 24-year-old amateur, an army veteran from San Francisco, led the Masters for each of the first three rounds and through 16 holes of the final round. He started out with a four-stroke advantage over Cary Middlecoff but collapsed to an 80.

At the time, the tradition at the Masters was to pair the third-round leader with Byron Nelson, the two-time champion, on the last day. Bobby Jones, the club's founder, wanted nothing more than an amateur to win his tournament – no amateur had won a major since Johnny Goodman at the 1933 US Open and no amateur has ever won the Masters. But Venturi was Nelson's protégé, the pair playing exhibitions all round the country, and there was concern that there should be no implication of impropriety. Instead, Venturi was allowed to pick his playing partner and chose Sam Snead, the one member of the great American triumvirate (the others being Nelson and Ben Hogan) that he had never played with. Snead could only look on helplessly as nerves consumed the youngster.

Just before the final round, someone asked Venturi: 'How does it feel to be the first amateur to win the Masters? You know you'll make millions.' Venturi wrote in his book *Getting Up & Down*: 'I brushed the guy off but the damage was done. He was right. I was going to win the Masters, which was being shown, for the first time, on national television. The victory would change my life. I would become the most celebrated amateur since Jones. I started to get tears in my eyes. With the business offers that were sure to come my way, I would be able to buy my parents new cars or a new house. I suddenly started to think about all the possibilities, when thinking about anything except my game was the last thing I should be doing on the final day of a major championship.'

Venturi three-putted the 1st hole for a bogey but then settled down and another bogey at the 9th still meant he had a five-stroke lead as Middlecoff also struggled on a windy day. But then Venturi bogeyed the 10th, the 11th and the 12th, a run eerily similar to Norman's. 'My lead, as well as my sanity, was slipping away even further. It is difficult even today, almost 50 years later, to describe what it felt like, and what little there was I could do about it. All I can say is that it is the most horrible feeling in the world. I'm sure Greg Norman knows what I mean.'

Venturi parred the 13th but dropped further shots at the 14th and 15th holes, though he still led until he bogeyed the 17th. Jackie Burke had started the final round eight strokes behind and his closing 71 was good enough to claim the green jacket – only Burke and Snead broke par on the day. It remains the greatest comeback in Masters history. Venturi reflected in his autobiography: 'I know it sounds absurd, but I didn't really play that poorly. I reached 15 greens in regulation. What killed me were six three-putts, while Burke didn't register one the whole tournament. I kept hitting the ball on the wrong side of the hole. Did I choke? Well, I suppose if you go by my score, you can make that argument. I chose to look at it differently. The day was tough for everyone.

'The flight back to San Francisco was the longest of my life. I replayed much of the final round in my head, and it wouldn't be for the last time. Over the following weeks, months and years, that round would come back to me in the middle of the night, and the result was always the same. I don't wish that kind of nightmare on anyone.'

Instead of making it big in business and staying as an amateur – he was later informed that had he won, a vice-presidency of the Ford Motor Company would have been his – Venturi turned professional and finished fourth at Augusta in 1958 and second in 1960. He was another player destined never to wear the green jacket, but on a broiling hot day at Congressional in 1964, playing the final two rounds on the same day, Venturi overcame heat exhaustion and dehydration to win the US Open. Injuries ended his career but he overcame a stammer to spend 35 years broadcasting on golf. He died at the age of 80 in 2013, just months after he was inducted into the World Golf Hall of Fame.

As the 1996 Masters unfolded, Frank Chirkinian, the legendary producer who pioneered the way golf was covered on television, 'recognising the parallel [with 1956], told everyone to let me run with it, and I did, describing Norman's frame of mind while everything was falling apart,' Venturi recalled. 'For me, it was very tough to watch. Afterward, Norman told me: "You got into my brain." He seemed surprised. "Greg," I reminded him, "I've been there." '

The sensitivity, born of Venturi's own experiences, shown to Norman on the CBS telecast, was not to everyone's taste but Chirkinian, a friend of the Australian who was working at the Masters for the last time, had no truck with any critics. 'There's no reason to say anything when a television picture is already telling the whole story,' he told Steve Eubanks. 'Some members of the print media criticised us for not saying on air that Greg Norman was choking. That really ticked me off. I mean, why say it? The viewers could see for themselves what was happening. It's obtuse.'

Chinese Fir

Hole 14
Yards 405; Par 4

At start	Hole	10	11	12	13	14	15	16	17	18	In	Status
	Par	4	4	3	5	4	5	3	4	4	36	
−13	G. Norman	5	5	5	4	4						−8
−7	N. Faldo	4	4	3	4	4						−10

AFTER MOVING away from the 13th green and, usually, its stunning backdrop of azaleas, the course turns back on itself for the 14th hole, Chinese Fir. It was Louis Alphonse Berckmans, a member of the Beautification Committee, who named the holes in 1932, working with Bobby Jones and Clifford Roberts. The committee had suggested 'concentrating in the vicinity of each hole a massed profusion of a distinctive variety of trees or plants that bloom during the winter season'. Remember, the course was intended only to operate in the winter.

Berckmans was 74 years old and no golfer but he became a member of the club and his younger brother, Prosper Jr, was the club's first general manager. Their grandfather, the Belgian Baron Louis Mathieu Edouard Berckmans, bought the old indigo plantation in 1857 and turned it into the Fruitland Nurseries, which imported plants and trees from various countries. Their father, Prosper Julius Alphonse Berckmans, who helped to popularise the azalea, continued the nursery until his death in 1910 and a few years later it ceased operation.

But many prominent features remain today, such as the azaleas and the long row of magnolias that guards the drive up to the clubhouse, known as Magnolia Lane. The clubhouse, which was built in 1854 and became the baron's home, was the first cement house constructed in the American South, while outside it is the country's first, and still the largest, wisteria vine. A big oak tree that stands next to the clubhouse on the golf course side also dates from the 1850s; it is here that people are referring to when they arrange to 'meet under the tree'.

Various pine trees dot the property, loblollies being the most common, with some more than 150 years old (particularly down the 10th) and others dating from the 1930s when the course was built, although more have been added in the last decade. A few of the plants after which the holes are named were already in place but most were planted specially. The Masters Media Guide estimates that more than 80,000 plants of over 350 varieties have been added to the course since it opened.

All of which goes to show that a hole without water, or even a bunker, such as the 14th, can still be visually stunning – and awfully difficult to play. Since 1952, when a bunker to the right of the fairway but not especially far from the tee was taken out as it only inconvenienced some of the older members, it has been the only hole on the course without sand, although the 5th, 7th, 15th and 17th holes started life without bunkers when the course was built. It is the contours on the green that make the 14th such a tricky proposition and where the hole is positioned makes a difference all the way back to the tee shot.

Still leading by two strokes, after the final pairing's first 'half' for six holes, Nick Faldo had the honour at the 14th and drove down the right side of the fairway, only to see his ball catch a slope and run down to the trees on the edge of the fairway.

Greg Norman hit a three-wood down the left side of the fairway, seemingly in better shape. But the pin was on the top left shelf of a green that essentially sweeps down in tiers from left to right, as well as containing a myriad of other slopes. Norman had to land his approach well up the left-hand side of the green but it pitched sufficiently short and right of the pin that it caught the slopes and ran down to the third of the tiers on the right-hand side of the green, leaving a monster putt. These were the very same slopes which helped him out on Thursday when the hole was on the right-hand side of the green but now each roll of the ball took it further from the target.

The 14th hole is a very gentle dogleg from right to left, not nearly as pronounced as the 2nd or the 13th, for example. Since a number of holes are shaped in this direction, Masters lore maintains that a right-hander who draws the ball (or a lefty who favours a fade) has an advantage at Augusta. As usual in these parts, it is a little more complicated than that. Few courses demand such an array of shots, fades and draws, with virtually every club in the bag.

In *The Making of the Masters*, David Owen refutes the theory that the right-to-left hitters have an inbuilt advantage. 'Although it is true that several holes on the course have fairways that bend to the left and therefore seemingly favour players who can draw the ball off the tee – the 2nd, 5th, 10th, 13th and 14th holes immediately come to mind – the matter is not so simple as it may at first appear. (And it doesn't help to explain the Masters success of Hogan, Nicklaus, Faldo and Woods, to name four notable faders.) One usually overlooked fact about Augusta National is that all of its notable right-to-left holes, including the 14th, have wide-open landing areas on the right but severely punish shots that are hit too far to the left.'

Take the 13th: how many players have overdone the draw off the tee and ended up hooking into the creek on the left of the fairway, or over it into the trees? Ian Woosnam was over there in 1991 but managed to make a bogey and went on to win. Others have not been so lucky. Such mistakes, according to Owen, 'violate a cherished piece of local knowledge: play away from the doglegs. On all the holes that seemingly favour players who can work the ball to the left, the only sure way to get into hopeless trouble off the tee is to hit a hook.' He adds: 'On holes where draws are seemingly favoured from the tee, the greens often demand approach shots that move in the opposite direction.'

A high fade is usually the best way of softly landing a shot onto the (usually) rock-hard greens. Faldo would spend weeks before the Masters practising his high shots and utilising them in the tournaments on the run-in to Augusta.

It depends, however, on where the flagstick is and with the back-left pin position on the 14th, getting close with any sort of shot is extremely difficult. Norman was just left of centre of the fairway with his tee shot and could not manage to get his approach close. Faldo's aim had been to open up the green by finishing in the right half of the fairway. And, as local knowledge avers, erring away from the dogleg does not lead to severe punishment. In fact, despite a tree a little way in front of him to the left, Faldo had a perfectly clear line to the green and safely found the heart of it, the contours again rejecting his ball from the top tier but leaving it on the middle plateau, 30 feet from the hole.

Norman faced a putt from more than 80 feet, up, down, and up again, and it was a brilliant effort. He got the pace almost exactly right and the ball came up six inches short and to the right of the hole. He tapped in for his first par since the 7th. Faldo, although from under half the distance, could not quite find the same touch and his lag putt came up three feet short. Still work to do, but he popped it in to maintain his two-stroke advantage.

It had been a golden decade for the Masters. From Jack Nicklaus winning the 50th edition at the age of 46 with his spectacular blast-from-the-past charge in 1986 through to Ben Crenshaw putting everyone through the emotional wringer with his victory for the recently deceased Harvey Penick in 1995. And the final round of the 60th Masters was proving one of the most incredible ever seen. But it was to be the end of an era. The next edition of the tournament, in 1997, would prove to be one of the most significant moments in the history of golf: the start of the age of Tiger Woods.

Woods played six rounds as an amateur in the Masters, finishing 41st in 1995 and missing the cut in 1996. After finishing his second year at Stanford, Woods made the cut at the US Open at Oakland Hills, finished 22nd at the Open Championship at Royal Lytham, where he won the silver medal as the leading amateur, claimed his third successive US Amateur Championship – not even Bobby Jones had done that – and then turned professional. 'Hello, world,' he said at the great unveiling, with a cheque for $40 million from Nike in his back pocket.

When Woods won on his fifth appearance as a pro, at the Las Vegas Invitational in a playoff over Davis Love, he qualified for the 1997 Masters. He won again two tournaments later, claimed the PGA Tour's Rookie of the Year, was voted *Sports Illustrated*'s Sportsman of the Year and featured liberally in the end-of-year musings in the golf magazines. Tiger was all the golf world was talking about, which must have been a blessing to Norman.

He began 1997 by winning the Mercedes Championship, the old Tournament of Champions which starts the year, for his third victory in nine events as a professional. Then came Augusta, where he made his third appearance – his first since turning pro. As the US Amateur champion, Woods was paired with Faldo, the defending champion, on the first day. Already one of the favourites for the title, there was much attention on the 21-year-old but at first his swing was out of sync.

He outdrove Faldo by 70 yards at the 1st, the only problem being he ended up in a greenside bunker for two and took a bogey. He went to the turn in 40 with four bogeys in all on the outward nine. With Faldo out in 41 and struggling as well, the massed gallery started drifting away to other groups. While the veteran Englishman could do nothing to rectify his problems, Woods seemed to flick a switch; on the 10th tee he adopted a new swing-thought which cured the faults in his action, and then started one of the best stretches of golf ever played at Augusta over the last 63 holes, making only three more bogeys for the rest of the tournament.

Now that he had his power under control, he was taking the course apart. At the 13th he hit a drive and a six-iron and two-putted for his birdie, but it was the 15th that really showed that Woods was playing a different game to everyone else. That day David Duval had a nine there and Norman had a double bogey on the way to a 77. Woods hit a monstrous drive of around 350 yards, getting a huge kick forward after landing on a downslope that few others could reach, and a second shot with only a wedge from 151 yards to four feet – eagle. 'It was a tough day initially but I got through it,' he said. He came home in 30, six under, for an opening 70. John Huston was leading on 67 but the story was all about Woods.

Faldo scored a 75 on the first day, eight strokes higher than his final round a year earlier, and although he was not playing with Woods on the second day, it was as if he was shell-shocked from being exposed to the ferocity of the new star's play. He scored an 81, his highest ever round at Augusta. It included a nine at that supposed drive-wedge par-five, the 15th. He missed the cut, as did Norman. Was the latter's collapse from 1996 still weighing on his mind? He was asked, of course, and, just as predictably, disagreed.

Woods added a 66 on the second day, moving into a three-stroke lead over Colin Montgomerie. This time he eagled the 13th, with a three-wood and an eight-iron to 20 feet, and it was there that he took the lead for good. Montgomerie had a 67 and was asked if he could win? 'It depends on how Mr Woods fares,' said the Scot, fresh off his lowest score at Augusta. 'The way he plays this course tends to suit him more than anyone else playing right now. If he decides to do what he is doing, well, more credit to him, we'll all shake his hand and say "well done". But at the same time, there's more to it than hitting the ball a long way. The pressure is mounting, more and more.'

Mostly on Monty. He puffed his chest out and had a smirk when he outdrove Woods off the 1st tee – Montgomerie had used a driver, Woods a three-wood – but for the rest of the day had a face like thunder. Experience might have been on the Scot's side, but it was no use to him and there was only one more day left before they would no longer be equal on number of major championships won. Montgomerie had a 74, Tiger a 65. Woods displayed his power at the 2nd, which was 555 yards long but downhill, when he hit a drive and a nine-iron over the green before chipping back to a foot for a birdie. He finished the round by hitting a sand wedge from 109 yards to a foot at the last. He now led by nine strokes from Costantino Rocca.

Montgomerie, 12 behind, pretty much stomped out of the recorder's hut at the back of the 18th green, up to the clubhouse and then on to the media centre and the interview room. He had not been asked to make an appearance, no official would have dared, but he had something to say. Before anyone could ask a question, the Scot declared: 'All I have to say is one brief comment. There is no chance – we are all human beings here – there is no chance humanly possible that Tiger is not going to win this tournament tomorrow. No way.'

With many writers on deadline, there were not many bodies in the room, but everyone else was still listening on the internal feed piped to their desks in the main auditorium. After a brief pause, one questioner in the room mumbled: 'What makes you say that?'

'Have you just come in, or have you been away?' Montgomerie asked, getting more than a little frayed at the edges by now. 'Have you been on holiday?' But, the questioner reasoned, everybody thought Norman was going to win the year before when he led by six strokes. 'This is very different,' Montgomerie opined. 'Nick Faldo is not lying second and Tiger Woods is not Greg Norman.'

Of Woods, Montgomerie added: 'I appreciated that he hit long and straight and I appreciated that his iron shots were very accurate. I did not appreciate how he putted.' The final question harked back to what Montgomerie had hinted at the previous evening, whether Woods was ready to win. 'He is' was the emphatic reply before the Scot made a swift exit stage right.

Montgomerie scored a flustered 81 the next day, matching Faldo from Friday. Paul Azinger, who played with Woods in the second round, had a 77 the day after. Rocca, alongside Woods on the final day, never threatened the leader and scored a 75. Woods posted a fairly conservative 69 and won by a record 12 strokes from Tom Kite. His total of 270, 18 under par, broke the previous record of Nicklaus and Ray Floyd by one stroke. He was the youngest winner at 21 and set records for the last 63 holes (22 under par) and the second nine (16 under for the week). He was the first player to win a major on his first appearance as a professional since Jerry Pate at the 1976 US Open.

And he was the first golfer not from a Caucasian background to win the Masters. The club had only admitted its first black member in 1991 and it took until 1975 for Lee Elder to become the first black golfer to play in the Masters – Charlie Sifford, who was excluded from the PGA Tour for years, had shamefully not been invited when he won two Tour events in the late 1960s. 'It's all over with now,' Sifford said. 'Lee Elder played, now Tiger has won it. I'm proud of them both.' Elder was in the gallery on the last day. 'I came to see history,' he said. 'To have a black champion of a major makes my heart feel very good.' Woods, wearing his already-traditional Sunday red, hugged his father Earl after putting out on the 18th green and said: 'I wasn't the pioneer. Charlie Sifford, Lee Elder, Ted Rhodes, those guys paved the way. Coming up 18, I said a little prayer of thanks to those guys.'

When Nicklaus came on the scene, Jones, sitting on a golf cart at his beloved Augusta, famously said: 'He plays a game with which I'm not familiar.' Now Nicklaus said of Woods: 'It is not my time any more, it's his. Tiger is out there playing another game. He is playing a golf course he will own for a long time. This young man will win many more Masters.' A year earlier, in 1996 when Woods was still an amateur, Nicklaus had predicted that the younger man would be the favourite at Augusta for the next 20 years, which has proved exactly the case.

Woods's golf reached a sublime peak in the summer of 2000 when he won the US Open at Pebble Beach by a record 15 strokes – at 12 under par when the best of the rest, Ernie Els and Miguel Angel Jiménez, were three over par – without ever three-putting. He then won the Open Championship at St Andrews by eight strokes, from Thomas Bjorn and Els, again, with a record score of 19 under and without going in a bunker all week on the Old Course. Nicklaus said: 'When he gets ahead, I think he is superior to me.

I never spread-eagled the field.' Then Woods won the US PGA at Valhalla, after a dramatic playoff against Bob May, the obscure golfer who came closest to halting Tiger's assault on history.

Having perfected a fade under the tutelage of Butch Harmon, Norman's old coach, Woods spent the eight months from August 2000 to April 2001 working a draw back into his game, especially for Augusta and the tee shot at the 13th hole. In 1953, Ben Hogan won the three majors he played in, while Jones claimed the original, old-school Grand Slam in 1930. No one had held all four of the modern Grand Slam events at the same time. Woods took the lead on the third day of the 2001 Masters and kept his nose in front on the last day despite being challenged by Duval, who finished second by two strokes, and Phil Mickelson, who finished three back. Whether it was a Grand Slam, a term usually used to refer to winning all four in the same year, or a Tiger Slam, the man himself could not care less. 'I've got all four trophies on my coffee table at home, that's pretty neat,' he said.

Woods in his prime was a combination of Faldo and Norman in theirs. He had the physical ability, power and panache of Norman but he also possessed the course management skills, the determination and the ability to play his own game and let others make mistakes that were the hallmarks of Faldo's game. Woods would never have let a six-shot lead go in the final round of a major. He would have been the one not making a mistake and forcing his opponent to play more aggressively than the circumstances could allow. Only once in 15 occasions when he led a major with a round to play did Woods not win. Although, all 14 of the majors that he has won to date came when he at least shared the lead with a round to go, while four times Faldo came from behind to win.

As Augusta made various changes to the course over the years, 'Tiger-proofing' became the nickname for the process. They were necessary as players were able to hit the ball farther, thanks in large part to improvements in the ball and driver clubheads. The Big Three of Nicklaus, Palmer and Gary Player used their annual trips to Augusta to preach the necessity of 'rolling back' the ball, stopping it from flying so far, otherwise 'we'll be teeing off downtown', as Nicklaus said. The most significant changes were the introduction of a second cut of fairway, a sort of semi-rough, in 1999, and the lengthening of nine holes in 2002 and six more in 2006, plus the addition of more pines in places to pinch in various fairways.

The philosophy that the difficulty of the approach shots needed to be returned to their former values was correct. When players could bomb a drive without thinking and then play a wedge for their second shot, it took away the subtlety of the design. But not all the changes were welcomed and when cold weather plagued both the 2007 and 2008 tournaments, the golf appeared to have become too attritional. Some intelligent massaging of the set-up has brought the thrills back for the players and the fans but is the end result that the course has indeed been Tiger-proofed?

Lengthening a course and making it more difficult should only play into the hands of a long hitter who happens to be the best player in the world by a country mile. So it was in 2001 and 2002, and again in 2005. But after collecting his fourth green jacket, Tiger's Masters run has stalled. Of course, he has not won a major at all since 2008 but his Masters drought predates his winning the 2008 US Open with a broken leg – perhaps drawing too deeply on his well of determination and perseverance in the process – as well as the scandal over his extramarital affairs which broke over Thanksgiving 2009.

It is not that his results have not been consistently high at the Masters since his last win; even when he is not playing well he has an ability to get the ball round the course in a tidy score. He was third in 2006, second the next two years, sixth in 2009, fourth in 2010, when the Masters was his first event of the season, and fourth again in 2011. Some of those years he had a chance to win, some of them he did not. In 2012 he certainly did not and finished tied for 40th place. In 2013, he had just got himself to the top of the leaderboard in the second round when his third at the 15th hit the flagstick and rebounded into the pond. He then took an incorrect drop and what initially went down on the card as bogey six turned into an eight overnight. He was lucky not to be disqualified for signing for an incorrect score had not the Masters rules committee admitted its own error in not confronting Woods about the incident in the recorder's hut.

Woods struggled that weekend, a common thread throughout his major performances in recent years, and finished four behind Adam Scott and Angel Cabrera. Two things have stopped Woods from getting nearer the tally of 11 green jackets predicted by Nicklaus and Palmer. His putting has not been as relentlessly reliable as in his earlier days but he has also put more pressure on it with his more erratic long game. In particular, with all the extra length at Augusta, driving the ball well is still a prerequisite. Woods has to hit the driver, which he tries to keep in the bag as much as possible elsewhere, and when he takes it out he fears the 'Big Miss', as his former coach Hank Haney calls it. Once, from the 1st tee at Augusta, he found the 8th fairway, waving to the 1st and 9th fairways plus various pines on the way.

And time marches on. He will be 38 at the 2014 Masters, the same age that Faldo won his third jacket, three years younger than when Norman had his best chance of joining the elite club. Neither contended nearly as often again as they imagined.

Woods was once asked if he felt it was strange that Norman was not able to enter the champions' locker room at Augusta? 'I do. It's amazing, for someone who's had such a great career and come so close, you almost feel like he has won the tournament, even though he hasn't, because he's been there so many times and especially on this golf course because it sets up so well for him. It's hard to believe he's not in the locker room.'

Firethorn

Hole 15
Yards 500; Par 5

At start	Hole	10	11	12	13	14	15	16	17	18	In	Status
	Par	4	4	3	5	4	5	3	4	4	36	
−13	G. Norman	5	5	5	4	4	4					−9
−7	N. Faldo	4	4	3	4	4	4					−11

A S THE LAST par-five on the course, the 15th hole offers a final chance to make a big move. Often it rates as the easiest hole (against par) of all at Augusta, although there is still plenty of danger to create another fine example of the risk-reward nature of the back nine. As Nick Faldo and Greg Norman teed off there was another small reminder of why it has been one of the most dramatic holes in golf since the very start of the Masters.

Playing ahead of the final pairing, Phil Mickelson, following a typically erratic spell in which he bogeyed the 12th, birdied at the 13th but bogeyed again at the 14th, made an eagle to jump back up to six under par. He was again now sharing third place with Frank Nobilo, two behind Norman and four behind Faldo. It was a textbook three, which is to say it was most un-Phil-like – a drive down the middle and an approach to the middle of the green before he added the characteristic flourish by holing the putt from 20 feet.

In fact, in 1996 the 15th played as only the fourth easiest hole on the course and among those helping to bump up the average was Colin Montgomerie. After his triple-bogey eight on Saturday he had another 'snowman' on Sunday. He played those two holes in six over and the other 70 in only two over par. He had laid up short of the pond in front of the green on Saturday so on Sunday he went for it in two. However, his three-iron clipped a branch and came down into the water. His next ran back down the bank in front of the green and back into the water. 'GOD. THIS. BLOODY. PLACE' gasped the world number two. He finished tied for 39th place, alongside Vijay Singh at eight over par, and ahead of only four other players who made the halfway cut: Jack Nicklaus, Steve Lowery, Seve Ballesteros and Alex Cejka. 'I've been coming here five years and I've not had an eagle and my best score is 69. I just can't get going.'

Augusta National was never a happy hunting ground for the Scot, but then nor was American golf generally. He never won on the PGA Tour but it was at the other two majors in the States that he had some of his cruellest near misses, particularly at the US Open. And he took some fearful stick from the galleries, particularly after being dubbed 'Mrs Doubtfire' by hecklers at Congressional in 1997. But the likes of Montgomerie and Lee Trevino, who could not get on with the course either, tend to be in the minority. Most players love the Masters. They may not love the fact that certain things on site are done differently to what they are used to at regular tournaments but they put up with that just to have a chance to play at Augusta.

And the chance to play in the Masters is not given to everyone. Fewer than 100 players get to contest the tournament each year. Qualification is like a longed-for Christmas present and the treasured invitations, for the first batch of qualifiers, arrives on the doormat around about that time of year. Part of the mystique is giving an invitation to every player who wins on the PGA Tour, so much so that when the qualification was dropped for a few years a part of the romance went with it. First-time winners on tour, or perhaps a veteran who has not got to play at Augusta in a while, value the ticket for the Masters as much as the oversized cheque with a long string of zeros. In the run-up to the tournament, players who have yet to qualify still have that last chance by winning that week. It makes defeat doubly hard to bear, as Ernie Els found out in 2012 when he had to sit at home – although three months later he solved the problem by winning the Open at Royal Lytham and earning a Masters exemption for five years.

No one quite knows how or why the Masters became a major championship in golf. It just happened, largely on the basis of knowing it when you see it. In 1950, Jimmy Demaret, who never won a US Open or a US PGA and finished tenth on his only appearance in the Open, became the first player to win the Masters for a third time and declared it the 'greatest championship in the world. Bar none!'

It helped that the best players won the Masters so it was obviously a major deal: in 1951 Ben Hogan won the Masters for the first time, the next year Sam Snead won for the second time, and the year after that, in 1953, Hogan won again (he also went on to win the US Open and the Open Championship, and is still the only player to win all three in the same season). The year after that, Snead won for a third time in a playoff over Hogan.

Arnold Palmer, whose charisma leapt out of the screen when golf was televised regularly for the first time, won four times in eight years and the game's new Big Three – for Byron Nelson, Hogan and Snead read Palmer, Jack Nicklaus and Gary Player – cleaned up every year from 1960 to 1966. Player went on to win three times, Nicklaus a record six. Tiger Woods joined Palmer on four wins, Mickelson joined Demaret, Snead, Player and Faldo on three. The best players of each generation kept winning the Masters.

In 1960, Palmer had won the Masters and thrillingly claimed the US Open at Cherry Hills, overcoming the still amateur Nicklaus and the veteran Hogan, and on the plane over to

Scotland for the Open at St Andrews got chatting with his friend, golf writer Bob Drum, about recreating Bobby Jones's Grand Slam. The modern professional equivalent, they quickly came to the conclusion, was the Masters, the US Open, the Open and the US PGA. And it has stuck ever since.

Yet when Jones heard a commentator at the Masters refer to it as a championship one too many times, he snorted: 'A championship of *what*?' To Jones, whose inclination was to dislike the name 'Masters' in the first place, it was always a tournament and not a championship. Fair enough, but everyone believes the winner is a major champion, and therefore it may only be the Masters Tournament but each year it provides a Masters champion.

Jones himself is the first reason the tournament has always been so highly regarded, even four decades after his death. He died in 1971 of an aneurysm after 23 years of living with syringomyelia, a degenerative disorder caused by a cyst destroying the spinal cord. He was named 'President in Perpetuity' of Augusta National. He founded the club after retiring in 1930 as the greatest golfer the world had ever seen who did not play the game professionally. He won the US Amateur five times and the British Amateur once, and against the best professional players of the day, including Walter Hagen and Gene Sarazen, he won the US Open four times and the Open three times.

He did not play many tournaments in a season but when he did it was under the pressure of being expected to win. Usually, he did. The lawyer from Atlanta was the most understated national hero. Hogan said of him later in life: 'The man was sick so long and fought it so successfully I think we've finally discovered the secret of his success. It was the strength of his mind.'

When the Augusta National Invitation Tournament was first played from 1934 onwards, his friends, who happened to be the best golfers around, came to honour the Emperor. They still do. A quarter of a century after his death, just before the 1996 Masters, *Golf Digest* published an extract of an Alistair Cooke essay from *The Greatest of Them All: The Legend of Bobby Jones*. 'Because of the firm convention of writing nothing about Jones that is less than idolatrous,' Cooke concluded, 'I have done a little digging among friends and old golfing acquaintances who knew him and among old writers who, in other fields, have a sharp nose for the disreputable. But I do believe that a whole team of investigative reporters, working in shifts like coal miners, would find that in all of Jones's life anyone had been able to observe, he nothing common did or mean.

'The sum of what can be said about his character, by me at any rate, is: that he was an incurable conservative frequently shown in the company of tycoons (more their photo op than his), which led to his reputation for gregariousness ('They say I love people, but I don't love people, I love a few people in small doses'); that he was a weekend golfer who rarely touched a club between October and March; that he showed a famous early streak of temper at St Andrews when he was 19 for which he proffered "a general apology" on the spot and was ever afterward restrained. In his instincts and behaviour he was what used to be called a gentleman, an ideal nowadays much derided by the young and liberated.

'What we are left with in the end is a forever young, good-looking Southerner, an impeccable, courteous and decent man with a private ironical view of life who, to the great good fortune of people who saw him, happened to play the great game with more magic and more grace than anyone before or since.'

Jones was persuaded to play in the first few Masters and kept going until 1948 but never finished higher than 13th in the first year. His magic had gone but he had imbued it in his golf course.

That became clear as early as the second year when Sarazen made his famous albatross and made headlines for the tournament around the world. With Craig Wood leading in the clubhouse on six under par, Sarazen had to play the last four holes in three under to tie.

'Paired with Hagen,' Charles Price described in *A Golf Story*, 'Sarazen elected to go for the green at the par-five 15th, ignoring the water in front of it. Hagen smiled and shook his head. But if Sarazen were to get any birdies at all, one of them would have to be here. There were not more than a dozen spectators by the green, one of whom happened to be Bobby Jones, who had wandered down from the clubhouse out of curiosity, possibly because of the friendly rivalry between Sarazen and Hagen. It was an interesting pairing apart from the tournament, now that it was all but formally over.

'Sarazen had started to choose his three-wood, but changed his mind to the four-wood before he pulled the three of out his bag. He then stepped into the shot with that one-piece swing of his, like a coach hitting fungoes to an outfielder. The ball struck the far bank of the water hazard abutting the green, skipped onto the putting surface, and softly rolled into the cup for a two.' The albatross, or double eagle, was the first at Augusta and there has now been one, and only one, at each of the par-fives. No one has since played a hole in better than six under for the tournament, as Sarazen did then, though in 2010 Woods did it at the 15th and Mickelson at the 13th, both with two eagles and two birdies.

With one stroke, Sarazen had caught Wood and after they tied at the end of 72 holes, Sarazen won the 36-hole playoff the next day. We now remember Sarazen for becoming the first player to achieve the career Grand Slam of winning all four majors, only matched since by Hogan, Player, Nicklaus and Woods. But at the time, it was 'the shot heard round the world' that made the bigger impact. Amid the Depression, six years after the stock market crash of 1928, the timing could not be bettered, according to Price. 'It would be hard to choose a year in the country's history when Americans were more eager to accept the element of luck,' he wrote. 'The nation had sunk to an emotional low point. It was without hope in the land of promise, without faith in the hard work that had made it so.

'The game of golf didn't have much to offer the man in the street, especially now that Bobby Jones was no longer performing the impossible. But it could offer up Eugene Saraceni, the son of an Italian immigrant, making a golf shot that was 40,000 to 1. That it happened on Bobby Jones's golf course and during his tournament – well, there was hope yet, some things you could still have faith in. Sarazen's double eagle didn't make the front pages, considering the aristocratic nature of golf and the thread-bare conditions of the public. But it came at a time when people would welcome anything lucky, anywhere they could find it, in the sports pages if they had to and about golf if they must, the closer to the impossible the better. Gene Sarazen's double eagle qualified as "impossible".'

The impossible keeps happening at Augusta. Simply looking at the last three decades: Nicklaus's late charge at the age of 46, Larry Mize chipping in to win a playoff, Sandy Lyle making a birdie at the last from the fairway bunker, Fred Couples getting a ball to stop on the bank at the 12th, Faldo overturning a six-shot deficit to Norman, Woods eagling the 15th with a drive and a wedge on the way to a 12-stroke win. A lack of Augusta's main currency, drama, in the second half of the 2000s was a serious concern for the current Augusta National chairman, Billy Payne, owing to course changes and cold weather producing less excit-ing fare, but then the event got back on track. Mickelson from the trees at the 13th in 2010, Charl Schwartzel closing with four birdies in 2011, Bubba Watson with his miraculous bendy escape from the trees at the 10th in 2012 and even an Australian finally winning a green jacket in 2013.

The Masters is the most anticipated major of the year because it is the first, coming eight months after the last. It means spring is here, or, at least, on the way. In the States the second Sunday in April is about the only time golf has the sporting landscape to itself. The National Football League is well over, college basketball, which induces mass hysteria every March, finished the weekend before, the new baseball season is only just getting going, professional basketball and ice hockey are two months away from their climaxes – and the weather in the northern half of the country is not gentle enough yet to have everyone outside for the afternoon. In Europe, the evening, feet-up time slot is perfect and in Britain we have been transfixed since that four-year spell when our boys could not lose it. In Australia, over a Monday morning breakfast, they kept watching because their boys couldn't win it.

Part of the reason the United States Golf Association chose to introduce a new broadcast partner, Fox Sports, from 2015 was that Glen Nager, the USGA president, was tired of only hearing about the Masters and its 'tradition unlike any other'. He felt that NBC was not promoting the US Open as successfully as CBS does the Masters. Nager told *Golf Digest* that while the 'US Open was considered the premier major championship in golf' in the 1970s, 'if we looked at indicia today, the Masters is considered the number one major in golf'. Golf's highest ever rated broadcast was Tiger's 'Win for the Ages' at Augusta in 1997, and his slam-completing 2001 Masters win was not far behind.

Though Woods has been the perennial favourite at Augusta for the last decade and a half, Mickelson, with his Normanesque impulse to go for broke, has been no less an important figure in providing drama at the Masters. Between them they dominated, claiming five titles out of six between 2001 and 2006. While there is no question Tiger is respected, Phil is loved. Part of the endearment is because he has messed up so many times. And he admitted when he screwed up. When he drove into the hospitality tents at Winged Foot in the 2006 US Open, and had a double bogey to lose to Geoff Ogilvy by one, he said: 'I am such an idiot.' For much of his first 46 majors, he held that unwanted tag of being the best player not to have won one. That changed at Augusta.

In 1996, Mickelson was playing in his fourth Masters. He had been seventh the year before and his eagle now at the 15th, combined with Nobilo bogeying the last to fall to fourth place on his own, gave Mickelson solo third place. 'It gave me a real good opportunity of experiencing being in contention,' said the 25-year-old. 'I had it last year, too. If I can keep putting myself in that position, the odds say I'll break through sometime.'

He had to be patient. His powerful yet sometimes wild game and his imaginative recovery skills seemed well suited to Augusta and he was already talked about as a champion-in-waiting. He finished 12th in 1998, sixth in 1999, seventh in 2000 and third in each of the next three years. It took his 12th attempt, in 2004, to get it right, after a thrilling ding-dong with Els, who was prowling the putting green waiting for a playoff when he heard the roar that meant Mickelson had holed from 18 feet on the final green and become only the sixth player to win the Masters by birdieing the last hole. 'Oh, my God!' he said as he hugged his wife, Amy, and their three children by the side of the green.

Mickelson won again two years later and for a third time in 2010, after a fine duel with Lee Westwood. The crucial shot came at the 13th, from the trees, off the pine straw, through a gap only Mickelson could see, from 207 yards with a six-iron, onto the green. This time the family celebration was all the more emotional since it was the first time Amy had been at a tournament since being diagnosed with breast cancer 11 months earlier.

Before the 2003 Masters, 40 years on since Bob Charles won the Open to become the only left-handed major champion, Mickelson was asked who would be the next lefty to win one. The American was more than a bit peeved and declined to answer. As great irony would have it, Mike Weir won that week to become Canada's first male major winner and Charles's successor. With Mickelson winning the following year, Weir sparked a run of five victories by left-handers at Augusta in the ten years up to Bubba Watson's win in 2012. Given the lack of lefties at the highest level, it marked a gross over-representation and brought forward theories that the course is suited to playing the 'wrong way round'. Martin Kaymer once said that he wished he 'could play the other way round' at Augusta. Mickelson, with a smile, retorted: 'I would love Martin to play this tournament left-handed.'

As seen in the last chapter, the idea that the course favours players who hit the ball right to left is exaggerated. But recent course changes that require greater precision from players bring in the old Trevino saying that 'you can talk to a fade but a hook won't listen'. Luke Donald told the *New York Times*: 'I certainly wouldn't mind having Mickelson's cut shot off many of those tees.'

'There are an awful lot of holes that look more inviting if you stand over the ball as a left-hander. The golf course may have always demanded a certain right-to-left ball flight for the right-handed player, but considering where they've moved the tees, it's exaggerated. It's a harder shot for a right-hander. It's just much harder to control a right-to-left draw. And when you have to hit it farther and control that shape longer like you do now on this golf course, well, the challenge is greater. It's easier to set up for a left-to-right fade.'

Mickelson loves the 13th hole but says the 12th is another that gives him an advantage based on his shot dispersion as a left-hander. 'If I pull a shot and aim at the centre of the green, it's going to go long right or short left, which is exactly the way the green sits. It's the opposite of a right-handed shot dispersion, which is why it is such a difficult hole. Long, left is trouble and short, right is in the water. You have to hit a perfect shot.

'But conversely, 16 plays the exact opposite. It's probably the hardest shot for me, whereas the average right-hander can aim at the middle of the green and if he pulls it, he still carries the water. If he comes out short, right, a lot of times it'll catch that swale and come down to give you a chance for a par. Whereas, for me, short, left is in the water and long, right is up top.

'So shot dispersion does make the golf course play differently depending what side you stand on. However, it seems to be a very equal test. It seems to me there are holes that favour one side but there seem to be an equal number of holes that favour the other.'

When Mickelson won the Open at Muirfield at his 20th attempt in 2013, with a closing 66 that included four birdies in the last six holes, his coach Butch Harmon said: 'I always thought when Greg [Norman] won in '93 it was the best round to win an Open. But I think this tops it. When you consider the course was playing so tough, so hard and fast, and the circumstances, to go out and suck it up in the way he did was phenomenal.'

Harmon enjoyed some of the biggest highs in golf working with Norman, Woods and Mickelson but the 1996 Masters was not one of them. Later that summer he parted company from Norman as the Australian tried his luck with Faldo's tune-up man, David Leadbetter, and Harmon himself concentrated more on Woods. He had few answers as to what happened to the then world number one on that Sunday at Augusta. 'It was devastating,' Harmon told Lauren St John in *Greg Norman – The Biography*. 'I walked around with Laura and Morgan-Leigh and it was one of those things where, as you watched it happen, you couldn't believe it. The man had played so well for three rounds. He just had such total control, not only of his swing but of his emotions. He had done everything right and to see it all start to come apart was very difficult for a teacher to watch. More difficult for the hurt that not only he was going through, but his family was.'

As Faldo and Norman approached the green at the 15th, they both received a standing ovation. Temporarily, the mood had lightened again. Both had driven into the fairway and had gone for the green in two. Neither had hit it. Faldo went first, from the shadows cast well into the fairway by the pines on the left. He had 212 yards to the flag and hit a four-iron. It landed at the front of the green but must have hit a patch of ground even harder than the rest of the course. His ball sped on through the green and came to rest down the incline behind it. Norman was hitting from 200 yards with a six-iron and went at the flag, which was on the right edge on the green. He came up a little short and right, just short of the bunker on the right and his ball started rolling back down a bank. The pond awaited but on the line his ball was travelling there was a little dell and it stopped in it, short of the water.

Both men now played delicate chip shots. Norman was first up. 'If we can make this for eagle, we'll be right back in it,' he told his caddie. An eagle would have put the pressure back on Faldo and made his chip look even harder. Norman's ball ran past the right edge of the hole but pulled up only two feet farther on. It must have looked good all the way because Norman buckled at the knees, fell to the ground and rolled over, a hand instinctively holding the Akubra hat in place. 'When that chip shot missed, I just went limp,' he said. 'My mind left my body and my body left my mind.'

Faldo's chip was a classic Augusta conundrum – too short or too timid and the ball would come back to his feet; too far and bold and it would never stop before charging down the bank at the front of the green and into the water. He played it as a bump-and-run and it came off perfectly. In *Life Swings*, he wrote, with all due modesty: 'With the adrenaline coursing through my veins and my throat like parchment, I made it look ridiculously easy by judging the chip to absolute perfection. The ball trickled ever so slowly towards the target, coming to rest three feet from the flag.'

Faldo popped in his putt for a birdie and Norman followed suit. As at the 13th, Norman had done his bit by birdieing the hole for the fourth successive day. Faldo, who played the 15th in two pars and two birdies for the week, had matched him again, however. There had still only been one hole where Norman had gained a stroke on Faldo and that was back at the 5th. Faldo was on 11 under, Norman was 9 under par. There had been no Sarazen magic for the Australian this time round.

Redbud

Hole 16
Yards 170; Par 3

At start	Hole	10	11	12	13	14	15	16	17	18	In	Status
	Par	4	4	3	5	4	5	3	4	4	36	
−13	G. Norman	5	5	5	4	4	4	5				−7
−7	N. Faldo	4	4	3	4	4	4	3				−11

WITH THREE HOLES to play, just one water hazard stood between Nick Faldo and victory at the 60th Masters. Alas, the pond at the 16th also needed to be cleared by Greg Norman in order to avoid total capitulation. It was not to be. For all that the scorecard said there had been nothing to split the pair over the previous three holes, Faldo had matched the Australian's two birdies at a time when Norman needed a big swing in his direction. Faldo had sensed how critical it was not to let Norman regain any momentum at the par-fives. By covering his opponent there, not giving an inch, his reward was a doubling of his lead from two to four strokes at the 16th. With a six-iron to the heart of the green, safely above ground, the job was done. Ladbrokes in London had Faldo 1-4 and Norman 11-4 after the 15th hole. After the 16th, they closed the book.

The last question at Norman's press conference that evening was to ask when he finally realised that it was not going to happen this year? He said: '16.' What else could he say?

What he really meant was the start of the 16th hole, not the end. He later admitted to Lauren St John that he knew it was over after the chip at the 15th had not gone in the hole for an eagle.

He was about to commit one of golf's cardinal errors – still thinking about the shot before the one you are actually playing.

After dropping five strokes in four holes, from the 9th to the 12th, Norman responded in the only way he knew how, by going in search of birdies. A two-shot deficit with six holes to play at Augusta is nothing. He was able to pick up a couple of birdies, but they did not do him any good. Had his chip at the 15th gone in for an eagle, who knows what that would have done to Faldo? There might have been a two-shot swing there and they would have been level. But it did not happen. It was a brilliantly played shot and he had just played his best sequence of holes of the day but he could find no encouragement.

In her biography of Norman, St John quoted him as saying: 'I hit the most perfect shot. I put all my energies into it. I visualised it. Everything I know that I'm good at – feel, not executing till you are ready to go. And then when it didn't go in, I thought, "Oh, shit." Then Faldo hit a great shot, too, so I didn't even make up a shot. So that's when I knew. And the next shot was indicative of the emotions going out of my system.'

A stream that cut in front of the 16th green was transformed into a pond in 1947 and nearly 50 years later it claimed one of its most celebrated victims. The pond covers the front and left-hand side of the green and the tee shot, due to the angle, is played all the way over the water. On practice days, players entertain the gallery by skimming shots over the surface of the pond, doing a 'Barnes Wallis', earning a cheer if a ball skips up onto the green, a groan if it runs out of pace, dies and sinks.

The pin was on the back-left portion of the green. One of the three bunkers around the green protects the back-left section from the pond but Norman's tee shot was so far left that it missed not just the green but the sand as well. It was the most awful-looking thing and Norman's eyes only tracked its path for a fraction of its flight before he ducked his head so as not to see the inevitable splash. 'I just tried to hook a six-iron in there,' he said, 'and I hooked it all right.'

Suddenly the brief spark of energy the gallery had tried to instil in Norman had dissipated. Everyone was stunned. Even Faldo lowered his gaze and scratched the back of his head as if trying to figure it all out. 'It was a riveting unravelling,' wrote Gary Van Sickle in *Golf World* (US). 'You didn't want to watch but you couldn't stop watching.'

A deathly hush descended. As the *Philadelphia Inquirer* stated: 'If you took any pleasure at all in witnessing that then your heart is as hard as a tombstone.' Bob Verdi wrote in the *Chicago Tribune*: 'It's quite a feat, strangling yourself in broad daylight while also attempting to swing a golf club.' The *LA Times*'s Jim Murray added: 'There is only one golfer on the planet that can regularly beat Greg Norman in a major tournament. That's Greg Norman.'

Norman walked forwards, swinging his club round and in front of him along the ground to clean the clubface of any debris. He dropped another ball and hit his third to ten feet, a fine shot under the circumstances but too little, too late.

The traditional Masters Sunday pin at the 16th is very accessible for a hole-in-one; Ray Floyd did just that earlier in the day. He hit a five-iron up the right side of the green, the ball beginning to run out of steam once it was level with the hole and then took a sharp left-hand turn, accelerating down the slope and making a sideway entrance into the cup. 'I aimed at the TV tower and it never left the line,' he said.

'When it first landed, I thought it would stay up on the right. But it got closer and closer, it teetered and teetered, and then there was this crescendo from the crowd, they could see the line. I saw beer, sodas and sandwich wrappers go flying. That's when I knew it went in. It's my first hole-in-one here. It's a nice memory to take home.' It was the seventh hole-in-one at the 16th in the Masters. It took eight years for there to be another one but then there were eight in nine years.

Faldo's tee shot at the 16th was on the same line as Floyd's but it was not long enough to reach the hole. Instead it rolled down the slope from right to left, leaving him a 20-foot putt for a birdie, the most straightforward putt on an otherwise complex green. He would not admit it until the final green but the worst was over now. He would have to do something spectacularly bad to lose it from here.

Norman had already done that for him. As he had stepped up to the tee, Frank Nobilo was being interviewed by Steve Rider on the BBC coverage, saying, 'I saw Greg on the range this morning. He is bleeding. He is honestly bleeding. His expectations are as high if not higher than everyone else's for him. He is in a totally unenviable situation. No one would like to be in this situation on this tee right now, blowing a six-shot lead. He's got to come up with a great shot but, saying that, he is probably the one guy who is capable of it.'

After the tee shot, the commentators threw it back to Nobilo, who added: 'Obviously, Greg's had a few bad tee shots today. It's not an enviable tee shot, when you look at where the pin is, all you really see is the right-hand edge of the trap and you have to hit all the way across the water. Normally, it's a very makeable shot for Greg. You have to feel for the guy. Right now, he is going through purgatory.'

Two putts from each man brought a par for Faldo and a double bogey five for Norman. Faldo was still at 11 under for the tournament, four under for the round, Norman had slipped back to seven under for the tournament, six over for the day.

Purgatory is what Australians call getting up early on a Monday morning to watch the Masters. It is a long history of disappointment. In 1950, Jim Ferrier led with a round to play but lost by two to Jimmy Demaret after dropping five strokes in the last seven holes. Ferrier started out as a sportswriter who was a successful amateur golfer, winning four Australian Amateur Championships and the Australian Open twice. He then emigrated to America, turned professional and won the US PGA in 1947. But he never prevailed at Augusta, with seven top-seven finishes in 15 appearances.

Bruce Crampton was another Australian who based himself in America. He did not drink or smoke and played every week, in 1964 missing only one tournament when his golf equipment was stolen. He finished second in four major championships, each time to Jack Nicklaus, including the Masters in 1972.

Peter Thomson, Australia's most successful major winner with his five Open Championships, played only eight times in the Masters, with a best result of fifth in 1957. He was a master of fast-running courses, imaginatively controlling the ball on the ground, but enjoyed less the game through the air and only spent a small part of his career playing in America. A feeling in that country that he was overrated fuelled a brief but devastating spell on the US Seniors Tour, when he swept away all before him, only to return to other matters such as golf writing and course design.

Kel Nagle won the centenary Open at St Andrews in 1960, stopping Arnold Palmer picking up the third leg of a potential Grand Slam, but in nine appearances at Augusta his best finish was 15th. Jack Newton earned a share of second place at the 1980 Masters with a last round of 68, finishing four adrift of the runaway winner Seve Ballesteros. As well as Norman's assaults in the 1980s and 90s, Craig Parry was the third-round leader in 1992.

But little went right on the final day and a 78 left 'Popeye' in a tie for 13th, seven behind Fred Couples.

More recently, in 2007, Stuart Appleby led by one from Woods and Justin Rose but a closing 75 dropped him to joint seventh, four behind winner Zach Johnson. And then in 2011, Australia had two runners-up for the price of one as Adam Scott and Jason Day both had their chances to win only to be pipped by Charl Schwartzel birdieing the last four holes to win by two.

Norman's three runner-up finishes at Augusta put him alongside Floyd, Tom Watson, Tom Kite and Johnny Miller, and one behind Ben Hogan, Nicklaus and Weiskopf. Weiskopf, Miller and Kite never had the compensation of winning the thing either. During the closing stages of the 1986 Masters, Weiskopf was asked on television what was going through Nicklaus's mind during his late charge and the 1973 Open champion admitted that if he had any idea he might himself be wearing a green jacket.

One of the consolations that Norman held on to after his 1996 debacle was that he still had 'a lot more tournaments to play here'. He would get another chance to win the Masters. He did, indeed, play in each of the next six years, and then again in 2009, but the clock eventually runs out for anyone who does not earn a lifetime exemption by becoming a champion.

After missing the cut the intervening two years, in 1999 he was back in the thick of it despite having undergone shoulder surgery the year before. José María Olazábal led after the second and third rounds but Norman was the sentimental favourite. On the Saturday, he overshot the green at the 12th into the flora on the bank behind and, after a frantic search, had to declare a lost ball. He walked back to the tee, put his tee peg right next to the divot from the previous shot, took aim exactly as before and this time fired the ball onto the green. When he holed the putt for a bogey the place went wild. It was the sort of roar Amen Corner reserves for Sundays. 'Is it from 1996 or just because I'm getting old?' Norman said later when asked about the outpouring of support from the gallery.

The Shark added: 'What happened here in 1996 changed my life. There is a huge amount of support out there from people on a global basis. My locker is full of letters this week. So you still get people writing to you from 1996. You can roll it into what happened last year with the surgery, roll it into the fact that you get to see and appreciate other things in life more than just the game of golf.'

On the Sunday in 1999, Norman was once more playing in the final pairing, starting out one behind. The vital moment came at the 13th, when Norman holed from 25 feet for an eagle but Olazábal managed a birdie from 20 feet to stay level. Norman then bogeyed the next two holes and the Spaniard's nearest challenger was now Davis Love, who chipped in at the 16th to get within one. Olazábal had watched it happen from the tee and responded with a six-iron to three feet. Norman hit it to six feet but missed the putt, whereas Olazábal holed his. Short it may have been, but the degree of difficulty was extreme. 'You can't imagine what a three-footer that was,' Olazábal said. 'Downhill and lightning quick with a left-to-right break. I don't know how the hell I made that putt.'

Olazábal made another brave putt at the 17th to save par and won by two from Love and by three from Norman. It was an emotional victory for the Spaniard as three years earlier he could barely walk and thought he might not play golf again before being treated for rheumatoid polyarthritis. Norman was genuinely pleased for a friend and, having entered the week more in hope than expectation, with his world number one crown long gone, he was in full philosophical mode afterwards. 'This is easier to take,' he said. 'I was more disappointed in 1996 – that one was a totally different animal. It was a successful week and a sad week rolled into one. I feel good I'm back in a position where I know I can contend again. I'm sad I lost but don't make a mountain out of a molehill on this one.'

Norman had become the eighth player to record at least six top-three finishes at Augusta but the first to do so without having won it. Others were also finding the green jacket elusive, albeit none quite in as harrowing circumstances as the Australian. Love was second in 1995 and 1999 and had six top-ten finishes. David Duval was second in 1998, sixth in 1999, third in 2000 and second again in 2001. Ernie Els had five years in a row when he finished sixth or better, a run book-ended by runner-up finishes in 2000 and 2004.

In the recorder's hut in 1999, as they signed their scorecards, Olazábal turned to Norman and said: 'Just keep trying because you deserve this jacket and hopefully you will get it.' He never did, just as Olazábal never won the Open. In *Golf International* in 2013, Robert Green observed that both men would be happier had they swapped an Open and a Masters title so they ended up with one of each, rather than two of the same colour.

Norman was sixth in the Open Championship that followed at Carnoustie in 1999, and that seemed as if it might be his last appearance on a leaderboard at a major as injuries took their toll and business and course design became his priorities. After 2005 at St Andrews, he did not even play in the Open but three years later he entered at Royal Birkdale. More than anything it was a warm-up for the following week's Senior Open Championship at Royal Troon and the US Senior Open the week after that. For a month before Birkdale Norman had other things on his mind anyway, getting married to former tennis star Chris Evert and honeymooning in the Bahamas and then at Skibo Castle in the Scottish Highlands, where the clubs came out again and he started to hit the ball well.

The weather in Lancashire was brutal, wet and windy. Links golf in such conditions is a great leveller and Norman's experience was a vital commodity. Two rounds of 70 put the 53-year-old part-time golfer a shot off the lead. 'My life is great,' Norman said. 'I feel great. I have a wonderful wife, my whole being is just beautiful. I enjoy playing golf, I enjoy spending time at home with Chrissie and my kids. I enjoy my business and what I'm doing. It's the first time I've got the most beautiful balance in my life.'

He added: 'My mind still salivates about playing golf.' But physically, after various surgeries over the years, his body was not up to the long hours of practice he used to put in. He was telling anyone who would listen that he played more tennis than golf and so his expectations were 'still realistically low'.

A two-over-par 72 in high winds in the third round was good enough to give Norman the lead by two strokes from Padraig Harrington and K.J. Choi. He had birdied two of the last five holes to become the oldest ever leader of the Open. Faldo was so excited he exited the commentary box at the end of the round and went over to give Norman another hug (12 years after the one on the 18th at Augusta). 'What you are doing is awesome,' he told his old rival. 'I'm rooting for you.'

But the fairytale had to come to an end at some point and three bogeys in the first three holes on Sunday hastened that point. Everyone else was struggling as well, however. Harrington had three bogeys in a row to end the front nine and with six holes to play Norman was only a shot behind the Irishman, but then at the 13th there was a two-shot swing. Harrington birdied there and at the 15th and then eagled the 17th after hitting a glorious three-wood onto the green. Walking down the 18th fairway, Harrington told Norman: 'I'm sorry it isn't your story being told this evening.'

Harrington said: 'I thanked Greg for his company. He's a super guy and the perfect gentleman to be playing with in the last group of an Open. He says "good shot" when it needs to be said, does his own thing as well. Of course, I wanted to win but it would have been a fantastic story if Greg had won. He has been a great champion and another win at this time in his career would have been the icing on the cake. It is never easy leading a tournament in very difficult conditions so you have to feel for him. But, gee, you'd be happy to drive the ball like him at any stage of your career, let alone at 53 years of age.'

For the eighth time Norman had taken the lead into the final day of a major and he had still only won on one of those occasions. This time he closed with a 77. 'I'm disappointed,' he said. 'Padraig played great and finished like a true Open champion. I hung in there and can hold my head up high and I'm sure I surprised a lot of people. I thought I got off to a pretty good start but the conditions were tough. If you haven't played a lot of golf it's hard to regroup. And I don't plan on playing too much golf.'

Norman moved on to become the captain of the International team at the Presidents Cup. He served in the post at Harding Park in San Francisco in 2009 and at Royal Melbourne in 2011, the Americans winning each time. One of the decisions Norman made for the 2009 match was to pick Adam Scott as a wild card. It did not go down well since Scott, the world number three a year earlier, had completely lost form, missing six cuts in a row during the season. 'It was easy for me to take the criticism,' Norman said, 'because I wanted to help my friend and to help a player who should be a lot higher in the game than he was get back up there. He needed a pat on the back from someone to realise he was not in as deep a hole as he thought.'

Scott was 15 when he watched Norman lose the 1996 Masters and was devastated for his hero. They first met around that time when Norman gave the youngster a lift on his plane. Over the years Scott often stayed at Norman's home in Florida and the Shark turned into a mentor. 'I love the idea of handing down what I've learned to someone like Adam,' Norman told *Golf Digest*. 'He's humble, he's kind, he's intelligent – but also a great listener who never sucks up all the oxygen in the room. All the things people like about him are real.'

Reflecting on his selection for the 2009 Presidents Cup, Scott said: 'Greg as the captain had a lot of faith in me and made me a pick. There is no hiding in a Presidents Cup and I used that as a real motivator and a way to make myself believe I was a great player again. It was a really big boost for me.' There was always a wonderful rhythm to Scott's swing, which looked uncannily like that of Woods when both were taught by Butch Harmon. The final key for Scott was sorting out his putting, which he did by turning to a long-handled putter early in 2011, initially trialling it on Norman's putting green in Florida.

He almost won the Masters that year and his confidence started to build. In 2012, he was four ahead with four to play in the Open Championship at Royal Lytham. While Els birdied the last hole, Scott ended up bogeying the last four holes to lose by one. Els was elated to win a second Open but sorry for his 'good buddy Scotty'. He need not have worried. Scott handled himself with great decorum, so much so that few could bring themselves to label his collapse as 'Normanesque'. Scott was adamant: 'Next time, and I'm sure there will be a next time, I can do a better job of it.'

And next time, he did. 'Lytham gave me more belief that I could win a major,' he said at the 2013 Masters. 'It proved to myself I could. The difference was that last time I played 14 good holes but this time I played 20 good ones.' Scott was one of three Australians, along with Day and Marc Leishman, battling to end the Augusta curse. When Scott holed his putt on the 72nd green, he roared: 'C'mon Aussie.'

'I knew it was time for me to step up and show how much I wanted it,' he said. 'I was pumped. I thought I'd won but only for a split second.' There was still a playoff to come but out of Scott's sight at the time, Leishman celebrated his countryman's putt with his own fist pump. When he found out later, due to a photograph taken from a particular angle which had Leishman in the background, Scott was touched that a player who had also hoped to earn a green jacket that day could be glad for his friend. 'I was just hoping he would hole the putt – for him, for Australian golf, for everything it meant,' Leishman said.

Angel Cabrera, the big man from Argentina who won the 2009 Masters, tied with Scott and almost won the playoff when he nearly chipped in at the 18th. 'My heart was about to stop and I was thinking, is this it, really?' Scott said. Norman tweeted at the time: 'The golfing gods can't be this mean to Australia.' He said later: 'It was the first time I was on the other side of the fence and praying for someone else to do something special.'

The golf over the last hole of regulation and the two play-off holes was spectacular and only ended when Scott holed for a birdie on the 10th green. 'I knew that was my chance, it was getting too dark,' he said. Not seeing the line clearly because of the gloom, Scott called in caddie Steve Williams, the New Zealander who was Tiger's long-time bagman, who advised that it was 'at least two cups outside the hole'. 'It was a great read,' Scott said. 'He was my eyes on that one.'

Scott was quick to give credit to Norman: 'A part of this belongs to him.' He added: 'What an incredible day. Everything fell my way in the end. I am so proud of myself and everyone who has helped me. I am a proud Australian and I hope this sits well at home and even in New Zealand – we were a trans-Tasman combo with Steve on the bag.' It did sit well. *The Australian* proclaimed a new national hero under the headline 'Scott banishes Masters hoodoo'. The *Sydney Morning Herald* said: 'In Australian pantheon, Scott's first among equals.'

When he returned home in November, Scott was feted everywhere he went. Not since Norman had the game Down Under enthralled to such a popular Pied Piper. Huge crowds came out to watch him win the Australian PGA Championship, the Australian Masters, the World Cup for Australia alongside Day, and he only just missed out on the Aussie Triple Crown when Rory McIlroy stole the Australian Open away at the 72nd hole. Mike Clayton, another Aussie player turned scribbler, wrote: 'Scott, as is his way, took the loss with grace. For a month he has signed autographs, spoken at dinners arranged in his honour, had hundreds if not thousands of photographs taken with green-jacketed arm around adoring fans. What is more impressive is he looked like he enjoyed every step of the journey. He never once looked like he was doing us a favour by being here when he could have been sunning himself in Bermuda.

'Scott is a throwback to the generation of Thomson and Nagle, outwardly modest men who understood their golf scores were not the most important things in the world, and he surely will win a lot more.'

Nandina

Hole 17
Yards 400; Par 4

At start	Hole	10	11	12	13	14	15	16	17	18	In	Status
	Par	4	4	3	5	4	5	3	4	4	36	
−13	G. Norman	5	5	5	4	4	4	5	4			−7
−7	N. Faldo	4	4	3	4	4	4	3	4			−11

B Y STRANGE coincidence, three months after overcoming a six-stroke deficit to Greg Norman at the Masters, Nick Faldo found himself starting the final round of the Open at Royal Lytham six shots behind Tom Lehman. Lightning did not strike twice. In fact, it would be a long wait for an Englishman to win a major championship again, although the European golfing success story continued with José María Olazábal winning the Masters in 1999 and Paul Lawrie winning the Open at Carnoustie the same year.

Tiger Woods took home many of the major titles as the new millennium got under way and it was not until Carnoustie in 2007 that Padraig Harrington got the ball rolling again in winning the Open. The Dubliner prevailed again the following year and added the US PGA a couple of weeks later. Now it was Northern Ireland to the fore with Graeme McDowell taking the US Open in 2010 – in the same year Germany's Martin Kaymer won the US PGA – and then Rory McIlroy winning the 2011 US Open and the 2012 US PGA, both by eight strokes, while Darren Clarke nipped in for the 2012 Open at Sandwich.

There was a time, after Faldo faded from the upper echelons, that England could barely muster a male golfer in the top 100 in the world. When Paul Casey became England's leading golfer according to the world rankings, he said: 'That's nice, but the problem is that England's best golfer is only 27th in the world.' In time a batch of players, all of whom got into golf when Faldo was the main man, rose to the very top. Lee Westwood and Luke Donald have both been world number one, while Justin Rose and Ian Poulter also hit the world's top ten. The major title, though, was lacking. Westwood, in particular, got close but his near miss at Muirfield in 2013 was his eighth top-three finish without ever being first.

By then, the drought had ended with Rose taking the US Open at Merion a month earlier. In a superlative performance on the final day, the 32-year-old South African-born golfer beat Phil Mickelson and Jason Day by two strokes. At the last, he hit a four-iron from beside the plaque celebrating Ben Hogan's famous shot at the 1950 US Open. Rose hit another beauty just off the back of the green and made his par. On Father's Day, he gave a nod to the heavens, acknowledging his dad, Ken, who died in 2002 but not before instilling the essential ingredients for golf and life in his son.

Rose was the teenage amateur who holed a wonder shot at the last to finish fourth in the Open at Birkdale in 1998 but then turned professional and missed his first 21 cuts. 'He's a classy guy,' Faldo said after having lunch with Rose two weeks before the US Open. 'No matter how many times he got knocked down, he still had self-belief.'

'I don't know why, but I could just tell that Justin was ready,' Faldo later told the *Daily Telegraph*. 'He had pieced it all together, got everything right in that relationship between swing and mind and, after being there a few times, was finally able to deal with it. You have to think that Justin's becoming the complete golfer and I expect him to win more majors.'

Rose had achieved something not even Faldo had managed, winning America's national championship. The list of English winners (barring early champions who had emigrated to the States as the country's first professionals, along with many from Scotland) is a short but impressive one: Harry Vardon (1900), Ted Ray (1920) and Tony Jacklin (1970). Since the days of Vardon, Ray and J.H. Taylor, England's golfers have usually been ploughing a lone furrow on the world stage – think of Henry Cotton, Jacklin and Faldo.

But Rose said: 'There's been a very strong crop of English players for quite some time now, with myself, obviously Westwood and then Donald and Poulter as well. Paul Casey was up there for a good while and is probably going to make a comeback, I think. I really hope it does inspire them.

'I think it was always going to be a matter of time before one of us broke through. I always hoped it was going to be me, obviously.' Casey, in fact, claimed his first win for two and a half years, most of them spent battling injuries, only two weeks later and admitted he was inspired by his old friend.

But the person who did most to inspire Rose was Adam Scott. When Rose texted his congratulations to the Australian for his Masters win, Scott wrote back that he was next. 'I feel like it's our time,' Scott added. The pair shared a joint celebration later in the year at their homes in the Bahamas. 'I couldn't be happier for him,' Scott said. 'You can see when a guy is ready and I saw that in Justin.' Just before the Masters, Rose had beaten Scott a couple of times in practice rounds. 'The good thing for him about me winning the Masters was that it probably fired him up even more. Sometimes that's all you need.'

Rose said: 'It's been a learning process and all the self-improvement over the years enabled me to get to the point where I believe in myself 100 per cent down the stretch. It's how you deal with the pressure in the moment. That's what Merion was all about. Me signalling up to my dad, before I'd even won, it was just that I felt I had done the job I needed to do. As a golfer that's all you can do – control your emotions and control your own game. That's how you become a tough competitor.'

No one was tougher than Faldo. But a second miracle rally from six shots down in 1996 was beyond him. To paraphrase Colin Montgomerie from his third-round press conference at the 1997 Masters, Greg Norman was not leading and it wasn't the same Nick Faldo who was lying second. At Lytham, baked hard by unbroken sun all week, Faldo had three rounds of 68 but Lehman, after two 67s, had a 64 on the Saturday to get half a dozen clear. 'Ground control to Major Tom,' as the headline in the *Independent on Sunday* summed up.

Faldo was not quite sending out the same positive signals as he had after three rounds at Augusta in April. 'It's a different time and a different course. I have to go out and shoot a great round and see what happens. Tom will be under enormous pressure. He is going for his first major, while I have it all to gain and nothing to lose. I will need at least a 63.'

While Lehman, who had finished 18th at Augusta and second at the US Open already that season, was not as heralded an opponent as Norman, he was at least able to smile when the scenario from Augusta was put to him that night. 'You mean like lightning striking twice? I feel like I'm playing very well, and I like my chances. I would rather be six strokes ahead than six strokes behind.'

This was different from Augusta. Despite what he had said, this time there was far more pressure on Faldo. He had done it once, he could surely do it again. If he could beat the world number one from such a position, what chance did a player have who had never won at the highest level and had struggled all around the globe just to get to the big stage? In front of a huge home gallery, it was a different Faldo from the one who had started the last day at Augusta so relaxed, setting out more in hope than expectation.

Expectation is the equivalent of Kryptonite to any golfer. It shows first in the putting, as Norman found at Augusta. At Lytham, Faldo hit a fine opening tee shot at the par-three 1st to six feet. But he missed the putt while Lehman holed from a similar distance to save par. It might have been a two-shot swing, the sort of early encouragement the Englishman got against Norman and needed now. He went on to miss from ten feet at the 2nd, six feet at the 5th, three feet at the 6th and six feet at the 7th. He could not take his chances and never got to feed on the momentum of the situation as he had at Augusta. The difference was cut by two to four strokes after four holes but Faldo only gained one more shot for the rest of the round.

'Faldo, as a big, blond Australian can confirm, is one of the few who can intimidate opponents,' wrote Michael Henderson in *The Times*. 'He really shook Lehman, make no mistake about that. As he marched ahead from tee to green in those crucial opening holes, he walked with a purpose that suggested that he, and not the Minnesotan, was defending a six-stroke lead. The mood was something like a revivalist gathering as spectators hailed him as the one true leader. There were ocean breakers of applause, wave upon wave, as even ordinary shots brought yells of encouragement. Alas, he was not up to it.'

Faldo ended up in fourth place, as Lehman won by two from Ernie Els and Mark McCumber. Faldo shot a 70, and only if he had holed more of those early putts could he have exerted the sort of pressure he had on Norman. He drove into a bunker at the 15th and knew his challenge was over, his shoulders sagging, his head dropping. 'I had so many chances but was unable to take them, as simple as that,' he said.

Lehman closed with a two-over 73. 'I didn't play well at all,' he said, 'but I stuck it out and I came through.' Bobby Jones won the first of his three Open crowns at Lytham in 1926, with a wonder shot at the 17th hole, but Lehman was the first American professional to win at the Lancashire course. At 37, and having overcome cancer two years earlier, Lehman was made of stern stuff. He became the world number one, albeit only for one week, but one or 331, who's counting? For four years in a row, from 1995 to 1998, he played in the last pairing at the US Open but could not win any of them. After one of the defeats, amid a gaggle of reporters, he was asked how he would get over the disappointment. 'How about hot sex all night long?' suggested his wife, Melissa. 'Yep, that'll do it,' he said.

After Lytham, David Davies wrote in *The Guardian*: 'In April Faldo destroyed Norman, not only overhauling a six-shot lead but turning it into a five-stroke win. On Sunday Faldo tried to stare his man down again, but failed. Lehman, one of golf's nice guys, is also one of its strong guys, and he stared right back. He admitted to nerves, that his swing lacked tempo and that his putting was poor. But the American dug as deeply as he needed into his reserves of will power and determination.'

It was a strange time for golf, the rest of the 1996 season after Augusta. Everyone was a little traumatised after the epic show-down between Faldo and Norman, and there already seemed to be a sense that everything would change once Woods turned professional. He finally did so in the autumn, making a grand entrance that culminated in his record-breaking Masters win the following April. The lull was over. A new cast list was assembling, headed by Woods but including Els, Mickelson, Vijay Singh and David Duval.

Faldo and Norman were like two heavyweight boxers who had punched themselves out. Neither won another regular tour event for the rest of the season. When Faldo won at Riviera on 2 March, 1997, it was to be his last top-flight victory. He was 39 and it was his fourth win in America, aside from the three Augusta victories, to go with 30 European Tour wins and a handful of others. Norman won the St Jude Classic and the old World Series of Golf at Firestone in 1997 to bring his tally of PGA Tour wins in the States to 20. His last significant victory turned out to be the Greg Norman Holden Invitational in Australia in 1998.

Neither stopped playing but all the ten-hour-plus practice days take their toll in the end – Norman has had multiple surgeries on shoulders, back, hips and knees. Neither took full-time to the Senior tours once passing 50, although Faldo, inspired by making a brief comeback for the latest Open at Muirfield, was planning to play a handful of events in 2014 around his television commitments. These days Norman is more likely to feature in the business journals than the golf magazines. *Forbes* profiled the Shark in 2013: 'The way you feel about Greg Norman probably says as much about you as it does about him. Define him by his major meltdowns or his go-for-broke playing style or the $300 million (revenues) business he built from scratch. It's up to you.

'But this much cannot be denied: the man has lived. Number one golfer in the world, international businessman, peripatetic adventure-seeker, personal friend of US presidents (remember when Bill Clinton famously fell down his stairs?), one-time husband of Chris Evert and folk hero to the Chinese.' The marriage to Evert was short-lived but he is now happily married for the third time, while he has been building courses in China and is an adviser to their Olympic golf programme. The sport returns to the Games in 2016 in Rio de Janeiro and the Chinese team may well include Guan Tianlang, who made the cut as a 14-year-old at the 2013 Masters.

Norman's first big coup came just months before the 1996 Masters. In January that year Acushnet bought out Cobra and Norman's initial $2 million stake in the latter realised a cool $40 million. A turf company proved another successful venture and he was off and running in the corporate world. From time to time, given his golfing and business pedigree, Norman's name crops up as a possible future commissioner of the PGA Tour.

It is an unlikely fit. He might like the challenge on one level but why would he want to work for a few hundred moaning golf pros rather than for himself? In any case, he has never got on with the incumbent, Tim Finchem. They clashed a number of times through his career, most recently over the format for the Presidents Cup, and in the autumn of 1996 Norman was irked when Finchem announced a series of World Golf Championships to start in 1999. A couple of years earlier, Norman had supported an idea to link up some of the best tournaments from all over the globe under one umbrella – effectively a world tour. He wanted the best players to play against each other more often, as this rarely happened outside the majors.

But Finchem, fearing loss of control and television rights, knocked down both the plan and Norman's involvement before responding with his own WGC proposal. Initially, the idea was to play them around the world but soon enough they became permanently situated in the United States. The effects of various scheduling changes and ever greater revenues from television and sponsors has led to a two-tier landscape where either all the top players are playing in the same tournament, or they are not, and the former are chiefly located in America. As Matt Kuchar said in November 2013, what Norman had suggested years ago had pretty much come about.

Faldo's business ventures all tended to be a bit more stop-start. But then his whole life seemed that way for a while. He broke up with his long-term coach David Leadbetter and his caddie Fanny Sunesson broke up with him. Management companies and business advisers came and went. His relationship with Brenna Cepelak came to an end, at which point she took a nine-iron to his Porsche, and then in 2001 he married Valerie Bercher, whom he met when she was working at the European Masters at Crans-sur-Sierre. They later divorced, though a daughter, Emma, was a joyful addition to the Faldo clan in 2003.

In 2001, in a profile of Faldo in the *Observer Sports Monthly*, Andrew Smith wrote: 'I put it to Faldo that if Steve Martin was to direct a farce about a man having the most monumental mid-life crisis ever, it might look something like his life over the last five years. Nothing was spared. Everything hit the fan. He looks perturbed, then decides that it might be true and laughs.'

Faldo's life is far more settled these days, built around the foundations of his television career, his course design work and his Faldo Series for junior golfers. All three reveal far more his passion for golf than appeared when he was playing in his prime. Frank Keating once wrote a column in *The Spectator* describing how it was necessary to reassess opinions of Geoffrey Boycott and Ian Botham once they had stopped playing and started commentating. Botham was by far the more popular performer but with microphone in hand Boycott reveals himself as the more passionate observer of his sport.

Faldo admitted to looking on the course like a 'miserable bugger, a head-down, boring old whatever with no life'. 'Because I wanted to win,' he said. 'I found I needed to stay in that ultra-focused mode to be successful, so that's what I did.' A more nuanced description of his play was provided by Lauren St John when she wrote: 'In actuality, every shot that Faldo plays reveals something about him. The most insignificant of putts and the most ordinary of five-irons show his careful routine, his perfectionism, his boyish enthusiasm for what would seem to be the dullest of challenges, and his stubborn refusal to give up in the worst of tournaments, on the most uninspiring of days. Even Faldo's soldier-like walk and quick, reluctant waves to the gallery illustrate his self-consciousness and uncomfortable awareness of being watched, as well as his awkward humour and shy pride when a shot comes off.'

Something had to fuel all those hours of practice and it was this: 'I've never been bored with this game at all, not for a single moment,' he said. 'I've been frustrated, but I've never been bored with it.'

Faldo's strengths as a television commentator are his never-ending fascination with any shot that is in front of him on the screen at any one moment and his ability to communicate the emotions whirling within a player when the pressure is on down the stretch on a Sunday afternoon. It is a shame he was never able to communicate as successfully with the written press. He was done over by the news hounds on the tabloids, of course, which made him retreat, but he could not get along with many of the golf specialists either, who could be critical if the occasion merited it but who were always there to record his many triumphs.

His instinct to stand alone was evident in his Ryder Cup captaincy in 2008. In an era when there are almost as many assistants to the captain as members of the team, Faldo only had

Olazábal to help him out as a solitary vice-captain. Faced with an American team inspired by another of his old rivals, Paul Azinger, it was a rare poor match for Europe. Some of Faldo's decisions were debatable, but he did not deserve to be pilloried quite so harshly in the newspapers, and by many who, not having been on the scene in his playing days, only knew him by reputation. His unease with the media became a self-fulfilling prophecy that week.

Yet get him going in the right circumstances, perhaps about one of his course designs, and there is no stopping him. Steve Rider, the former front man for BBC golf and author of *Europe at the Masters*, interviewed Faldo many times. 'Nick has always been a player on and off the course whose enthusiasm for the sport knows no bounds,' Rider once said. 'He is genuine. His Junior Series and everything he does for youth golf is genuine and I have the highest regard for him as a player and a personality. For me, Faldo has always been one of the more compelling interviewees. He always comes up with something fresh and surprising. I remember once we did a documentary with him at Muirfield, going over his final round of 18 pars in 1987. He had a vivid recollection of something on every shot, a movement in the gallery, what his caddie said, his mental processes. Absolute awareness of the situation.'

The Faldo Series was launched towards the end of 1996 as an attempt to 'give something back to the game that has given me so much,' he said. It has done that. More than 7,000 youngsters aged 12 to 21 benefit from the programme each year and in 2013 the Grand Final was staged at The Greenbrier. There are European and Asian sections and the Series is supported by the R&A and the European and PGA Tours, among others. Rory McIlroy and Yani Tseng are former overall winners while Nick Dougherty was one of the first to emerge as a winner on the European Tour. Faldo is very much hands-on in passing on his tips for success.

'He was very friendly to me right from the start,' Dougherty said. 'I've seen him stand out in the rain all day giving lessons to kids and no one ever hears about that stuff. Every young golfer should aspire to be like him.'

In *Life Swings*, Faldo wrote: 'The youngsters on the Faldo Series must have grown weary of hearing me go on and on about it but it is a message worth repeating time and again: when you play in the four majors, I believe you must treat every shot as history in that your opening drive is as important as your final putt on the 72nd.'

A sixth major championship was about to put Faldo one ahead of Seve Ballesteros as the best of his generation and one behind Vardon as Britain's greatest ever. Woods is the only player since to go past him (having stalled in his pursuit of Nicklaus on 14), while Mickelson reached five with his Open win at Muirfield. Frank Nobilo, still sitting in on the BBC coverage as Faldo and Norman played the 17th hole, said: 'A player like Nick seems to thrive on this sort of situation. Deep down he is feeling it but he deals with it better than anyone else. His record proves that.'

Faldo's drive flirted with the Eisenhower tree on the left of the fairway but missed it and finished in the middle of the fairway. His approach with a wedge finished eight feet from the hole. Not much encouragement for Norman there, but the Australian hit a fine approach himself, to just over six feet. Faldo's putt was always heading right of the hole and then he marked and stepped back to allow Norman to putt.

In contrast to some of today's sportsmen (it is usually men) who have made themselves believe that sledging – or 'silly macho bravado laden willy waving', as cricket blogger Lizzy Ammon tweeted during the 2013–14 Ashes series in Australia – is somehow vital to the outcome of the actual game, rather than merely a loss of dignity by the perpetrator, Faldo had not needed to utter a word out of place or act in any way unbecoming. His physical presence in the contest was established simply by the excellence of his play and his determined demeanour.

Peter Alliss said on commentary: 'Faldo does not appear to be taking any pleasure from the way Norman is struggling. Many of the modern players in all sorts of sports, when someone suffers a misfortune, have a not-so-sly smile, punch the air, give the thumbs up to the crowd, but Faldo at this moment certainly, and all throughout, has shown steely nerve but also great courtesy.'

Norman missed his putt for birdie, the ball moving left-to-right in front of the hole, not hit with sufficient conviction to find the cup. It was the sort of putt that he had holed for three days but not on this Sunday. Both men tapped in for their pars but Faldo was not taking anything for granted. 'Greg could have holed that putt on 17,' he said. 'I could have hit a tree on 18, I could have taken six, he could have had a three. I wasn't counting my chickens until I hit that last shot out of the bunker onto the green at the last.'

Rick Reilly wrote in *Sports Illustrated*: 'The last 20 minutes were unlike any seen in the previous 59 Masters. Norman became a kind of dead man walking, four shots behind and all his dreams drowning in Augusta National ponds behind him. Spectators actually looked down, hoping not to make eye contact, as Norman passed among them on his way to the 18th tee.'

Holly

Hole 18
Yards 405; Par 4

At start	Hole	10	11	12	13	14	15	16	17	18	In	Total	Status
	Par	4	4	3	5	4	5	3	4	4	36	72	−7
−13	G. Norman	5	5	5	4	4	4	5	4	4	40	78	
−7	N. Faldo	4	4	3	4	4	4	3	4	3	33	67	−12

THE FINISH of the 60th Masters could not come quickly enough. Greg Norman's loss of a six-stroke overnight lead was now the biggest in major championship history and the turn-around brought back memories of Arnold Palmer losing seven strokes to Billy Casper over the back nine of the final round of the 1966 US Open, Casper winning in a playoff the next day. Not even the possibility of a playoff remained as a lifeline for Norman. Nick Faldo, four behind on the 8th tee, now led by four. Both men just wanted to get the last hole out of the way.

Faldo drove into the second bunker on the left and then did a 'Sandy Lyle' – hitting his second shot on the green and holing the putt for a birdie. In 1988, Lyle hit a one-iron into the first of the two fairway bunkers – the ones Ian Woosnam flew when he won the Masters in 1991 – and struck a seven-iron onto the green, the ball rolling back off the ridge in the middle of the green. Then, Lyle had needed to make the putt to become the first Briton to win the Masters, whereas Faldo had the luxury of a huge lead. Still, the relief was palpable when his nine-iron safely found the green, the ball again trickling up the bank towards the top tier but then rolling back gently to 15 feet.

Norman hit a huge drive past the bunkers but, typical of his day, missed the green on the right fringe. As both men climbed the hill towards the green and the clubhouse, a deep-blue, late-afternoon sky above, the atmosphere remained muted, polite applause greeting the victor and vanquished. Faldo acknowledged the gallery with measured waves of the hand. 'He took those final steps quietly, giving only the smallest of nods, keeping his head low,' wrote Malcolm Gladwell in his *New Yorker* essay 'The Art of Failure'. 'He understood what had happened on the greens and fairways that day. And he was bound by the particular etiquette of choking, the understanding that what he had earned was something less than a victory and what Norman had suffered was something less than a defeat.'

'It was a weird sensation,' Faldo wrote in *Life Swings*, 'for having won my previous two Masters on the 11th green in playoffs, I had always dreamed of marching up the 18th at Augusta with my arms raised in triumph knowing I had won the title. With Greg being such a popular competitor, the crowd were understandably confused about how to react; on the one hand they wanted to treat the vanquished with the respect worthy of a great champion, on the other hand they wanted to whoop and holler at such an unlikely victor.

'I could sense the waves of sympathy pouring down upon Greg from the bleachers as I made my way up the fairway, so it would have been entirely inappropriate to engage in any demonstration of triumphalism. I tried to acknowledge the cheers in a dignified manner, with a smile and a nod of the head, but inside I was exultant for the 18th green at Augusta is a sight like no other – the greenest of grass, the whitest of bunkers, the bluest of skies, the clubhouse shimmering in the distance.'

Norman putted up just short of the hole and holed out for a four. He had scored a 78. He had opened the week by equalling the course record with a 63. Each day after that his score had got higher but on the second and third days his lead had extended regardless. But not on the final day. Only seven players scored as high or higher, and five of them were, or would be, Masters champions.

Jack Nicklaus, Bernhard Langer, Craig Stadler and John Daly all had 78s, Woosnam and Alex Cejka had 80s and Vijay Singh had an 82. On seven under par, Norman finished alone in second place, one ahead of Phil Mickelson, who had a 72 on Sunday, and two ahead of Frank Nobilo, whose fourth place was his best ever major result. Norman had hit only eight of the 18 greens in regulation: he was in the water twice, at the 12th and 16th holes; did not save par from sand twice, at the 1st and the 4th; could not get up and down from off the green at the 9th and the 10th; and three-putted the 11th. He made three birdies but these were more than wiped out by the five bogeys and two double bogeys.

There was only one stroke left to be played in the 60th Masters, Faldo finishing it with a single putt for his sixth birdie of the day. He raised his arms above his head, wanting to enjoy the moment even though his first thoughts were not of his victory but for his opponent. He put his arm round Fanny Sunesson, then remembered to take his ball out of the cup. He marched towards Norman, looking all stiff and angular as any unemotional Brit is meant to be. But as Faldo took Norman's hand he did something that surprised everyone, including the Australian and perhaps even himself: Faldo wrapped Norman into a bear hug.

Faldo had always been the very opposite of unemotional, but he just never found the right way to express those emotions, either keeping them locked up or losing it a bit, Muirfield style. Here he did it perfectly. 'The Hug' changed perceptions about Faldo, showing him in a new light. Even when Norman briefly uncoupled to kiss Sunesson, Faldo pulled him back so they started to leave the green with their arms round each other's shoulders. Only at the last minute did Faldo break away to turn back to the crowd and salute them.

'Throughout the long round, while Greg Norman had fallen deeper into the abyss, Faldo had maintained a composure that could not fairly be described as robotic control, but was that of an ordinary man with an extraordinary talent, thinking clearly under the most terrible pressure, and retaining, through it all, enough humanity and humility to understand what Norman was going through and to react with compassion and grace,' wrote Lauren St John in a profile entitled 'The New Man' for *Golf World* a few months later. 'It is ironic that the major that Nick Faldo least expected to win may be the one that earns him love, not just respect, and the only thing he has ever wanted: greatness.'

A year later, Al Barkow wrote in *Golf World* (US). 'The hug Nick Faldo gave Greg Norman on the 18th green at the conclusion of last year's Masters was one of the warmest gestures ever seen in golf. No matter that the hugger and the huggee were evasive about what was said between them during that embrace. The hug was enough, and beyond mere good sportsmanship. It said much about empathy, sympathy, the depth of human feelings. That the hug was clearly initiated by Faldo made it surprising to many. Here was a champion athlete whose public image was that of an icy, emotionless, totally absorbed mechanic at work – Robo-Pro. So sharply etched was that image, you might wonder if the hug was not so much thoughtful as thought out, that it was a pre-conceived act. "Oh no," says Faldo, taken slightly aback at that suggestion. "You don't plan something like that."'

'It was very special,' Norman said afterwards. 'I'm not going to tell you what he said. It was a very emotional thing. There were tears in our eyes. I'm going to leave it up to him if he wants to tell you. He's gone way up in my estimation.'

When Faldo was asked what he had said that had so moved Norman, the Englishman said: 'If he didn't, I'm not going to tell you.' Told Norman had said it was up to him, Faldo added: 'I just said, "I don't know what to say. I just want to give you a hug." Simple as that. There's a few other bits but you ain't going to know.'

Essentially, it was this: 'Don't let the bastards get you down.' Norman wrote in *The Way of the Shark*: 'He didn't have to point at the media centre. I knew exactly what he was talking about. He was genuinely concerned about how I would handle what happened that day, and how others would handle it. That gesture on the 18th green by Nick Faldo was pure class.'

As Norman headed for the media centre, Faldo made for the Butler Cabin and the television presentation of the green jacket. 'I am genuinely sorry for Greg,' he told the Augusta National vice-chairman, Joe Ford. 'Credit to the Masters for what you put us through out there. You had to play precise golf.' Ben Crenshaw, the 1995 champion, handed Faldo the jacket (Faldo's own, in fact, since he already had one) and said: 'Congratulations, it was a magnificent round of golf.' Jim Nantz, the CBS host and now Faldo's partner on the Masters telecast, told the champion: 'I've been in here for all three of your victories and each time there has been so much passion and emotion, your voice cracking.' Faldo replied: 'Well, it's kind of tricky out there, it gets to you.'

Norman took a conscious decision in the recorder's hut not to scurry away into the night like a couple of players he could think of. He declined to name them to sports reporter, Jimmy Roberts, but did tell him: 'I thought to myself that I ain't going to be that guy. I've got to suck it up. I'm going to take my medicine.

The best thing I did was go straight into the press conference.' So he arrived in the interview room and stayed there until every last question, every last way of asking basically the same thing, had been asked. 'Well, I played like shit,' he opened up. 'I don't know. That's probably the best way of putting it. With all my mistakes today, I didn't do the right things. Nick did a good job and I really just got a good old ass-whipping.'

How does it feel? 'Of course, I'm very disappointed. Of all of them I let get away, this one I did let get away. Even if I had played half-decent, it would have been a good tussle with Nick. I let it slip. I made a lot of mistakes today. Call it what you want to call it, but I put all the blame on myself. I hit a couple of poor iron shots and you pay the price.'

What do you call it? 'What I said right at the beginning. I played like a bunch of shit. That's all I can say. I just didn't get the job done. It's not going to stop me. You learn from your mistakes. You know, I'm disappointed. I let this one get away. It's not the end of the world for me, I'll wake up tomorrow morning and still breathe, and I'll get ready to go to Hilton Head [the next week's tournament] and the other major championships. No one likes to lose major championships. I had a chance to win one this week, and I didn't. Maybe I can convert something at the end of the year.'

He was asked about some of the particular moments from the day, the second at 9, the chip at 10, the tee shot at 12, the lay-up at 13. Was the lead a problem? 'My lead? No, I came out starting as if everything was on the same score and just played as good golf as I could.'

Greg, how do you keep from being fatalistic about everything that's happened in the past? 'That's golf, you know.' About Faldo, after his comment from the previous day about people making good shots against him in the past: 'Oh, Nick played great golf. There's no two ways about it. He played great and I played poor.'

Is it humanly possible not to dwell on a day like today? 'Watch.' How are you able to do that? 'I guess because to me there's not a whole lot of anguish. As I said earlier in the week, my life is pretty good. I'm happy. I've got pretty good control over the situation. Things work on the golf course. Sometimes they work the way you like them to work, and sometimes they don't. You know, I have a pretty good life and... it's not the end of my world, losing this Masters championship. You learn, and you try to understand why and what happened. But sometimes, in a situation like today, I may not want to learn about this one. Maybe this is one I just screwed up bad enough with my own mistakes that you just put that one down, that it was just poor play.'

Could this be the most disappointing single round of your career? 'Yeah, it probably would be at the end of it all.' How so philosophical? 'I've developed it from playing the game and seeing what the game gives you and what the game takes from you. I've done that in business, the business side of life, too. Not everything's perfect your whole life. Maybe these hiccups that I have inflicted on myself are meant for another reason. I think there's something waiting for me down the line that's going to be good for me.'

Ever wonder how history will look at your record? 'No. My life's not over yet. So, as I said, I have a strong belief in myself that something good's going to happen to me before my career is over. I really do believe that. And all of this is just a test.'

Someone asked: 'In a *Sports Illustrated* article I just read about you, it came through that perfectionism is certainly something you strive for as a characteristic of yours. How can you have that attitude and not win?' Answer: 'How can I not win? Well, I am a winner. I just didn't win today. I am a winner. I'm not a loser. I'm not a loser in life. I'm not a loser in golf tournaments. I win golf tournaments and I've won more than my share.'

Just at this moment, a television in the corner of the interview room was showing Faldo being helped into the green jacket. 'I wish I'd won what Nick Faldo's won,' Norman continued, 'but I haven't. I'm a winner. I think I am a perfectionist. That's how I've always been in my life. I feel confident in my belief and my approach to whatever I do that I can do it. If I wanted to be a brain surgeon and take the time to study that, I could. Anybody could be if you dedicate yourself enough to it. It depends on what you want out of life. I want to win the Masters. I didn't win the Masters. Nick Faldo won the Masters, so he's got something I haven't got.' About the brain surgery, Dan Jenkins later wrote in *Golf Digest*: 'Maybe so, but he wouldn't operate on this cowboy – not on a Sunday anyhow.'

Greg, I read you collected, is it $40 million in stock shares? So financially, this is just peanuts to you? 'Well, you could say that. Is it $40 million? Something like that. So there's a good thing about life, see?'

Do you have a feeling of wanting to go out of the room and just screaming and letting it all out? 'I don't know if I can convince you guys... I know I screwed up today, but it's not the end of the world for me. It's really not. God, I'd love to be putting this green jacket on here but it's not the end of the world for me. I'm not going to fall off the face of the earth because of what's happened here. If I had won today and all those other championships, my life might be totally different, but I didn't win. It's not going to affect my life. I get upset inside, but I'm not going to run around and be like a Dennis Rodman and head-butt an official.' At this point Billy Morris, the Augusta member moderating the interview, swayed to his left, out of reach, while Norman played along by raising his right fist. It raised a laugh. 'I'm not that way. I'm really not that way. I respect the game of golf we play. I love the game of golf. It's given me a lot, and it's going to give me a lot more.'

Greg, what are you going to do with all the money? 'All the money?' The $40 million and the other millions. 'Keep going, don't just stop. Well, my kids are secure for the rest of their lives. My kids' kids will be secure. That's what hard work's all about. People might be envious of an athlete making a lot of money but... there's smart business decisions. The way you approach life, the way you play the game, the way you capitalise on things, I've done those. I've done them rather successfully.'

Is it ironic that the things you want most now are things you can't buy? 'Well, there's a lot of things in life that I can't buy. Don't forget, money's not everything.'

His performance at the microphone was scrutinised as much as his play on the course. 'The generous interpretation of Norman's lengthy, post-round press conference,' Bill Fields wrote in *Golf World* (US), 'is that Norman is what he says he is, a man more buoyant than a fishing cork, most satisfied that his family is financially secure beyond imagination. The harsher view is that Norman's reputation, and all its bluster, precedes his achievements, as his critics have contended it always has. Norman is fond of saying better days are still ahead but he would need to achieve in his 40s what no golfer ever has in order to fulfil his competitive promise.' By that measure it would go unfulfilled.

There was later time for more solitary reflection down by the beach by his home in Florida but first there was the flight home on his private jet, one of his 'toys'. His agent at the time, Frank Williams, who had bet $10,000 on Norman at 14-1 at the start of the week and refused Dunhill owner Johan Rupert's attempt to buy it off him for $100,000 on the Saturday night, recalled the scene.

'Everybody was very upset,' he told *Australian Golf Digest*. 'I was with his wife and daughter, who are crying, I'm crying – I had a big bet, too, mind you and was going to make a lot of money, but that's another story. So Greg comes on to the plane and we're all in tears, we're all devastated. "I don't understand you people. I get paid a lot of money to hit a little white ball from A to B better than anybody else. I've got millions of dollars, I own this plane, I've got an ocean-going boat that is second to none, I've got two helicopters, I've got a home in Florida you'd die for and I've got no education. What are you all crying for?"

'He said, "I'll tell you what we're going to do – we're going to stay on this plane until we've drunk it dry." We used to carry a lot of booze. We took off, landed at West Palm Beach, taxied into the hangar and sat on the plane for four hours until every drop of booze had gone. He was fantastic! And I know it was probably one of the biggest disappointments of his life but he handled it so well, cheered everybody up.

'It was a very interesting time in my life to be working for him and with him and I considered it an honour and I still do. I hear negative things about him but I also know all the positives and there is a lot more to Greg Norman than people realise. He's the best father you'll ever meet. I've seen him sit at his kitchen table with the kids and just explain certain things to them that I wouldn't know how to do with my own kids. He's terrific.'

Faldo was next in the interview room. 'I guess I don't know where to begin after that,' he said. 'We've had an amazing day. I honestly and genuinely feel sorry for Greg, what he's going through. But as I said last night, I set out with a goal to shoot 65-66 and I shot 67, which is still the best round of the day and then things turned around. And by the time we went through 12, I had a two-shot lead. Then it was mine to lose. I was doing my huffing and puffing exercises and concentrating hard on what

I was doing and tried to just play as well as I could, as hard as I could, as solid as I could.

'So I'm pleased with the way I played. I obviously didn't think it was going to happen this week. My true goal was to come in and have a really good week. I thought that would be good after a couple of years of sharing the heat in the majors. I played well, only made a couple of mistakes yesterday. I went out today and thought about being really smart with my club selection. You have to steer the ball in the right places this week. I obviously putted well, only three-putted once. If I was chipping, I was chipping well, never left any scary ones.'

How does this one compare to the other five majors, he was asked? 'Well, they're all different. This one's an amazing one, isn't it? I mean, I guess... I hope I'm remembered for shooting a 67 on the last day and storming through and not what happened to Greg. I'm obviously pleased with what I've done. But it's going to be remembered for what happened to Greg.

'To come back and finally be in contention for a major again and pull it off, it's really pulling your nerves out there. I feel this has been more of a physical preparation. We've worked well, I've worked hard on how to practise and what I need to practise. It's a process of putting all sorts of little things together and going out and doing it. But the big thrill, really, is to go out and do it on the day. You never know when you've got another win in you. It's a great feeling to know you still have.'

Without tempting fate, how many majors do you think you might be capable of winning? 'I'm just delighted to have scratched another on the board. You can't say, can you? You can't say what is going to happen. I like to think this is a springboard, that the game is going to go well at last and I can compete. If I can be competitive out there, then finishing them off is a different matter.'

Did you ever think what most of us were saying, I can't believe this is happening? 'To be honest, not really. I was out there doing my own thing. I'm in control of my golf ball and that's it.'

Obviously, Greg's had a lot of near misses. What do you think of his resilience? He keeps coming back. 'I think he's fantastic. He'll go back and assess it all. The man's got the drive and commitment, he'll be back.'

To another question about Norman, he said: 'He's a great player, great competitor. He really is. Great guy, everything. He's a credit to the game. And the game needs him out there all the time. You know, we're all in charge of our own house. That's the thing, isn't it? It's as simple as that. He'll be alright. I'm sure he'll be alright.' Do you actually feel sorry for him? 'Yeah, I honestly, genuinely do. What he's been through is horrible. As I said, it's hard to be plastered and repair that. If it happened to me like that... as I said, I feel sorry for him. He's had a real rough ride today.'

Because of the circumstances of the day, are you more low-key about this championship than the others? 'You can imagine, it's kind of difficult. Emotionally, I was feeling for Greg. We've had a very strange day. I'm pleased with what I've done but it's obvious it was a strange atmosphere out there the last few holes.'

Faldo was, of course, right about the day being remembered for what happened to Norman but an appreciation for his own performance grew with time. A year later, he reflected: 'Oh, I'm more than happy that the way I played has been recognised, more than happy. A lot of people are saying it was one of the best rounds in a major.' And his assessment: 'I think as a total package, it may be right there. In a way it was a perfect round. Some people think the perfect round's going to be a 60 or whatever. But you've got to piece together the score and play across the board and go through all the emotion. That's as good as it gets.'

Faldo's point was that it was not just a birdie-fest in the open-ing round of a relaxed tournament at a resort course. This was the final round of the Masters at Augusta National. This was hardly 'less than a victory', to use the Gladwell phrase, because of Norman's blow-up. It was enhanced because of what happened to the leader, because Faldo showed how the course had to be played on that day and, in the process, was not put off by the distraction of Norman's collapse.

He missed only two greens, one of them by only inches, and one fairway, and dropped only one shot. For the week, he was sec-ond in fairways hit (52 out of 56) and tied for fourth in greens hit (51 out of 72). He was fifth on the putting table, with 112 putts for the week, partly because he took 31 putts on Sunday – he did not need to take fewer as often solid two-putting was the order of the day. His 67 was the lowest score achieved at the weekend.

On Sunday, Larry Mize and Davis Love, who finished joint seventh with Corey Pavin and Jeff Maggert, had 68s, while Nobilo and Maggert had 69s. On Saturday the best scores had been the 69s of Duffy Waldorf and David Duval. While Norman had played the first 36 holes in 132 strokes, Faldo played the last 36 holes, with the course playing ever more tricky over the weekend, in 141 strokes, one better than Nobilo and Waldorf, with Norman taking 149 for the second half of the tournament.

In *Life Swings*, Faldo wrote: 'I had felt anything but confident before that last round against Greg at Augusta. As it turned out, the round proved to be my finest in terms of sustaining the men-tal stamina you need to commit to your routine before each and every shot as the pressure and atmosphere grows. This is some-thing I am very proud of.'

In his 1999 book *Beyond the Fairways*, David Davies wrote: 'In a career that is not yet over, nothing can be the absolutely defini-tive performance but it is safe to say that anything that beats the final day of the 1996 Masters will be something the like of which has not yet been seen on a golf course. On that day, Faldo did superlatively the thing that he does best. He set himself to play fault-free golf, play to the absolute limits of his concentration, bear down relentlessly on his opponent and give him not a glimmer of encouragement.

'He knew that if he did all these things, and that if a few putts were to drop as well, he might have a very distant chance of catching and maybe even forcing a playoff with the world number one, Greg Norman, who led the championship after three rounds by six shots. Norman had been brilliant all week; Faldo by his standards merely humdrum. Norman confessed he wanted nothing more in the whole world than a green jacket; Faldo already had two of them. Norman's game might have been made for Augusta, Faldo has won there in spite of not being, ideally, long enough.

'On that Augustan Sunday, Norman disintegrated but Faldo stayed steadfast and ignored the burning building, the crashing car, the sinking ship that was alongside him and simply played his own game. No one in world golf was better suited to that task and without hitting any scintillating shots, but without making a mistake, Faldo got round in 67 and won by five shots. It was a stunning upset, achieved mostly in silence, not because people did not appreciate what Faldo was doing but because they were distressed at what Norman was doing to himself.'

'There was in the years of his prime something quietly beautiful about the relentless, slow-burning courage with which he played golf,' Hugh McIlvanney wrote of Faldo in *Golf International*. 'His balls were unbreakable.'

It is an oversimplification to attempt to sum up two whole careers in a single day. Yet the final round of the 1996 Masters offered so many insights into the lives of Nick Faldo and Greg Norman. The one thing it lacked was a glimpse of the most scintillating player in the game from the mid 1980s to the mid 1990s. But that was the point about Norman: when it came to grabbing hold of the very biggest titles, he was too often left grasping at thin air. Something was missing in his game, as were the trophies and a certain green jacket that should have sat beside his two claret jugs. This was his eighth and last runner-up finish in a major championship and only Arnold Palmer, with ten, and Jack Nicklaus (19) have recorded more. His conversion rate of chances into victories was at the opposite end of the spectrum from Faldo's six wins from nine top-two finishes.

What happened that day? The mystery will remain whether Norman's back was so much worse than the previous three days of the tournament, and not even he may be able to evaluate that now, being susceptible to hindsight. Tension was evident in his swing from the opening tee shot and in his regripping and fidgetiness the rest of the round. A couple of high-tariff shots, the second at the 9th, the chip at the 10th, were only marginally out but he had allowed himself no room for error. Then came the miserable splashes at the 12th and the 16th.

All the above were compounded by the unrelenting manner in which Norman was pursued by Faldo. The pressure the Englishman exerted was irresistible. It would be no consolation to the Australian that only an opponent of his calibre could have inspired Faldo's performance. His round was the perfect one for the circumstances, very nearly flawless in terms of shot execution and spot on in his unyielding demeanour. Anything less and he would not have been able to force the long-time leader into a duel that, however subconsciously, Norman must have hoped would be unnecessary.

But it was no devil-may-care, nothing-ventured-nothing-gained, leaderboard-ignoring effort from a player coming out of the pack with no expectation and little attention and posting a number well before the leaders finished. No, Faldo knew exactly what was happening and what he had to do. The control of himself and his game needed to be all the greater for the element of calculation involved.

In contrast to his image of being blinkered and isolated from everything around him, it was his ability to feed off the situation and the signals of unease coming from Norman that enabled Faldo to complete such an epic comeback. And crucially, while many pursuers are spent by the time they draw level with their prey and allow the leader a second wind, Faldo was aware there would be a response from Norman at the two par-fives on the back nine and he was ready for him. With his magnificent two-iron at the 13th he outdid Norman at his own game and turned up the pressure on his opponent another notch.

It was the ultimate performance from a professional golfer on the ultimate stage, strategy and execution in perfect harmony. In victory he showed due compassion for the loser and changed perceptions of himself as an emotionless machine. Norman, too, felt that the day changed how people thought of him, thanks to the dignified way he handled his bitter disappointment. With his business empire, Norman moved past being a professional golfer, in the sense of no longer needing to earn money from the game, and could play like an amateur. That is not to decry his dedication to the game but to suggest that a love of competing drove his golf and still drives the way he attacks much of his life. Some you win, some you lose. Whatever happens, you dust yourself down.

Not long after the 1996 Masters, Faldo said: 'When my day is done I want people to say: "I saw Nick Faldo play."' There were many days that people were excited and thrilled to see Norman, or others such as Seve Ballesteros, play golf. But on certain days, when it mattered most, when the test was at its sternest, when technical precision needed to be married with artistic flair, when, it goes without saying, determination, perseverance and concentration were essential requirements, when the game's 'little cups' were up for grabs, those were the days to say, 'I saw Nick Faldo play.'

Such a day was Sunday 14 April 1996, the final round of the 60th Masters, an epic contest that defined an era of the game dominated by a larger-than-life Australian and an Englishman with an unshakable belief in himself.

SCORES

1996 Masters Tournament
April 11–14
Augusta National, Augusta, Georgia

			R1	R2	R3	R4	Total	Prize money
1	Nick Faldo	–12	69	67	73	67	276	$450,000
2	Greg Norman	–7	63	69	71	78	281	$270,000
3	Phil Mickelson	–6	65	73	72	72	282	$170,000
4	Frank Nobilo	–5	71	71	72	69	283	$120,000
5	Scott Hoch	–4	67	73	73	71	284	$95,000
5	Duffy Waldorf	–4	72	71	69	72	284	$95,000
7	Davis Love	–3	72	71	74	68	285	$77,933
7	Jeff Maggert	–3	71	73	72	69	285	$77,933
7	Corey Pavin	–3	75	66	73	71	285	$77,933
10	David Frost	–2	70	68	74	74	286	$65,000
10	Scott McCarron	–2	70	70	72	74	286	$65,000
12	Ernie Els	–1	71	71	72	73	287	$52,500
12	Lee Janzen	–1	68	71	75	73	287	$52,500
12	Bob Tway	–1	67	72	76	72	287	$52,500
15	Mark Calcavecchia	E	71	73	71	73	288	$43,750
15	Fred Couples	E	78	68	71	71	288	$43,750
17	John Huston	+1	71	71	71	76	289	$40,000
18	Paul Azinger	+2	70	74	76	70	290	$32,600
18	David Duval	+2	73	72	69	76	290	$32,600
18	Tom Lehman	+2	75	70	72	73	290	$32,600
18	Mark O'Meara	+2	72	71	75	72	290	$32,600
18	Nick Price	+2	71	75	70	74	290	$32,600

			R1	R2	R3	R4	Total	Prize money
23	Larry Mize	+3	75	71	77	68	291	$25,000
23	Loren Roberts	+3	71	73	72	75	291	$25,000
25	Brad Faxon	+4	69	77	72	74	292	$21,000
25	Ray Floyd	+4	70	74	77	71	292	$21,000
27	Justin Leonard	+5	72	74	75	72	293	$18,900
27	Bob Estes	+5	71	71	79	72	293	$18,900
29	John Daly	+6	71	74	71	78	294	$15,571
29	Jim Furyk	+6	75	70	78	71	294	$15,571
29	Jim Gallagher Jr	+6	70	76	77	71	294	$15,571
29	Hale Irwin	+6	74	71	77	72	294	$15,571
29	Scott Simpson	+6	69	76	76	73	294	$15,571
29	Craig Stadler	+6	73	72	71	78	294	$15,571
29	Ian Woosnam	+6	72	69	73	80	294	$15,571
36	Fred Funk	+7	71	72	76	76	295	$12,333
36	Jay Haas	+7	70	73	75	77	295	$12,333
36	Bernhard Langer	+7	75	70	72	78	295	$12,333
39	Colin Montgomerie	+8	72	74	75	75	296	$11,050
39	Vijay Singh	+8	69	71	74	82	296	$11,050
41	Steve Lowery	+9	71	74	75	77	297	$10,050
41	Jack Nicklaus	+9	70	73	76	78	297	$10,050
43	Seve Ballesteros	+11	73	73	77	76	299	$9,300
44	Alexander Cejka	+14	73	71	78	80	302	$8,800

The following missed the 36-hole cut (146):

	R1	R2		Total	Prize
Tommy Aaron	71	76		147	$1,500
David Gilford	69	78		147	$1,500
Jeff Sluman	74	73		147	$1,500
Ted Tryba	72	75		147	$1,500
Tom Watson	75	72		147	$1,500
Fuzzy Zoeller	74	73		147	$1,500
Mark Brooks	72	76		148	$1,500
Bill Glasson	71	77		148	$1,500
Jumbo Ozaki	71	77		148	$1,500
Curtis Strange	71	77		148	$1,500
Hal Sutton	72	76		148	$1,500

Michael Campbell	73	76	149	$1,500
Sandy Lyle	75	74	149	$1,500
Gary Player	73	76	149	$1,500
Steve Stricker	80	69	149	$1,500
Neal Lancaster	76	74	150	$1,500
Arnold Palmer	74	76	150	$1,500
Payne Stewart	74	76	150	$1,500
*Eldrick 'Tiger' Woods	75	75	150	
Ben Crenshaw	77	74	151	$1,500
Ed Dougherty	76	75	151	$1,500
Satoshi Higashi	76	75	151	$1,500
Sam Torrance	80	71	151	$1,500
Kirk Triplett	76	75	151	$1,500
Gay Brewer	75	77	152	$1,500
Tim Herron	76	76	152	$1,500
Tom Kite	75	77	152	$1,500
Kenny Perry	75	77	152	$1,500
Paul Stankowski	74	78	152	$1,500
Woody Austin	79	74	153	$1,500
Brad Bryant	78	75	153	$1,500
David Edwards	79	74	153	$1,500
Costantino Rocca	78	75	153	$1,500
Mark Roe	74	79	153	$1,500
Billy Mayfair	77	77	154	$1,500
Steve Elkington	76	79	155	$1,500
Brian Henninger	76	79	155	$1,500
*Gordon Sherry	78	77	155	
D.A. Weibring	74	81	155	$1,500
Ian Baker-Finch	78	79	157	$1,500
Paul Goydos	74	83	157	$1,500
*Chris Wollmann	79	79	158	
Charles Coody	82	78	160	$1,500
*Jerry Courville Jr	78	82	160	
*Buddy Marucci	79	81	160	
Mark McCumber	78	82	160	$1,500
Billy Casper	75	86	161	$1,500
Doug Ford	81	88	169	$1,500

*amateur

Prizes

Nick Faldo	Gold Medal
	Sterling Silver Replica Masters Trophy
	Crystal Vase (Low score, R4, 67)
Greg Norman	Silver Medal
	Sterling Silver Salver
	Crystal Vase (Low score, R1, 63)
Phil Mickelson	Pair of Crystal Goblets (Eagle, Hole 15, R4)
Duffy Waldorf	Crystal Vase (Low score, R3, 69)
	Pair of Crystal Goblets (Eagle, Hole 8, R3)
	Pair of Crystal Goblets (Eagle, Hole 2, R4)
Davis Love	Pair of Crystal Goblets (Eagle, Hole 15, R4)
Cory Pavin	Crystal Vase (Low score, R2, 66)
	Pair of Crystal Goblets (Eagle, Hole 13, R2)
Mark Calcavecchia	Pair of Crystal Goblets (Eagle, Hole 8, R3)
David Duval	Crystal Vase (Low score, R3, 69)
Tom Lehman	Pair of Crystal Goblets (Eagle, Hole 8, R3)
Loren Roberts	Pair of Crystal Goblets (Eagle, Hole 15, R1)
Ray Floyd	Crystal Bowl (Hole-in-One, Hole 16, R4)
	Pair of Crystal Goblets (Eagle, Hole 15, R1)
Jim Gallagher Jr	Pair of Crystal Goblets (Eagle, Hole 15, R2)
Vijay Singh	Pair of Crystal Goblets (Eagle, Hole 8, R3)
Jack Nicklaus	Pair of Crystal Goblets (Eagle, Hole 15, R3)
David Gilford	Pair of Crystal Goblets (Eagle, Hole 13, R1)
Tom Watson	Pair of Crystal Goblets (Eagle, Hole 8, R1)
Fuzzy Zoeller	Pair of Crystal Goblets (Eagle, Hole 13, R2)
Hal Sutton	Pair of Crystal Goblets (Eagle, Hole 13, R1)
Paul Stankowski	Pair of Crystal Goblets (Eagle, Hole 2, R2)
Woody Austin	Pair of Crystal Goblets (Eagle, Hole 15, R2)
Costantino Rocca	Pair of Crystal Goblets (Eagle, Hole 13, R1)
	Pair of Crystal Goblets (Eagle, Hole 13, R2)

ACKNOWLEDGEMENTS

My thanks are due to so many people without whom this book would not have become a reality, starting with everyone at Elliott & Thompson, including Lorne Forsyth, Olivia Bays and Jennie Condell. I am particularly grateful for the endless dedication and patience of my editor, Pippa Crane.

In obtaining specific source material on the 1996 Masters, I am indebted to Steve Ethun and Melissa Lyles at Augusta National, Brian Eldredge at T3Media and the BBC's wonderful Hazel Irvine. Thanks to all.

This book would not have got finished, or even started, without the love and support of family and friends, while so many colleagues have made a contribution, directly or indirectly, along the way. Among them: Tony Adamson, John Barton, Hugh Bateman, Ken Brown, Colin Callander, Iain Carter, Matthew Chancellor, James Corrigan, Peter Corrigan, Bob Davies, Patricia Davies, Peter Dixon, Carolina Durante, Mark Garrod, Kevin Garside, Tim Glover, Robert Green, Glenn Greenspan, David Hamilton, Michael Harris, John Hopkins, James Lawton, Lewine Mair, Michele Mair, Paul Newman, Richard Simmons, Alan Page, Paul Trow.

Last, but by no means least, it would be remiss not to mention the much-missed Bev Norwood, friend, mentor and editor on a myriad of projects over two decades. It was Bev who first offered me the chance to try longer-form journalism and he was characteristically encouraging when I first outlined this project during the 2013 Masters. It was to be the last time we met in person, he was unable to travel to the Open at Muirfield and died shortly afterwards, though not before editing the *Open Championship Annual* for a 30th year. Many memories remain, especially of sharing digs at many recent Opens, along with his childhood friend, Vernon Averett. Good times. Thanks, Bev.

INDEX

Also by Andy Farrell:

THE 100 GREATEST EVER GOLFERS

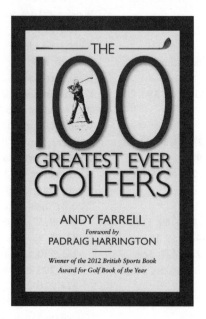

What makes a great golfer? Is it innate talent, unstinting dedication, hard graft or inner strength? Can it be measured by championships won or prize money earned? Is the perfect technique more important than an engaging personality?

Since the birth in 1860 of the Open Championship, every era of golf has produced its iconic great players, and here Andy Farrell selects his candidates for the top 100. Sure to inspire endless debate for its selection, this fascinating treasure trove of stories is essential reading for any golfer.

"A book to argue with as well as to learn from.
I recommend it wholeheartedly."
Brian Viner, *The Independent*